The State
We're In

The State
We're In

WILL HUTTON

JONATHAN CAPE
LONDON

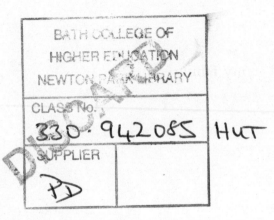

First published 1995

7 9 10 8

© Will Hutton 1995

Will Hutton has asserted his right
under the Copyright, Designs and Patents Act 1988
to be identified as the author of this work

First published in the United Kingdom in 1995 by
Jonathan Cape
Random House, 20 Vauxhall Bridge Road, London SW1V 2SA

Random House Australia (Pty) Limited
20 Alfred Street, Milsons Point, Sydney,
New South Wales 2061, Australia

Random House New Zealand Limited
18 Poland Road, Glenfield,
Auckland 10, New Zealand

Random House South Africa (Pty) Limited
PO Box 337, Bergvlei, South Africa

Random House UK Limited Reg. No. 954009

A CIP catalogue record for this book
is available from the British Library

Papers used by Random House UK Limited are natural,
recyclable products made from wood grown in sustainable forests.
The manufacturing processes conform to the environmental
regulations of the country of origin.

ISBN 0–224–03688–2

Printed in Great Britain by Clays Ltd, St Ives plc

for
my family

Contents

Acknowledgments

In a book of this type there are many to thank. Neil Belton, my editor at Jonathan Cape, has more than justified his reputation. He read every chapter and every redraft, and his comments – sometimes critical, sometimes praising – were essential to the construction of the book. He then went on to edit every page of the final draft. This is an old-fashioned relationship between editor and author, and was excellent. Jenny Cottom navigated the book through to publication against tough deadlines with great dedication. My father, William Hutton, and my colleague at the *Guardian*, Andie Beven, read the book for sense, grammar and content. Their contribution was invaluable.

I was also fortunate in enlisting any number of friends to read chapters, sections and early drafts. The small seminar at the halfway point, where Paul Ormerod, David Marquand, David Miliband and Colin Mayer gave me feedback and criticism was an important juncture – my thanks to them all. David Miliband even managed to offer further comments on the final draft of chapters 11 and 12. Yvette Cooper's comments, particularly on chapters 2, 11 and 12 were perceptive and helpful, prompting the rewriting of a number of sections. Paul Gregg's statistics and comments on the two labour market chapters provoked important revisions, while David Held, Jonathan Perraton and others at the Open University offered detailed and intelligent insights which I hope they will feel I have taken on board. Anthony Barnett provided, literally, a last minute set of comments which were typically acute. Others, too numerous to mention, have made contributions through chance remarks or being unsuspecting guinea pigs for some of the ideas, and James Nicholson was a tireless chaser of facts and statistics.

And of course there is the *Guardian*, where my weekly column has given me the chance to explore some of these ideas. I would never have started the book without an eight-week term at St

Antony's, Oxford, as a Senior Associate Member, and my thanks go to Archie Brown and Avi Shlaim for negotiating my admission so painlessly – and to the Warden, Lord Dahrendorf, for his keen support and interest.

The term at St Antony's and a sabbatical month a year later were the keys to the book's completion. They gave me the opportunity to think, read and write – but for that you need a generous employer, an enlightened editor and supportive colleagues. The *Guardian* provided all three, and I owe particular thanks to Peter Preston for his support and generosity.

Last but not least there is my family, who have lived with an increasingly distracted father and husband for over a year. It's over and I won't do it again – at least not until you're grown-up. Thanks above all to Jane; you were – and are – just great.

W.H.
November 1994

Preface

This is a book of political economy. Europeans will recognise it, I hope, as written in the tradition of political economists like Keynes, Polanyi and Shonfield; Americans will see it in the tradition of a Galbraith, Reich or Thurow – and Friedman, on the right of the political spectrum. It has economics and the economy at its heart, but attempts to link them to the wider operation of the social and political system. My deeply held contention is that the attempt to isolate economics from other disciplines – notably politics, history, philosophy, finance, constitutional theory and sociology – has fatally disabled its power to explain what is happening in the world. There is too much ideology passing itself off as science, and the results have been lamentable.

But over 100,000 words later I am keenly aware of how difficult the task is. Many of the chapters could have been expanded into books in their own right, and I am all too conscious of the lively debates in each area, which necessarily could only be touched upon. The aim of the book, after all, is to show how the economic, political and social relate to the whole of British society.

The central *economic* argument is that the weakness of the British economy, particularly the level and character of investment, originates in the financial system. The targets for profit are too high and time horizons are too short. But British finance has not grown up in a vacuum. Behind the financial institutions stand history, class, a set of values and the political system. The City of London and Whitehall and Westminster are symbiotic; one could not exist without the other, and none could have become what they are today without the others' support.

Complementing this economic thesis is the book's *political* argument that the semi-modern nature of the British state is a fundamental cause of Britain's economic and social problems. Markets, whether we like it or not, are embedded in a country's social system and values. It falls to the state to govern both the economy and society, and the character of the state's political institutions themselves shape the democratic character and the efficiency of governance. The constitution, which defines the responsibilities and institutions of government, is thus a central determinant of how the country is governed.

Yet Britain has no written constitution. During the twentieth century it has been content to work with the legacy of previous centuries and govern the country through its unwritten constitution, which can be defined in a sentence: whatever the Crown assents to in Parliament is law. This, I argue, was barely adequate in the past and it is certainly not adequate today. Arrogant executive discretion, official secrecy, centralisation of power and the lack of engagement with the multiplicity of concerns and groups that make up civil society have their origins in the semi-autocratic system of government that Britain possesses. The country needs and must have a modern constitutional settlement.

The urgency of addressing the country's financial and constitutional system grows by the year. Ungoverned British capitalism's lethal demand for some of the highest financial returns in the world has encouraged firms relentlessly to exploit their new freedom to hire and fire. As a result there is a mounting and quite proper sense of crisis spreading across all classes about the character and availability of work and its implications for every aspect of society – from the care of our children to the growing dereliction of our cities. Official unemployment figures, alarming enough, only tell part of the story. Insecurity, low wages and wasted talent are widespread, and the problem touches professions and occupations once thought inviolable.

This does not mean that change should be resisted; but it does mean that the British need better institutions with which to survive and prosper. We need a decent political system as much as a proper financial and welfare system; we deserve a better structure for our firms, resources for education and training, and economic institutions that go well beyond the boundaries of the nation state. What is happening in Britain, after all, is only a more acute version of what is happening elsewhere – and the world needs to equip itself with an international financial order that is more conducive to growth, employment and equity. Here Britain must look to European initiatives to secure what a single state can no longer secure for itself.

This book is critical of the purist free market orthodoxy, both at the level of economics and as a political philosophy. Its exponents are hardly likely to surrender, but I hope that they recognise the force of the concerns expressed here about growing inequality, Britain's lack of a tradition of citizenship, the impact of financial short-termism on investment and the labour market, and the destructive consequences on human relations of an exclusive emphasis on the primacy of market forces. I do not believe that the best of them set out to construct as deeply divided a society and underperforming economy as Britain now has; and some at least are refreshingly honest and will confront these realities head on.

My greatest hope is that the book will offer a way forward that is neither a return to the bastardised Keynesian corporatism of the 1960s and 1970s, nor the forced march towards a wholly deregulated market. There are other options besides becoming a huge version of Hong Kong with American levels of wages for the millions at the bottom of the pile. Our people deserve better than that. What is required is creative institution-building and a democratic opening – and confidence that men and women can shape their world.

1. The State We're In

The British are accustomed to success. This is the world's oldest democracy. Britain built an empire, launched the Industrial Revolution and was on the winning side in the twentieth century's two world wars. The British believe that their civilisation is admired all over the world. A Briton does not boast openly, but is possessed of an inner faith that he or she is special. To be born in these islands is still seen as a privilege.

Yet in the last decade of the twentieth century the record of success is tarnished and any sense of privilege is evaporating. The country's great industrial cities are decaying and listless, while in the new industries and technologies Britain is barely represented. Even its unique economic asset, the City of London, is sullied by malpractice and a reputation for commercial misjudgement.

The country is an inveterate consumer, but the rise in consumption has done little for indigenous industry. Production has stagnated while the inexorable tide of imports has steadily outpaced the growth of exports. No longer can the economy, with its ageing and inadequate stock of factories, machines and industrial infrastructure provide work for all those who want it.

For two decades unemployment has been a grim fact of British life, bearing particularly hard on men. As well as those included in the official count who want work and can't find it, there are millions more who are marginalised – prematurely retired or living off inadequate savings or sickness benefit. One in four of the country's males of working age is now either officially unemployed or idle, with incalculable consequences for our well-being and social cohesion.[1] The numbers living in poverty have grown to awesome proportions, and the signs of social stress – from family breakdown to the growth of crime – mount almost daily.

As the economy weakens the country's international prestige is waning. Its capacity to cling on to its privileged position in the

world pecking order – as a nuclear power with a permanent seat
on the UN Security Council and at the centre of a web of special
relationships with the US, Europe and the Commonwealth – is
plainly ebbing.

British institutions, burnished with an age-old legitimacy and
once seen as impregnable, are cracking under the pressure as pre-
tension meets reality. The Queen suffers the indignity of watching
her three children's marriages end, two in spectacular scandal, and
with the threat that Australia – once the most reliable member
of the Commonwealth – sees so little reflected glory in sharing
fealty to the Windsors that it may declare itself a republic. The
Prince of Wales has acknowledged his adultery and desire to be
'defender of [many] faiths', opening up profound questions about
whether he as king could maintain the current relationship between
church and state. The deep divisions fissuring national life ensure
that apparently innocuous royal remarks are loaded with political
significance, further disabling the monarchy as a national institution.

The royal family's difficulties have become symbolic of the
age. The last British-owned car company was sold to the Germans.
The American government seems more attentive to its relationship
with China and Germany than with Britain. The Channel Tunnel
is completed but of course the trains run more slowly on the
British side of the channel. The former workshop of the world is
now Europe's fourth economic power after Germany, France and
Italy and in some branches of production it is being overtaken by
Spain. One in three of the nation's children grows up in poverty. In
1991 one twenty-one-year-old in five was innumerate; one in seven
was illiterate.[2] The prison population is the highest in Europe. The
British are failing.

Above all, we live in a new world of us and them. The sense of
belonging to a successful national project has all but disappeared.
Average living standards may have risen but have not generated a
sense of well-being; if anything there is more discontent because
the gains have been spread so unevenly and are felt to be so evanescent. The country is increasingly divided against itself, with an
arrogant officer class apparently indifferent to the other ranks it

commands. This privileged class is favoured with education, jobs, housing and pensions. At the other end of the scale more and more people discover they are the new working poor, or live off the state in semi-poverty. Their paths out of this situation are closing down as the world in which they are trapped becomes meaner, harder and more corrupting. In between there are growing numbers of people who are insecure, fearful for their jobs in an age of permanent 'down-sizing', 'cost-cutting' and 'casualisation' and ever more worried about their ability to maintain a decent standard of living.

The rot starts at the top. The political system is malfunctioning, bringing politicians and civil servants into disrepute and discrediting the very notion of the public realm in which national renewal might be attempted. Instead the state is the handmaiden of the process of loss. The proud House of Commons regards itself as the cockpit of the nation, but it is no more than the creature of the government of the day. Once the courtesies of a nineteenth-century debating chamber have been observed, the government can make laws almost at will.

Yet this is only the tip of the iceberg. An unwritten constitution organised around the principle that the law is whatever the monarch assents to in Parliament has no clear democratic rules. Monarchical power has passed in effect to the majority party in the House of Commons. There are no limits to the centre's capacity to take power away from the regions and local authorities. The executive branch is held only nominally accountable to Parliament. There is no formal independence of the judiciary. There is no codified bill of rights. There is no presumption that the activity of the state should be open and transparent. There are no rules about the funding of political parties or the giving of honours. There aren't even rules governing the working of the House itself; there is 'custom and practice', but no formal code. The entire public realm can easily be captured by the partisans of the majority party in the House of Commons and its supporters outside.

The only formal check on executive power is the notion of a government-in-waiting – Her Majesty's Opposition – but four

successive Conservative election victories have devalued even that
threat. The Conservative Party has found itself in charge of a
ruleless state, handed down virtually intact from the settlement
of 1688 with universal suffrage bolted on, and has been willing
to toss aside even unwritten custom and practice in pursuit of its
objectives. In some respects the concentration and centralisation of
power resembles that of a one-party state.

But the incapacity of the constitution to offer any check
to discretionary executive government has even corrupted the
Conservative Party, with the contagion spreading to the state.
Honours are routinely awarded to party contributors; funds are
accepted from foreign donors of questionable character and motive
in return for undeclared favours; defence contracts and the flotation
of privatised public utilities are awarded to government supporters
in industry and the City. What has been constructed in Britain,
using the ancient and unfettered state, is a form of Conservative
hegemony in the literal meaning of that word: a system of supremacy over others.

This hegemony has infected the impartiality of the Civil Service, whose independence was an informal check and balance in
the British system. The already confused boundaries between
public, government and party interest have been blurred even
further, with senior officials as committed to partisan policies
as their ministerial bosses. Britain's lack of a written constitution
means that the public interest can only be expressed as the interest
of the majority party in the House of Commons. This is a weakness
that has been thoroughly exploited – as the ministerial and official
testimony to the Scott Inquiry showed so dramatically.[3]

Partisanship, executive discretion and secrecy saturate the public
domain – so that the so-called 'reform' of the public services has
involved the extension of the same principles into almost every
sphere of national life. Lines of democratic accountability have
been broken as schools, hospitals, and housing have been removed
from their former control by local government or Parliament
and placed under the management of new trusts and agencies.
By 1996, the *Guardian* has estimated, there will be a staggering 7,700 new quangos (quasi-autonomous non-governmental

organisations) dispersing some £54 billion of public money.[4] This is a bizarre achievement for a regime committed to removing the burden of government – a triumph of double-speak that Orwell would have admired.

The stewardship of this money has passed to an oligarchy of Conservative placemen, with a patchy record of increased efficiency more than offset by the loss of accountability. The Public Accounts Committee has identified twenty-four cases in the new executive agencies where public money has been squandered or wasted. As it warned, the state is regressing to a system of patronage and privatised carelessness with public money such as existed prior to the Northcote-Trevelyan reforms of the late-nineteenth century.

Parliament, in the popular view, has become the place where politicians score meaningless points off each other in the style of Oxford or Cambridge Union debates while the business of government is conducted by a flawed bureaucracy. At the same time there is growing scepticism about the capacity of the British judicial system to administer justice. The three biggest terrorist trials in British history – the cases of the Guildford Four, the Birmingham Six, and the Maguire Seven – ended with all the convictions being quashed. With lawyers' fees climbing to ever more outrageous levels (up to £500 an hour) justice has become the privilege of the better-off, while the legal aid budget designed to create equal access to the law has been squeezed. Meanwhile there is a crisis of identity in the police, their legitimacy undermined by their admission that they have cut corners in trying to get convictions of serious criminals. The police, which in the past had been moving from a 'force' to a community 'service' (liaising with victims, the elderly and the mentally ill) has been told to concentrate wholly on 'catching criminals' and maintaining public order.

Public institutions are not the only victims of the new corruption. The City of London has become a byword for speculation, inefficiency and cheating. Given the power to regulate their own affairs, City financial markets and institutions have conspicuously failed to meet any reasonable standard of honest dealing with the public or their own kind.

Lloyds – the London insurance market – failed to prevent rank exploitation of its individual investors or 'names'. Losses of billions of pounds have been run up, impoverishing thousands of external names, while insiders have feathered their nests.

Insurance company salesmen have wrongly advised as many as 400,000 members of occupational pension funds, who bought individual pension schemes which were no good to them at all. As many as 2 million more were persuaded to cash in their rights to the state earnings related pension scheme (SERPS) and to buy personal pensions – again to their disadvantage. Insurance companies sell policies they know are unsuitable and calculate their profits on the certainty that buyers will cash in their inappropriate policies early, for a fraction of their proper value.[5]

The Stock Exchange has been unable to prevent systematic manipulation of share prices for individual profit by insiders with market-sensitive and privileged information, while the Serious Fraud Office has spectacularly failed to make its prosecutions stick – and even when it gets a result the sentences are notoriously light.[6] Here again there is a feeling that the balance of advantage in the courts lies with the rich.

The whole system of financial regulation and accountability has been found wanting. Leading firms of accountants have been unable to see fraud under their noses, signing off accounts as representing a 'true and fair view' of companies that were about to go bankrupt or be exposed as fraudulent. The system of self-regulation has been irretrievably compromised by the financial services industry's own interests. Even the majestic Bank of England, despite warnings, was unwilling or incapable of taking early action to prevent the infamous Bank of Credit and Commerce International from trading fraudulently. Its collapse caught unwitting depositers by surprise, losing them millions.

The sense that the aim of financial and corporate life is personal enrichment at any price is accentuated by the extravagant remuneration packages for senior executives, even in cases where they have served companies for only a few months or have failed to do the job. David Dworkin of British Home Stores resigned after six months to pocket £3.2 million; Bob Horton, sacked as chairman of BP, collected £1.5 million, and is now part-time chairman of Railtrack.[7] They are just two of many.

The professions – notably lawyers and accountants – have not been far behind. Barristers' fees have become legendary, while accountants and solicitors are practised in charging their clients excessive amounts. Fees for advising on takeovers, privatisations and receiverships have reached embarrassingly high levels, often seriously diminishing the returns to the people who are supposed to benefit from the advice. The avarice of the professions has begun to weigh down the bodies politic and economic.

The privatised utilities are particularly offensive in this regard. The directors of these natural monopolies (for who else can supply water or gas?) granted themselves share options at keen prices which have made them millionaires many times over. The rise in profits which has driven up share prices has not been created by risk-taking or by genuine entrepreneurship; it has simply been achieved by massive lay-offs and exploitation of the companies' position through mechanical price rises. The water industry, writing off two-thirds of its initial £1.2 billion investment outside the industry, while its prices rise and executive salaries balloon, is the most noxious example of a general trend.

Commercial mistakes of the first magnitude have been made, without any apparent impact on the salaries or career prospects of those who made them. The clearing banks, who lent massively on property during the late 1980s property boom, have seen few heads roll despite collectively writing off more than £20 billion of bad debts. Executive pay has risen by 50 per cent in real terms over the decade; but despite these massive incentives Britain is unable to boast bold, new, growing companies, technical innovation or investment. Great personal wealth has not translated into wealth for the community.

Personal enrichment has in fact been accompanied by a weakening of the long-run growth rate. In the twenty years up to 1979 growth had averaged 2.75 per cent; in the twenty years up to 1994 growth has averaged little more than 2 per cent. If this in part represented a general weakening in the growth rates of all industrialised countries, it is none the less true that Britain's

international trading position and competitiveness have deteriorated over the same period. In 1983 UK trade in manufacturing
went into deficit for the first time since the Industrial Revolution;
in 1990 the UK was the only European state with a trade deficit in
merchandise. Devaluation in 1992 arrested the trend temporarily
but with the capital stock per worker so low, future growth must
see the deficit become even larger.

Over the 1980s research and development undertaken by private companies declined as a proportion of national output; in
1994 only thirteen British companies appeared in the world's top
200 spenders on R & D. Moreover, while the world average spend
on R & D was 4.85 per cent of sales, the thirteen British companies spent only 2.29 per cent of their sales, and without the
contribution of four drug companies the average would have been
even lower.[8] British companies' priorities are overwhelmingly
financial. In manufacturing, for example, investment rose by 2 per
cent per annum during the 1980s, profits rose 6 per cent a year,
while dividends jumped by 12 per cent per year![9] While the world's
top 200 companies spent three times more on R & D than on
dividends, Britain's top innovators' research spend was a miserable
two-thirds of what they handed out in dividends.

Despite the imperative to develop what economists call 'human
capital', 64 per cent of the British workforce have no vocational
qualifications, compared with 26 per cent in Germany. Britain in
1993 had 250,000 people on apprentice schemes compared with
more than 2 million in Germany. Efforts at improvement are
hamstrung by lack of resources and an inability to build a national
consensus on training.

Instead the country looks to foreign investment to provide
new industries and training. By 1995 the Japanese will be
boosting the UK trade balance by £4 billion. British regions
engage in unseemly attempts to outbid each other in attracting
the foreign multinationals that bring jobs and wealth; 25 per
cent of UK manufacturing capacity is now owned by foreigners
who employ 16 per cent of British workers. British companies
offer little except retrenchment, redundancy and rationalisation.

The media are the mirror for the economic and social disintegration of the country. The focus of the newspapers, notably the
tabloids, has narrowed to a right-wing populism that pays scant
attention to accuracy, the brew leavened by sexual titillation and
obsessional royal family watching. The power to form opinion
has been accompanied by a more careless attitude to the way
such power is exercised. The Labour Party has been the first
casualty consistently misreported by most of the press, a service
for which most of the editors in question were knighted. But
now every national institution can expect the same treatment,
with the growing conviction that an honest hearing in the press is
the exception rather than the rule unless what is being said chimes
with the transient preoccupations of editors and proprietors.

The upholders of differing standards and values have been
unable to mount an effective rearguard action. Organised religion
is on the defensive in its assertion of the values of community and
co-operation. Trade unions have been emasculated by legislative
and populist hostility to their aims and the welfare state has been
transformed by the introduction of market competition. The
National Health Service is developing into a two-tier structure,
with a third tier available to those who can buy treatment. The
state pension, indexed to prices rather than wages, increasingly
fails to offer even a minimal income in old age. If the public sector
was bloated in the 1970s, it has now become the twilight zone of
the second-best. Its employees are poorly rewarded and its services
under-resourced. Education has become a creator of class division,
with opted-out schools in the state sector and private schools offering access to qualifications, prestigious universities and, for some,
lucrative careers.

These changes have affected the deepest parts of the British
psyche. The notion of a fair day's work for a fair day's pay, the idea
that success will attend hard work and that society should support
basic institutions like families and children – all are evaporating.
Individuals are compelled to look out for themselves. Businessmen seem fixated on their personal remuneration; politicians seem
incapable of reaching out beyond their own tribal loyalties. Jobs
can be lost quickly and never found again; lifetime savings can be

stolen; home buyers can be trapped by debt in houses worth less than the price paid for them. There is a general sense of fear and beleaguerment.

Abroad, Britain is increasingly isolated. Unwilling to pool sovereignty any further with its European partners or adapt its idiosyncratic institutions to the modern world, it is marginal to the process of constructing a more integrated Europe. It clings to its role in Nato despite the collapse of communism and continues to spend more on defence than its European allies without any clear strategic idea of what to do with its military hardware. It desperately wants a special alliance with the US, but in the aftermath of the Cold War the Americans have become industrial and trade competitors with Europe, no longer subordinating their immediate interests to wider strategic objectives. The US is increasingly unmoved by its 'special relationship' with a third-class state.

Without privileged American support or firm European allies, Britain stands isolated, a fading middle-sized economy protesting its Great Power ambitions. Unwilling to face up to reality, choices over defence priorities are continually fudged, resulting in a calamitous drop in morale in the armed services as costs are pared and privatisation and contracting-out are introduced. It is not easy to motivate men and women to train for combat and possible violent death if military values are suborned and it is no longer clear what they might be fighting for.

Britain in the 1990s has lost its sense of direction and its people are at odds with themselves. It needs to revitalise its economy, modernise its institutions, rewrite the contract between the members of its society and recover its self-esteem. It needs to do what the Conservative government promised in 1979.

The failed Conservative promise

None of this was ever meant to be. But a description of Britain in the late 1970s would have been nearly as despairing. Parliament, in a famous phrase of Lord Hogg, had become an 'elective dictatorship'. The government of the country and management of the economy could only proceed, it seemed, by grace of the trade union movement withholding strike action in pursuit of high wage claims. The economy languished, apparently locked in a spiral of high inflation, currency depreciation and low investment. Internationally the country's stock was falling. In 1976 it suffered the indignity of being the first advanced industrialised country to be bailed out by the International Monetary Fund. Public spending outran economic growth, and it seemed that the sinews of British industry were being gnawed away by inflation, wage demands and a collapse in entrepreneurship. Public intervention was synonymous with subsidy and nationalisation.

The incoming Conservative government had a programme of action to put Britain back on its feet. The task was the revitalisation of British capitalism and the method was the adoption of the free-market nostrums of the newly assertive free-market economists. Britain had to rediscover the verities of the age of Adam Smith; the state was to be rolled back; and the felicitous invisible hand of market forces was to be ungloved. At a stroke this would curb inflation and make the economy more competitive.

The story of the Conservative years has been the single-minded application of this philosophy. The nationalised industries have nearly all been privatised. Effective strike action by trade unions has become very difficult, and membership of unions has declined remarkably. Spending on programmes such as housing and industry has dropped dramatically. Public spending as a proportion of national output, despite the increase in social security payments, was still lower in the recession of the early-1990s than it was in the recession a decade earlier. Real interest rates have reached unprecedentedly high levels as the only acceptable means of lowering inflation.

The financial system has been freed from almost all forms of regulatory restraint, and regulations in many other areas have been greatly reduced. The top rate of income tax has been cut from 83 to 40 per cent and corporation tax has been cut from 52 to 33 per cent.

The market principle has been extended into almost every walk of life. The targets are as disparate as television, with the auctioning of TV franchises, and health, with the establishment of an internal market between purchasers (doctors and health authorities) and providers (hospitals). Contracting out and market testing has exposed everything from the collection of refuse to the collection of statistics to the iron laws of supply and demand.

Defenders of the policy can point to the near defeat of inflation which, after a quarter century in which it averaged 9 per cent, has reached very low levels. There has been a decade of high productivity growth in manufacturing. Labour relations have improved and strikes have been virtually eliminated. The public sector is more efficient economically. These are not gains, say the apologists, to be treated lightly.

Yet they have been bought at high cost, and not all of them can be attributed directly to the government's efforts. Inflation has fallen worldwide, and Britain's performance has only improved marginally against the average; nor is it clear that the improvement can be sustained if the country's economic weakness provokes an inflationary fall in the value of sterling. Low inflation is earned through economic strength; that is not the British position.

The improvement in labour relations has been achieved through a massive diminution of workers' rights and high structural unemployment, but wage inflation is scarcely more sensitive to unemployment than it ever was (as Chapter 4 will demonstrate); and although labour productivity has risen sharply in manufacturing, no upsurge in production and investment has accompanied it. Productivity growth in the wider economy has just kept pace with historic trends. The privatised industries have achieved efficiency gains, but so far they have come mainly from shedding labour. Their record on innovation is indifferent.

The overall judgement on the market experiment must be at best mixed, at worst negative. The economy has been taken on a ferocious switchback ride; a period of deep recession in the early 1980s, then an unsustainable boom and then a second chronic recession. As an exercise in economic management it is scarcely credible – and it has made the business sector understandably cautious about undertaking new investment. In area after area implementation of the market principle – itself based on a theoretical model of the economy which (as can be seen in Chapter 9) is deeply flawed – has failed to benefit the community.

The deregulation of credit triggered the most enormous credit boom the country has ever seen which, together with income tax cuts, produced three consecutive years in which personal consumption grew by more than 6 per cent per annum. In 1979 consumption stood at around 60 per cent of national output; by 1994 it had risen to 64 per cent – an all time high. This is unsustainable, and managing its decline is one of the major policy challenges of the 1990s.

The capital stock in manufacturing has shrunk, while investment has exploded in financial services and consumer-related industries to match the spending generated by the credit boom. Britain has underproduced, underexported and overimported; the trade deficit is only another way of expressing the fact that consumption rose while production stagnated.

The unwillingness of industry to invest is disappointing, especially given that the share of profits in national output has risen from the depressed levels of the 1970s and the share taken by wages fallen.[10] Lowering top tax rates, reducing subsidies, weakening unions, increasing profits and strengthening management should have combined to unleash an entrepreneurial revolution – at least according to the predictions of free market economics. But here again the revolution has not delivered the goods.

For the key issue in a capitalist economy is the conditions that banks and financial institutions set the companies to which they lend and in which they invest (see Chapters 5 and 6). Although profits have risen, the paradox is that the required rate of return on investment has risen even faster. But this is no accident. The financial system, already biased to thinking only of the short-term, has been further deregulated and this has of course intensified its greed for high, quick returns. The more market-based the financial system, the less effectively it mobilises resources for investment (as can be seen in Chapter 10, in an international comparison of various capitalist systems).

One ray of hope was the high level of business start-ups in the late 1980s, but this proved to be a temporary phenomenon and many of the new businesses have already failed. Throughout the 1980s and 1990s there was no sign that Britain had succeeded in creating the equivalent of, say, a fledgling Honda or Apple computer. Information technology, which promises to play the same role in the next century that cars and consumer electronics played in the second half of the twentieth, is under-developed in the UK. The compass of R & D, innovation, and patent applications – the real measures of entrepreneurial vitality – remains pointed uncompromisingly in the wrong direction.

Creativity in Britain has instead been of the destructive kind. Firms, anxious to meet their shareholders' requirements for high returns, have taken advantage of the deregulation of the labour market to impose more casualised, part-time, 'flexible' patterns of work and so increase their capacity to modify their costs to the changing pattern of demand. Only around 40 per cent of the work-force enjoy tenured full-time employment or secure self-employment, roughly equivalent to J.K. Galbraith's 'constituency of contentment'; another 30 per cent are insecurely self-employed, involuntarily part-time, or casual workers; while the bottom 30 per cent, the marginalised, are idle or working for poverty wages.

While a labour market of this divisive kind may seem rational for firms cutting their costs or a government trying to control inflation, the wider economic and social impact has been disastrous. The growth of inequality and poverty created by this labour market structure has inflated public spending, in particular on the welfare state. Together with the lowering of top tax rates that was mistakenly supposed to be the chief means of stimulating incentives, this was the principal cause of the public borrowing crisis that defined the early 1990s. The gap between current public sector spending and revenue (the so-called current balance, which excludes all capital spending) plunged into the red to the tune of 6.5 per cent of national output in 1993–94: the highest current deficit in post-war history.

For all the malfunctions of the economy are related, fused by the government's overweening desire to establish the market principle as the basis of every policy. Tax cuts have encouraged excessive consumption and the promise of further cuts fuelled still more spending, while financial deregulation made borrowing against the promise of tax cuts and rising wages more attractive still. The same financial deregulation weakened the growth of productive investment and employment; this in turn inflated spending on social security, which interacted with the structural fall in tax revenues to create the deficit in current public spending and receipts. The penetration of imports and the dismal performance of our exports has inflated the balance of payments deficit.

The perversity of the process does not stop there. The extension of the market principle deep into society has destabilised many areas of national life. The emerging two-tier National Health Service and the three-tier education system (described in Chapter 8) are only a few of the ways in which social inequality has been superimposed on the already deep patterns of income inequality. Herein lie the origins of family stress, the crisis of parenting and the general communal decay which are at the root of so many of Britain's social problems. Altruism and the civilising values of an inclusive society have been sacrificed on the altar of self-interest, of choice, of opting out and of individualism.

The global experiment

But Britain has not been alone, even if it has been in the vanguard of the market experiment. Since 1979 there has been a worldwide growth in the belief that markets are the solution to economic difficulties. Privatisation has spread across the industrialised world and into the less developed countries. Everywhere there is a loss of faith in state intervention, regulation and ownership as instruments of economic improvement. Instead the emphasis is on deregulation, flexible prices and private ownership.

The pace may vary, but the direction is the same. The *impasse* in which British Keynesianism found itself in 1979 (discussed more fully in Chapter 2) seemed to be the forerunner of a general governmental incapacity in economic management, which the later collapse of communism simply confirmed. Social democrats and socialists alike have been on the defensive. The great ideological contest of the twentieth century has been settled. Free market capitalism has won; state planning and communism, of which social-market capitalism is alleged to be a subset, has lost.

The policy offensive has been organised at many levels. Tax and social welfare systems are seen not as instruments of social cohesion and public purpose; rather as burdens in the fight for competitiveness. The leading industrialised countries have fostered the growth of a global financial market by scrapping capital controls. Production is increasingly multinational and hostility to inward investment by multinationals has been replaced by an intense competition for the factories, skills and jobs they bring.

The old faith in Keynesian instruments of economic management is in decline. States no longer commit themselves to full employment; they do not believe it to be possible. Instead they crave price stability and the approval of the global bond markets for their fiscal rectitude. Independent central banks are worshipped as guardians of monetary order and low inflation. It is no surprise that if the unemployed in the industrialised world numbered 35 million in 1994, a record post-war high, then inflation, at under 3 per cent, was at a thirty-year low. This is the conscious choice of the world's leading industrialised countries.

There is scarcely a Western country that cannot tell at least one tale similar to Britain's. Financial deregulation prompted wild credit booms in the US and Sweden during the 1980s. In Sweden this led to the first attacks on the welfare state since the 1930s as a social democratic government tried to contain inflationary credit growth by curbing the rise in government borrowing. The French retreat from pro-active management of the economy through nationalisation and planning in the early 1980s, and Mitterrand's later embrace of 'competitive disinflation' and economic 'rigour', lowering French inflation below the German rate, was one of the more spectacular turnabouts of modern times. Youth unemployment in France is even higher than in Britain.

Spanish socialists and the New Zealand Labour Party have been no less enthusiastic about budget cutting, privatisation and restructuring their welfare states than, say, Canadian Conservatives. Everywhere the ideological edge of political competition has been blunted. Different parties, when in government, offer similar programmes.

Yet democracy depends on parties being able to develop distinctive policies that correspond to some coherent political vision. If the only choice – forced on political parties by the new power of veto of the global capital markets, which threaten a run on the currency of countries whose policies they dislike – is some variant of the new conservatism, then political debate becomes a charade. President Clinton is reported to have raged that the constraints imposed by the bond markets on US economic policy reduced political debate in the US to little more than a contest between the Eisenhower and Reaganite versions of Republicanism.[11]

Economic success has been elusive, except in East Asia where there has been a decade-long boom. Running capitalism, it seems, is a more subtle process than just turning over economic and social life to the market and insisting that the only policy goal is keeping down prices. The argument in the chapters ahead is that as well as the flexibility and competition that the market provides, successful capitalism needs careful economic management and institutions that foster co-operation and commitment, although the form they take may differ from country to country. East Asian capitalism has such institutions and values in abundance (see the detailed analysis in Chapter 10) and its governments are active sponsors and regulators of the economic process.

Yet such thinking has until recently made little impact on the West, particularly on the financial markets. Indeed the free market model has been so magnetic that Eastern Europe and Russia's transformation into market economies have been organised around its teachings. The accent has been on liberalising prices, on budgetary austerity and on deregulation; there has been little attempt to build longterm banking institutions and structures of corporate governance, or to use government procurement and the institutions of social solidarity that have accompanied success historically in the West and now in East Asia. Capitalism is socially produced and politically governed; it does not spontaneously arrive

at the best outcomes. Great risks are being run in Russia in the
name of an ideology which completely neglects such insights; for
civil turmoil in the former Soviet Union will pose a greater threat
to the world than any failure of the market in Britain.

While acknowledging the scale of that crisis, this book is about
Britain – for the British experience offers a salutary warning to
others. While individual countries may have at least one horror
story of radical marketisation similar to Britain's, only Britain can
tell them *all*. The process has gone further and faster here from an
already weakened condition, and the failures and shortcomings
that followed bear close examination. The British credit boom
generated the biggest rise in personal debt of any industrialised
country in this period. The growth in inequality has been the
fastest of any advanced state. The drop in the relative importance
of manufacturing has been the most marked. The economy has
been more volatile. The privatisation programme was among the
most aggressive of any advanced state. The attack on the welfare
system has been more comprehensive. The deregulation of the
financial system was the most complete; the assault on labour
market regulation the most all-encompassing. The cuts in the
top rate of tax were the largest. The market principle has been
driven deeper into society. No Western industrialised country in
the twentieth century has been subjected to such fast and extensive
marketisation.

This is not to say that markets universally bring perverse
results; for the states in the CIS or the command economies in
the less developed world, a dose of privatisation and of market
principles are long overdue. Yet each step in the process has to
be carefully sequenced, skilfully executed and above all actively
managed. Markets are living organisms, and they malfunction
very easily.

Above all they must be placed in the social and political institutional complex in which they work. It is no use, for example,
invoking the dynamism of the US economy in generating jobs as
proof that such policies would work in all circumstances, in all
countries. The US is a continental economy that grew around the
realities of geographic, economic and social mobility. If it creates

jobs very rapidly, it destroys them equally quickly. In 1988 2 per cent of Americans became unemployed in a month compared with 0.4 per cent of Europeans.[12]

Nor are the social consequences of US labour-market policy notably beneficial (see Chapter 10). Job insecurity is endemic, and wages for the bottom 10 per cent of the labour force are around 25 per cent lower than they are for the same group in Britain. To reproduce the American labour market here, average wages for the bottom 10 per cent in Britain would have to fall by close to £100 per week – and workers would have to become accustomed to holding jobs for months rather than years.

The effect of such poverty wages in the US has been profound. Nearly one job in every five in the US does not carry sufficient income to rear a family of four.[13] The impact on families is notorious; violence, crime and despair disfigure American society. Poverty wages are an incentive to many unskilled people, especially black workers, to leave the orthodox labour market altogether and look for higher incomes in the rough economy of the streets.

The volatility of the US labour market is reflected in the instability of the financial system. The 'hollowing out' of US industry, so that much production is undertaken abroad, is due to the intersection of two things: a growing pool of unskilled casual labour and firms hungry for high returns. Yet the climate of risk and insecurity also brings advantages; if the financial system is oriented to high returns, it is also willing to take substantial gambles on new technology and new products.

In trying to copy the USA the British have ended up with the worst of both worlds. We have neither the dynamism of the US or of East Asia, nor European institutions of social cohesion and longterm investment. Britain has imported the mechanisms by which risk and insecurity are increased for those least able to bear it, while retaining a financial system that combines demands for high returns with minimal acceptance of risk. With European levels of unemployment and American levels of working poor, Britain has unleashed the processes that have hollowed out American industry without any compensating dynamism.

Why is the British experience so poor?

The British experience shows that while it may be true that markets are necessary conditions for efficiency and wealth generation, by themselves they are not sufficient.

Markets are embedded in a network of social and political institutions which give them values and priorities. In this respect capitalist economies must all be seen as inter-related systems facing a similar problem; there are contracts which can be mediated by the classic incentive of price but there are also aspects of business relationships which cannot and should not be mediated by price. The relationship of trust, for example, between a banker and an entrepreneur; the belief that a supplier can meet an order; the capacity to sustain a team of people around a business objective: all require trust, commitment and co-operation. The degree to which an economy's institutions succeed in underpinning trust and continuity is the extent to which longterm competitive strength can be sustained. Above all, the structure of the collectively-organised institution *par excellence* – the state – is a determinant of economic performance as important as the flexibility of prices. (In Chapters 9 and 10 the theoretical underpinning of this argument is explored in more detail.)

Whether it is contemporary East Asian capitalism or the German model of the social market economy, the behaviour of the economy can only be understood in terms of the whole of each country's social and political system and where it stands in the global order. Japan's longterm banking institutions, its system of lifetime employment, creative sub-contracting and extraordinary manufacturing productivity fit together – and its phenomenal export growth could not have been achieved without the access to US markets encouraged by the Americans during the Cold War to hold Japan in the western orbit. The German system of vocational training, decentralised democracy, its longterm banking and strong welfare state also work as a whole.

So while there is always a tension between the need for adjustment in a market economy and the need for continuity and commitment, both the Germans and Japanese have found ways of reconciling this tension successfully. Despite widespread criticism in Britain of both countries for their apparent inflexibility during the recession years, it is more likely that their institutions will continue to succeed in resolving this tension better than their counterparts in Britain, which make little or no attempt to capture gains from co-operative effort. The German and Japanese commitment to investment, and their workforces' depth of skill, are sources of inbuilt competitive advantage.

In this respect the New Right reforms since 1979 have tackled the consequences, rather than the root causes of Britain's decline. The attack on trade unions and the public sector was addressing a second order problem; the real problem was the systematic failure to invest in ideas, people and innovation. This shortcoming was not based on over-mighty unions or excessive public expenditure, although both magnified the underlying problem, but on the fact that the British private sector has always demanded too high a real rate of return on its investment. So it is that Britain's capital stock per worker is the lowest of the leading industrialised nations.

The British economy is organised around a stock-market-based financial system and clearing banks averse to risk. Disengaged, uncommitted and preoccupied with liquidity, the financial system has been uniquely bad at supporting investment and innovation. The New Right reforms did not address this issue at all; indeed financial deregulation and liberalisation made it worse. Herein lies the chief economic reason for Britain's disappointing performance.

Bound up with the financial system is the system of company law and corporate governance, organised to emphasise the pursuit of short-term profit as companies' sole operational goal. Companies are the fiefdoms of their boards and sometimes just of their chairmen; and companies are run as pure trading operations rather than productive organisations which invest, innovate and develop human capital. The structures that favour lean production and co-operative relationships between workers, suppliers and financial backers are extraordinarily weak.

What binds together the British financial and corporate system is a particular value system – 'gentlemanly capitalism' – that places particularly high social status on the less risky, invisible sources of income generated in trading and financial activity rather than production.[14] The ideology of the free market has been interpreted through this social filter. Footloose institutional shareholders and boards alike demand business strategies that boost the short-term share price.

This uncommitted financial system could not have survived without Britain's unique unwritten constitution and its quasi-feudal state handed down intact from the seventeenth century. Its lack of checks and balances has produced the most centralised state in the industrialised world. The effects of the market experiment have been most pervasive in Britain because the political system allows a determined government to do what it will without let or hindrance.

More than that, British public authority is incapable of being anything other than top-down and centralised. Constructive forms of intervention and public/private partnerships, used in other capitalist countries to capture the gains from co-operation, have worked much less well in Britain. The state has developed a rentier culture that complements 'gentlemanly capitalism', in which the state stresses the financial virtues of balanced budgets and financial targets over investment and production. The market becomes the engine of economic and social organisation because the state is incapable of delegating authority. Britain has been unable to construct the dense skein of intermediate public institutions between the centralised state and the market that other successful capitalist economies possess.

This political and financial structure is uniquely exposed to the vagaries of the international economy, in particular the development of a global financial market and the demands of trans-national producers, and this is the final reason for Britain's unique experience. The City of London developed its historic role within the empire to become the premier international financial centre. It kept this role when the Cold War offered it the chance of replacing British free trade and the gold standard, under which it had flourished in the nineteenth century, with Gatt and the dollar standard. When North Sea oil came on stream, allowing sterling to resume hard-currency status, the City was perfectly poised to exploit international financial deregulation to help create and become the centre of the new global market.

The profits from the City's international role explain its arms-length relationship with British industry and give extra weight to its demands for deregulation. The powerful voice of the international financial community has helped to sanctify the New Right's calls for budgetary austerity, free trade, and price stability. Economic analysts from the great City investment houses regularly broadcast the capital markets' incantations on TV and radio.

The UK's flows of inward and outward investment are the highest in relation to national output for any industrialised country. Britain invests more overseas than others, but also receives more inward investment. Therefore its own business community continually emphasises the virtues of free trade and minimal regulation, and regards intervention in its affairs as obstructive. There are few business voices calling for British versions of the structures that work well in other capitalist economies; the country's role is to be a free-market, offshore financial centre and base for trans-national production. A disproportionate number of national newspapers are foreign-owned and also call for minimal intervention, low taxes and less involvement in Europe.

This cocktail of policies has set in train a self-reinforcing downward spiral. The City's domestic and international roles reinforce each other with their emphasis on short-term trading and bias against longterm investment. Even sectors that have hitherto been strong, like financial services and pharmaceuticals, are beginning to suffer from the same demands for high returns and quick pay-offs. The pre-modern state is the guardian of the whole, paradoxically using its centralised power to license the operation of the system which, because it has evolved from market choices, is said to represent the 'best' alternative.

The moral economy

Britain's national affairs are reaching explosive levels of stress. The individualist, *laissez-faire* values which imbue the economic and political élite have been found wanting – but with the decline of socialism, there seems to be no coherent alternative in the wings.

The Conservative response is to intensify the policies sending the economy and society towards the ultimate free market. The New Right lobby in the party, the press and the business establishment holds up some combination of Hong Kong and the US as the ideal economic model – and urges that a minimal welfare state, low taxation and little business regulation would allow the economy to take off into a virtuous circle of capitalist dynamism.

However, for a European country of 60 million people, this is a chimera. Capitalism requires the profit motive and a go-getting individualism if it is to function, but it also takes place within inherited social and political boundaries. It is not just that capitalism needs rules to function effectively; the firms that are its life-blood are social as well as economic organisations. They are formed by human beings with human as well as contractual claims upon each other, and behind this social world lies the moral domain. Unless this is recognised economic performance is likely to be unsatisfactory.

For what binds together the disorders of the British system is a fundamental amorality. It is amoral to run a society founded on the exclusion of so many people from decent living standards and opportunities; it is amoral to run an economy in which the only admissible objective is the maximisation of shareholder value; it is amoral to run a political system in which power is held exclusively and exercised in such a discretionary, authoritarian fashion. These exclusions, while beneficial in the short-term to those inside the circle of privilege, are in the long run inefficient and ultimately undermine the wealth-generating process.

Like a Russian doll, the task of reform has many layers. We need employment, which requires more capital stock and higher investment, which will be the most effective instrument for the social objective of bringing the marginalised back into the fold. And that in turn will involve the redistribution of income, perhaps even of work. Yet all these measures depend upon a recognition that rights – to consume now, to pay as little to the commonweal as possible, to satisfy desires instantaneously –

must be accompanied by responsibilities if we are to live in a good society. Without lower consumption there can be no investment for the future; without taxation there can be no infrastructure of public support from which all benefit.

Corrective economic and social policies and institutions that embody them presuppose a system of values; and that demands a political constitution in which public values and common interests can be defined.

This implies nothing less than the root and branch overhaul of the Westminster version of democracy. If markets require boundaries and rules of the game, they must be set by public agency – but if such intervention is disqualified by the belief that any public action necessarily fails, then the initiative cannot even reach first base. The state must act to assert common purpose; but unless the state enjoys legitimacy and expresses the democratic will, it can make no such claim.

The constitution of the state is vital not only for its capacity to express the common good but also as the exemplar of the relationship between the individual and the wider society. The extent to which the state embodies trust, participation and inclusion is the extent to which those values are diffused through society at large.

What is needed is the development of a new conception of citizenship. If a well-functioning market economy requires skilled workforces, strong social institutions like schools and training centres, and a vigorous public infrastructure, these cannot be achieved if the governing class cannot understand the values implicit in such bodies. And if creative companies orchestrate the voices of all stakeholders into a common enterprise, embodying such a conception in company law is impossible if the state is genetically programmed to view the business of governance as the exercise of sovereignty, and the duty of the governed to obey. Unqualified shareholder sovereignty and parliamentary sovereignty are two sides of the same coin.

To break out of this cycle of decline and to build co-operative institutions, Britain must complete the unfinished business of the seventeenth century and equip itself with a constitution that permits a new form of economic, social and political citizenship. Economic citizenship will open the way to the reform of our financial and corporate structures; social citizenship will give us the chance of constructing an intelligent welfare state based on active solidarity; and political citizenship opens the way to political pluralism and genuine co-operation. This idea of citizenship could subsume differences of gender and race, and instil a sense of obligation to our natural environment – a victim of uncontrolled economic forces.

This national effort will have to be matched by an international economic and political architecture more conducive to such developments. The burgeoning international marketplace – destabilising currency flows, using offshore havens to avoid tax – is hostile to expressions of common and public interest. Private interests have too easily slipped the national leash and have used the ungoverned world beyond national frontiers to undermine what they regard as tiresome, inefficient and bureaucratic efforts to assert the moral and social dimension in human affairs.

This escape from responsibility cannot and should not be allowed to become permanent. Unless Western capitalism in general and British capitalism in particular can accept that they have responsibilities to the social and political world in which they are embedded, they are headed for perdition. Paradoxically, the most likely consequences will be the closure of the very open markets that business most needs as societies seek to protect themselves from the destructive forces that unregulated capital can release – a reprise in the early twenty-first century of the conditions Karl Polanyi described in the early part of this century. Societies were atomised by free markets that were then policed by centralised states and willed into being the supposedly protective forces of communism and fascism. That kind of breakdown, and those desperate authoritarian attempts to repair it, must be avoided today. The demand for a moral economy is not simply the assertion of a different value system. It is a call to arms in a world in which time is running short.

2. The Conservative Supremacy

Mrs Thatcher was the conviction politician whose good fortune was to become leader of the Conservative Party at the right time. Fifteen years earlier and her prejudices would have disqualified her from running a state still committed to Keynesian economics and attempted social consensus. Fifteen years later and the exhaustion of the bounty from the North Sea along with the evaporation of the intellectual climate in which she flourished would have made her contribution irrelevant to the tasks of lowering consumption, raising investment and refashioning social integration that are the central British dilemmas. She was a creature of a very particular time. But that does not diminish her status or political achievement. She combined the instincts of the old Conservatism in which classic Toryism is rooted together with the New Right belief in markets and competitive individualism. As a result she invented a rhetoric which appealed as much to the England of ducal estates as to suburban Basildon, constructing an alliance which won three successive elections and proved durable enough to allow her successor to win a fourth in exceptionally unpropitious circumstances.

Moreover the policies she forged seemed apparently successful in addressing Britain's problems – notably inflation and deteriorating international competitiveness. In the late 1980s it really looked as though her programme of deregulation, privatisation and tax cuts had begun to transform the British economy. Her aggressive assertion of British interests in Europe and in the Falklands War, together with her status as broker of the Cold War *détente* added to her lustre, appealing to the ancient British totems of empire and Britain as a great power.

In the process she managed to serve the interests of both wings of her coalition. Although her admirers like to believe that she launched an assault on the old establishment, this radical exponent of the New Right left the old Tory network of the military, public schools, the law, the City and the landed interest immeasurably stronger. The liberal professions, affluent council house tenants and homeowners all benefited from her tax cuts, credit boom and privatisation programme. The powerful forces of social change in which people became more questioning of tradition and hierarchy and more ready to assert their individuality happily complemented the Thatcherite attachment to freer markets, greater choice and rampant individualism. The top-down, monolithic organisations of the Keynesian welfare state – from trade unions to compre-hensive schools and public housing estates – no longer met the spirit of the age; nor commanded the same allegiance. They were institutions from which the upwardly mobile wanted to escape – and Thatcherism was their ally.

There were powerful international forces compelling the econo-my to be managed in the manner she favoured. The rapidly developing global capital market wanted tight control of budget deficits and the dismantling of exchange controls that would enlarge the power of finance over industry. Both chimed with her instincts. She wanted to limit public spending as part of the larger aim of rolling back the state, created in the England of the post-war settlement. Freedom for finance was but the restoration of ancient privileges. Whether her allies came from home or abroad was a matter of indifference to her.

Her particular talent was that she spoke to a longstanding individualistic tradition in English life – so much so that one admirer, the late Shirley Letwin, claimed that Thatcherism must be understood less as a free-standing ideology than as the bind-ing of the English 'vigorous virtues' of self-sufficiency, energy, adventure and independence into a coherent political programme – and she deployed it in an effort to rejuvenate island capitalism. Impressed by the allegedly beneficial impact of individualism on the US economy Thatcher wanted to use the same life force to dynamise Britain, slaying the dragon of collectivism wherever she found it and aiming to create a situation in which entrepreneurship, the best of the old order and the upwardly mobile working class could happily co-exist.

Inflation, poor growth, and the disintegration of the nuclear family were all seen as the results of a degenerate collectivism, and in particular the restrictive institutions of the labour movement. Her object was to best it and reinvent a Britain that was true to what she imagined to be 'itself'.

This was a very special political philosophy. By laying simultaneous claim to tradition and market radicalism it was facing two ways at once, without addressing the reasons for Britain's poor economic performance. Indeed, as the prominent Cambridge sociologist Tony Giddens has argued, the free play of market forces has unleashed fundamental detraditionalising forces. These have undermined the institutions which are essential to the social solidity of conservative England – ranging from the royal family to the position of women as housewives and mothers – which the traditional Conservative sees as the basis for the Conservative Party's support. What is worse, the implementation of the project has perversely deepened the economy's failure.

That the high priestess of freedom gave herself more centralised power to implement her market reforms than any other prime minister this century is not a paradox. Post-war Conservatism had settled for continuing with Labour's 1945 settlement in a kind of 'grand bargain'; it allowed the essential structure of authority to be maintained whilst serving the Conservative project of preserving society's 'little platoons' (as the conservative philosopher Edmund Burke described them), even if it meant accepting such social democratic reforms as consultation with trade unions, the National Health Service and high marginal rates of tax. Mrs Thatcher was to have none of that. She used the state aggressively to attack the post-war settlement in the name of 'freedom', revoking her predecessors' bargain, which she regarded as 'wet' and a betrayal of conservatism. That required a state that could lend itself to such a task, and again she was fortunate that the British state was such a perfect instrument. For Mrs Thatcher shamelessly exploited the extraordinary powers that Britain's unwritten constitution gives the majority party in the House of Commons to achieve her ends. She pushed the system to its limits, using the traditional legitimacy offered by 'parliamentary sovereignty' (the doctrine that the power of Parliament – or rather the 'Crown-in-Parliament' – to make laws cannot be qualified by any other power) for her very untraditional ends. That the British system is a kind of plebiscitary democracy conferring near absolute power upon the office-holder neither troubled her conscience nor impeded her actions. She relied on another strength – the weakness of her parliamentary opponents and the British variant of socialism they espoused. By the late 1970s British Labourism, bringing together the disparate elements of non-conformism, trade unions, and scientific Fabianism, was a spent political force. It had succeeded neither in transforming society and economy along pure socialist lines nor in successfully using Keynesianism and consensual corporatism to manage capitalism well. Although it had particular British weaknesses, the Labour Party's problems were shared in the 1980s by most European socialist parties. If planning and public ownership were deemed to be inefficient, as seemed to be the case in an age in which the belief in markets carried all before it, it was no longer clear what a socialist party should aim to do nor how it should do it. On this issue the Labour Party split, a group of MPs rallying to the banner of what they saw as a genuinely social democratic party. In the British system a split of this kind is tantamount to political suicide. Only in 1994, with the election of Tony Blair to the Labour leadership, has the issue been resolved with Labour explicitly committed to developing a British social democracy.

Mrs Thatcher, for all these reasons, was therefore in a uniquely powerful position in 1979. Yet despite the claims of her propagandists at the time and her apologists later, her actual achievement was modest, even destructive – for in economic and political terms she did no more than entrench the vicious circles in which the country is trapped. She was only able to mask the full implications temporarily with a credit boom.

She may have had a strong desire to do the right thing, as Shirley Letwin argued, and wished to create the public good of a revitalised Britain. But whatever the motives, from the moment she took office she made a series of moves that strengthened the hegemony of her own party while reducing the political base of the Labour Party. The imperatives of party and economy coincided neatly, and unlike in other democracies there were no means of redress.

After more than fifteen years there is now an astonishingly low level of popular support for the policies she inaugurated. After a long period in office the Conservative Party has been corrupted by not having to win arguments, relying instead on its control of Parliament and a Conservative press to allow it to do what it will. As a result an increasing body of law, even in the government's own terms, is poorly designed – with the 1994 Criminal Justice Bill a notable example. Absolute power has become corrupting.

Much more seriously it is proving impossible for the Conservative Party to manage the inbuilt contradictions of Mrs Thatcher's political legacy. Conservative opinion is aware that the traditional institutions which it wants to protect, and which are the basis of its own support, are under irreversible assault. But it can do nothing to protect them without turning its back on the economic liberalism of the New Right and instead using the state in a more consensual paternalistic fashion. It knows that the free market programme has at best only partially succeeded, with increasingly destructive effects on social cohesion – but it is trapped by its own past into continuing the drive to subordinate everything to the market. It would love to relegitimise the traditional institutions of state and society, but is locked into a policy which involves the opposite.

There is thus a growing tension between the two wings of the Conservative coalition. The New Right wants to carry the revolution forward; an older and more cautious right wants to stop the clock and build a stable Conservative order around the current unstable position. Neither argument carries sufficient conviction to win a majority in the party or country.

European integration has become the stress point for this tectonic fault, with the New Right wing of the party increasingly persuaded that the Brussels system represents an obstacle to the aim of marketising Britain, a threat to the Thatcherite achievement. The older Tory viewpoint, aware of Great Power interests, the need for a hinterland in which the City can prosper and less troubled by the consensual aspirations of European conservatism, is prepared to arrive at an accommodation with whatever economic and political construction the mainland Europeans

propose – whether it is a single currency or a strengthened
European Parliament. Between these two wings there is no
longer a basis for an enduring compromise. The nature of Conservatism and the future of the state are scrambled in an unholy
brew.

The shortcomings of Britain's constitutional arrangements derailed the attempt at establishing a Keynesian social democracy
and divided the Labour Party. The Conservatives were tempted
by Labour's stalemate to impose market forces on society. This
too has failed, and now the Conservatives are dividing. A state
that in its heyday encouraged remarkably united major parties to
compete for office has now ceased to work. The parties that were
its pillars have become its victims.

Establishing the Conservative hegemony

There has not been such a determined effort, since the advent
of universal suffrage to use the machinery of the British state to
prosecute a particular party programme as that undertaken by the
modern Conservative Party. Every nook and cranny of the constitution has been exploited to consolidate the party's hold on power;
as far as possible implementation of its policies has been delegated
to those inside and outside government who actively support it.
The New Right has enlisted not just the British state structures but
the deep-seated conservatism embodied in Britain's economic and
political institutions and wider value system to support its cause.
The cachet of knighthoods and honours once bestowed on build-
ers of empire has been exploited to reward loyal back-benchers,
contributors to party funds or industrial tycoons.

In the early years of her administration Mrs Thatcher had to
move cautiously, not daring to instal her harder right-wing allies
(the so-called dries) beyond the key economic ministries but by the
fourth Conservative administration her successors could rely even
on nominees for executive agencies like the Funding Agency for
Schools to be Conservative supporters: pro-market, pro-choice,
against the post-war settlement, and using their position to exclude

other views.[1] As a self-conscious exercise in political hegemony Britain has witnessed nothing like it, and a kind of free market *nomenklatura* now runs affairs. Without the British constitution it could never have happened.

Only one thing is necessary to control the British state; a majority in the House of Commons. Even so debates must be negotiated, Bills must be processed and select committees must be hazarded. From the outset the Thatcherite Conservative Party set out to enlarge the executive's control of Parliament in every way it could. The so-called payroll vote of office-holding MPs who are compelled to support the government rose to over a hundred. The promise of honours and a sinecure on retirement or electoral defeat was offered, with a mushrooming range of executive agencies providing jobs to those who gave loyal service. When Keith Best MP, for example, was disgraced by using false names to apply for BT shares, he none the less became director of the Immigrants Appeal Panel through an appointments board headed by a former Conservative MP.

But as the executive tightened its grip on Parliament, so the quality of legislation deteriorated. The 1990 Broadcasting Bill, which unintentionally destabilised the entire ITV system by providing for the auction of TV franchises at widely varying prices, was voted against by only three Conservative members. That is only one of a long line of ill-drafted laws, stretching from the poll tax to the 1988 Social Security Act, that sailed through the legislative process more or less unscathed. As the Hansard Society reports, Bills are increasingly brought to the House of Commons so poorly drafted that they are partially rewritten as they progress through Parliament – a process reaching its apogee in the casual amendment in the House of Lords to the 1993 Trades Union Reform Act. This allows employers to discriminate against trade union members in pay and conditions, and was tagged on to the Bill only because the *Daily Mail* had lost a case to the NUJ at the time and wanted the law changed.

The use of the so-called 'Henry VIII amendment' in the 1994 Deregulation and Contracting Out Act, empowering the Secretary of State for the first time to repeal primary legislation relating to business regulation without referral to Parliament, is further evidence of the strengthening of the executive and the party's attitude to the parliamentary process.[2] Parliament as a deliberate legislative assembly and check on the executive has been reduced to a charade. A new breed of parliamentary consultants now specialise in mapping their clients' route through the parliamentary maze in order to tailor legislation to their own ends. And, as the MPs David Tredinnick and Graham Riddick showed in July 1994, useful questions can be planted to promote specific company interests – if the price is right. In October 1994 the practice proved to be even more widespread as two ministers, Tim Smith and Neil Hamilton resigned amid allegations that they too had asked questions in exchange for favours.

Conservative hegemony has radiated outwards from this unassailable position. The House of Lords as a revising second chamber has delivered the odd rebuff, but alongside the role of second chambers in other democracies its democratic credentials and pretensions are laughable. Hereditary peers still cast close to half the votes, with three-quarters voting regularly in support of the Conservative government – and half of the life peers vote the same way.[3] Thus the Lords' essentially pro-Conservative bias has ensured the passage of even the most controversial legislation. The famous occasion of the backwoodsmen turning up to vote for the poll tax, registering the second largest turn-out ever in the modern history of the House, is a sharp reminder of where the second chamber's sympathies lie.

The locus of executive decision-making in the British constitution is the cabinet, but it has proved to be a pliable instrument – used by the prime minister of the day either to tie ministers to government decisions or exclude them by delegating decision-making to various cabinet sub-committees. Cabinet government under Mrs Thatcher was a farce, in which substantive issues were almost never discussed. The debate and decision over ERM membership, for example, never went to full cabinet,[4] while the decision to allow the use of British bases for the US bombing of Libya was made by Mrs Thatcher in consultation with just three ministers.[5] Mr Major is more disposed to use the cabinet than his predecessor but largely because of his political weakness and the need to minimise the chance of party dissent. A collective cabinet decision binds all strands of opinion to the government, preventing dissenting ministers from taking an independent line. Cabinet government in Britain neither broadens the political base of decision-making beyond the regional and electoral constituency of the party in power nor improves its efficiency; it is but one more component in the smooth running of the hegemonic machine.

The Civil Service has offered little resistance to these developments: indeed the constitutional fiction that it serves the Crown means in the British context that it serves ministers of the Crown – and if ministers are minded ruthlessly to bend the state to serve hegemonic party ambitions the Civil Service must go along with them. There is no constitutional protection of a public interest that transcends party concerns because no conception of the public interest exists independently of what the government defines it to be.

Examples of the compromises made by public servants abound – ranging from the Treasury's payment of part of Norman Lamont's legal fees in the dispute over the letting of his house to a sex therapist, to the use of officials to cost Labour's spending plans in the run-up to the 1987 and 1992 general elections, to the willingness to use official immunity to shield ministers from legal probing in the Matrix Churchill affair. Yet all this forms the tip of the iceberg of politicisation, in which senior officials have become activists for highly partisan policies. The Permanent Under-Secretary at the Department of Health advocated publicly the creation of hospital trusts before the 1992 election. More than thirty changes to the definition of unemployment have been devised by officials at the Department of Employment. They have served ministers well in designing successive Employment Acts – amongst the other objectives is the weakening of the ability of trade unions to finance the Labour Party. Officials may complain that under current constitutional arrangements they have no choice; but that is precisely the point. Current constitutional arrangements are what allows the establishment of party hegemonies.

Nor has the judiciary – the third branch of government –

thrown up many obstacles to a party with hegemonic ambitions. 'The judges', as Sir Ian Gilmour writes, 'were lambs under the throne.' The longstanding tradition of Britain's judiciary being more executive-minded than the executive, in Lord Atkin's famous dictum, came into its own in the 1980s with the law providing almost no refuge from the ambitions of the Conservative Party to enlarge the centralising powers of the state. The judges went along with the government's efforts to ban *Spycatcher*, and local authorities found that they had no redress for the various initiatives that curtailed their autonomy, entrenched by custom and practice but not by law.

The Lord Chancellor, a member of the cabinet, appoints the judges who come from the same milieu as his party colleagues while the government's chief law officer, the Attorney General, is also drawn from the ranks of the governing party. The lack of a formal separation of powers is compounded by the judiciary and Conservative Party hierarchy largely sharing an education, culture and outlook. Judges appoint other judges in their own image, while the criminal justice system is increasingly involved in maintaining public order. The 1994 Criminal Justice Act increased central government's control of the police, weakening their accountability to local authorities and giving them enhanced discretionary powers over Britain's public spaces. It is the culmination of a fifteen-year process.

With the core organs of the state under party control, the business of economic and political transformation could proceed apace. Royal commissions were forgotten, and those few attempts at soliciting information beyond the ranks of the New Right ideologues acting as advisers to ministers were packed with appointees who would produce the 'right' result – the Peacock Inquiry into broadcasting being a classic of the genre.

Intermediate institutions that even faintly expressed an alternative political agenda have been summarily subordinated to the will of the centre. The capacity of local authorities for revenue-raising and autonomous spending decisions has been whittled away so that they are ciphers of central government, with areas such as education and housing progressively transferred to opted-out trusts.

The Greater London Council and other metropolitan counties were simply abolished, with Norman Tebbit openly acknowledging that the reason for disbanding the GLC was because it was 'Labour-dominated, high-spending and at odds with the government's view of the world.'[6] Contracting out and the surrender of the remaining authorities' operations to outside contractors have been forced through, whatever the political complexion or track record of the authority concerned – and Lord Bridge made it clear in a famous case that the law could and would not offer any defence of local autonomy.

'No similar challenge', he said, referring to Hammersmith and Fulham's attempt to contest the legitimacy of capping local authority spending, 'has any prospect of success unless an authority is in a position to show that the Secretary of State has acted in bad faith or for an improper motive or can point to some failure to comply with the procedural requirements which the Act clearly spells out.'[7] In short, once the majority party in the House of Commons has passed an Act that is the end of the matter. There is no countervailing principle to contest its legitimacy however absurd, undemocratic or partisan the result. The will of the minister is absolute.

This power is monarchical even if it is legitimised by the winning of periodic elections; and the restless search for hegemony has explored every loophole of the constitution to ensure that the Conservative Party wins general elections – the only remaining barrier to a complete one-party state. Local authorities have been deterred by lack of finance from ensuring that their electoral rolls, depleted by voters failing to register and so escape the poll tax, are complete – so reducing the Labour vote. This, it is estimated, cost Labour a minimum of six seats in the 1992 election and the Liberal Democrats two. On the other hand some millions of pounds are spent in organising the registration of the much smaller number of British voters living abroad, who are generally Conservative – and their votes are diverted if possible to a handful of marginal constituencies, worth possibly two seats in 1992. The ability to time elections to maximise party advantage, the gross imbalance in party funding permitted by secret contributions which favour the Conservative Party, and the loyalty of the press all contribute to the same end. Even small matters like the availability of the best poster sites are not left to chance, they too are usually reserved for the Conservatives by supporters in the advertising business.

The neat coincidence between ideological conviction and party advantage has also proved its worth in the attack on the nationalised industries – the more the privatisation programme extends from the utilities into the marrow of central government, the deeper the purge of the old cadre of 'one-nation' managers serving some notion of the public interest. The party has invented a new cohort of managers loyal to economic efficiency, as measured by a calculus of profit and loss, and aware of every implication for the share price of their company and thus their own share options. The privatised utilities, once a lobby for public investment and the common good, are now members of the Conservative business establishment – even contributors to Conservative Party funds – while public sector unions have been reduced in stature and influence. The crucial mirror image of the consolidation of Conservative hegemony has been the undermining of its Labour counterpart.

In London, for example, the Labour Party calculates that 272 new quangos now govern in place of the old Labour-controlled Greater London Council – and their complexion is openly Conservative. There are 1,675 quango members in London; and only 1,900 local authority councillors. Lord Sheppard, the chairman of London First, a group of businessmen charged with representing London's interests to the government, is a major contributor to the party. And Wales, a country in which the Conservatives hold only six out of 38 parliamentary seats, is run by a Conservative Secretary of State appointing 1,400 people to 80 quangos.

On one estimate there are over 70,000 public appointments which now can be made at the discretion of government ministers[8] and the number is set to explode further. The chief executives and chairmen of these bodies are nearly all conservative, with their 'non-political' business members tending to be conservative as well. A survey of 185 National Health Service Trust chairmen, for example, found that 62 were Conservative councillors, former Tory MPs, Conservative workers or had strong links with the party.[9] Businessmen and women chair three-quarters of all

NHS Trusts. The country is returning to the nineteenth-century tradition of rule by a private oligarchy of unelected Conservatives discharging public duties – what Professor John Stewart of Birmingham University has described as 'the new magistracy'.

Where honours are not available, there is always the chance of business favours. The chief beneficiaries of the foreign orders generated by the overseas aid programme turn out to be the large contributors to the party. There are pickings from privatisation to be made by investment banking supporters in the City.

Accusations of electoral gerrymandering are resurfacing for the first time since the nineteenth century. The district auditor has said that the sale of council houses by Westminster Council in the late 1980s was organised to produce in-built Conservative majorities in key wards, while in Scotland the Secretary of State is changing the constituency boundaries to protect the vanishing electoral fortunes of his party.

The partisanship of the press at election times, and in between elections the denigration of public institutions and the celebration of market solutions, has been hugely useful to the regime. The editors of the tabloids, whose 'political' coverage has become ever more indefensible in terms of any standard of journalistic independence or integrity, have been knighted by Mrs Thatcher and well-paid by their proprietors for their services.

The key signal was given in 1981 when Rupert Murdoch was allowed to buy the *Sunday Times* and *The Times* without any reference to the Monopolies Commission on the spurious grounds that they were loss-makers and that Mr Murdoch's purchase could not be delayed – even though the purchase meant that News International, the Murdoch holding company, would control nearly a third of the circulation of the British national press.[10] In a ruleless state there can be no rules that qualify foreign ownership of British newspapers. *The Times*'s system of 'national directors' aimed at supporting editorial independence was quickly buried – the Companies Act does not provide for strong non-executive directors, so they had no legal standing at *The Times* any more than they had anywhere else. Mr Murdoch, as Harold Evans describes, duly delivered his papers to the Conservatives. Later in the decade he was to be allowed to own a satellite station, Sky TV, and allowed to ignore the regulatory regime applying to land-based broadcasters. This Australian-turned-American now enjoyed unique extra-terrestrial favours.

Conservative newspapers account for 70 per cent of all newspapers sold, a result produced not by competition in the market but by manipulation of the ownership rules by Conservative press tycoons. Television has hardly provided a robust counter-weight. The appointment of Marmaduke Hussey as chairman of the BBC was an important move in the securing of Conservative control of the media. A pro-Thatcherite Euro-sceptic, he quickly installed John Birt as deputy director-general with a brief to clean up the corporation's news and current affairs output – code for removing any lingering anti-government bias. Under the guise of reinventing the BBC's impartiality Birt, who became director-general in December 1992, moved its coverage rightward to harmonise with the centre of gravity established in the written press. Kept on short rations, with its licence fee indexed to the growth of prices rather than wages, and kept guessing about the terms of the renewal of its charter, the BBC has not been eager to demonstrate its independence. And if it had any doubts, the five new governors nominated in 1993 were all carefully selected by the Prime Minister – after the first round of nominees had been rejected.

Meanwhile, the independent TV companies, shaken by the consequences of the franchise auction and the aggressive appetite of the franchisees for big audiences, are progressively abandoning any objective other than growth of audience share, as plans for the relegation of News at Ten to the early evening highlighted – though public disquiet caused them to be shelved. Television's mission to educate and inform is in decline; the fourth estate's critical scrutiny of the government in the name of the citizen is ever less evident.

Meanwhile old Conservative allies in finance and industry have rallied ever more openly to the cause. The former director-general of the National Economic Development Office, Sir Geoffrey Chandler, has described graphically how the CBI was a reliable ally in neutering every constructive attempt to advance a purposeful approach to manufacturing industry and training.[11]

'Its diverse membership, the contribution of some member companies to Conservative Party funds, the seduction and flattery of senior industrialists by private meetings with ministers, and, for some, the hope of honours, all helped to muffle the CBI as an independent industrial voice,' he writes. The CBI fully deserved its reputation as the 'Tory Party at work' by its public support for the party during the 1987 and 1992 election campaigns, he adds. By the late 1980s, 'having not barked, let alone bitten, for years', the then Chancellor, Nigel Lawson, could safely 'pat its titular leader on the head', praising the organisation for understanding the climate needed for business success.

The rival Institute of Directors, based more on the service sector, the self-employed and small business, has been a powerful advocate of low taxation and the minimal state – while the City finance houses have supplied pundits by the score intoning the virtues of sound money and spending cuts. The hegemony is almost total. No non-Conservative can expect any influential public appointment, and this rule extends to those factions in the Conservative Party critical of its current ideological bent. Similar strictures apply with almost equal force in the private sector: for the economically and socially ambitious there is only one route to the top.

The party of nature

The social buttresses of Conservatism have established it across swathes of middle-class England as an essentially non-political party. Support for Labour or the Liberal Democrats is regarded as *political* because both parties advocate change – and Labour in particular is an outsider, whereas support for Conservatism is like supporting the Townswomen's Guild or the Chamber of Commerce. Nothing could be more natural. Helena Kennedy recounts that early in her career as a barrister, she was advised not to mix law and politics; her interlocuter was a Conservative MP.[12] Loyalty to Conservatism is not political, it is the instinct of the upper middle class.

The Conservative Party is part of the bedrock of English life and its object is widely understood as finding middle England's centre of gravity and ensuring that no other party endangers middle England's pleasures and privileges. At least part of the historic point of Conservatism is to occupy office to prevent others from making changes. It is an essentially negative project.

In this the party is helped immensely by its possession of a series of cultural icons to which it lays exclusive claim. It remains the gentlemen's party, with its representatives not merely resonating competence and a good-mannered sense of obligation to the common weal, but above all believing that they are born to rule. Indeed, to the extent that the object of upward mobility in Britain remains one's acceptance as a gentleman (or lady), loyalty to the Conservative Party is one sign of success. Almost everyone wants to be a gentleman; the Conservatives are gentlemen; ergo aspiring to gentlemanliness means being Conservative.

The gentlemanly ideal reaches far back into British life, with historians like Cain and Hopkin arguing that it was the animating force in the rise of British capitalism. The landed aristocracy used the seventeenth-century constitutional revolution to secure their hold on Parliament and the state, so that their social prestige and economic power was combined with growing political muscle. The ambitious and the energetic naturally wanted to join their ranks, which meant not only having a source of income that was gentlemanly in its origin but adopting the same manners as that class.

A gentlemanly income was necessarily one for which the recipient did not labour too obviously. Ideally it came from land, but the next best thing was income from interest, dividends and professional fees so that money made from finance and commerce in the City was nearly as good as acres in the shires. Manufacture was less socially desirable, and although manufacturers and inventors were briefly celebrated in the middle of the nineteenth century the old values quickly reasserted themselves. Those who made money in trade were anxious to distance themselves from its source, and ease their way into the ranks of gentlemen.

In this social configuration the monarchy remained a central element, the focus of the social world and the fount of prestige. The Lords-Lieutenant in the counties, the monarch's representatives, were another magnet of local gentlemanly ambition. The army attracted gentlemen to man its upper echelons, and it too reached out into the Court and county society. The Church of England as the monarch's church personified a gentlemanly Christianity, and its bishops and prelates, by their presence in the House of Lords and inter-marriage with the gentry, had both political and social weight.

The legal system too is an essential wellspring of Conservative domination. From the courts to London's chambers of barristers, the system is bound by elaborate rituals and encrusted with tradition. Almost alone, the law was untouched by the nineteenth-century wave of reforms. The first loyalty of these archaic bodies is less to justice than to the maintenance of order interpreted through the seamless web of English case law accumulated over centuries.

This self-reinforcing network – monarch, church, the law, the City, the army and the landed aristocracy – came to represent the gentlemanly ideal and thus England itself. Educated in the main at the great public schools, its denizens were above and not part of society. They shared a similar world view and spoke a common language whose accent – received pronunciation – was the hallmark of good breeding and of the self-confidence that comes from being groomed to rule. Manufacturers and rich immigrants aspired to join their ranks, and their party was the Conservative Party.

This was the tradition which Mrs Thatcher inherited in the mid-1970s, which had its heartland in London, the Home Counties and across the south of England. Here were 261 constituencies which, even in the middle of the longest post-war recession at the 1992 general election, were ready to return 209 Conservative MPs – the backbone of the parliamentary Conservative Party. They are lineal descendants of the great tradition and, although they may not be very gentlemanly any more, their electorates recognise the integrity of their Englishness and their essential nationalism – expressed in everything from their accent to the schools they attended. At the end of the twentieth century the Conservative nexus retains its tribal grip on the imagination and institutions of the English.

The apex of this system remains the Court, where the aristo-cracy continues to serve the Queen in a series of functions whose ridiculous Ruritanian names – Silver Sticks, Crown Equerries and so on – mask the political and social importance of the informal Conservative networks at whose centre these positions place them. For example, Lady Susan Hussey, woman of the bedchamber, is the sister of a Conservative cabinet minister (William Waldegrave) and the wife of Marmaduke Hussey, the chairman of the BBC.[13] The military, great landowners and old City families congregate at the informal centre of Conservative England; their networks – all tied into the party – offer them advancement in regiments, City investment houses, the Inns of Court and boardrooms alike.

In the counties the Court's social power is replicated in minia-ture through the networks of Lords-Lieutenant. Invitations to their social events are eagerly sought. They are almost universally conservative – some actively tout for contributions to Conserva-tive Party funds. They act as directors of companies, oversee local charities and now manage the new executive agencies, policing the unspoken code. What could be more non-political, after all, than a Lord-Lieutenant?

The social depth of these icons, and their political significance, are often missed – above all by the British left. Their occasions and places range from the sports events of the English summer Season – Ascot, Wimbledon, Henley, Derby Day, Lords and Badminton – to the Royal Opera House or the Court of the Bank of England. What gives the sports events their distinction is their combination of excellence and their links to the world of Court and county, which in turn confers aristocratic English grace on them.

The upper echelons of each milieu are inhabited by gentlemen and gentlewomen whose reflex actions are the same. Educated apart and socially apart, they have no republican sense of civic responsibility. Their world is private. Their manners are culti-vated. A studied and amused disinterestedness is their hallmark. Above all they are self-confident. Long before opting out was exalted to the status of a political philosophy, these were the opted out.

The two key entrance tickets to this world are education and family. The public schools remain nurturers of Conservative gentlemen, combining the intense intellectual and social training that permits both examination success and the badge of gentle-manliness. After Oxford or Cambridge – 96 of 111 applicants from Eton to Oxford gained admission in 1993, for example[14] – there are the professions, the City or even a career in the party itself. You do not even have to be a party member to understand that the party's job is to protect your position, manage the economy in your interests and so serve middle England.

During the twentieth century, it has done remarkably well. The Conservative Party has a good record of avoiding economic traumas, generating nice economic booms and preserving English institutions. Until Britain's expulsion from the ERM on Black Wednesday it had managed to avoid responsibility for the three great devaluations of 1949, 1967 and 1976 which were all carried out by the Labour Party. The 1950s, early-1960s, early-1970s and mid-1980s were all years when consumption grew unsustainably and it fell to Labour governments to organise the necessary adjust-ment after each period of unsustainable consumption growth.

There is also an implicit understanding that the great institu-tions of the state are at heart more comfortable with Conservative masters. The Treasury and the Bank of England are both lobbyists for the financial over the producer interest, benefiting the southern rentier – now often in the form of the great financial institutions – rather than the northern manufacturer. These values are so deeply engrained and legitimised by free-market economics that they are taken as accepted truths. Their practitioners no longer recognise their partisanship, how closely their ideas serve the Conservative interest – or even how their values are embedded in a wider conservative culture. Competence has been the prerogative of Conservatives. They govern, they manage the economy, and they set social standards. Such are the foundations of Conservative hegemony.

The weakness of Labour

That this entire structure has remained in place despite universal suffrage and three post-war Labour governments is tribute to the political innocence of the Labour Party and the poverty of its strategic thinking. It has sought to empower trade unions, extend public ownership, build a welfare state and organise a viable British Keynesianism as a means of transforming Britain but has left the wider social and political order intact, together with its value system. In effect social democracy has been bolted on to a fundamentally conservative constitution and wider institutional structure, which has blocked Labour's objectives. In 1979 true Conservatism could emerge from its canny post-war dormancy with revitalised energy.

Labour's inability to confront Britain's central political reality had two complex roots. The first was that the prospect of achieving majority control of the House of Commons seemed to offer the same pleasures of absolute government as the Conservatives enjoyed, so that the problem seemed to be not to reform the state but to gain control of it to serve Labour's purposes. The second was intellectual: Labour saw its objective as constructing a variant of British socialism, complete with public ownership of the means of production and entrenched rights for trade unions, before which British capitalism would necessarily retreat and change.

In this socialist perspective property rights and class interests were the determinants of power; and the constitution, social and cultural institutions were essentially the superstructure that depended upon private property relations. The Labour Party was never Marxist, but it allowed its thinking to be dominated by economic determinism. The state and its institutions were simply means to economic and social ends, whether in the form of public ownership or Keynesian tools of demand management. That the structure and culture of those state institutions might have a large bearing on the success of the economic and social enterprise was never considered.

The problem begins with the fluidity of the socialist ideal

which, as Berki has remarked, stands variously for the values
of 'freedom, equality, community, brotherhood, social justice,
the classless society, cooperation, progress, peace, prosperity,
abundance, happiness'. Within this pantheon of ideas capitalist reformers and revolutionaries alike can pitch their tents,
each claiming to be true guardians of the socialist flame. All
socialist parties are as a result haunted by sectarianism and
a permanent competition to be more socialist than each
other.

But this ambiguity reveals a deeper flaw and the failure to
resolve it still bedevils the British and European left. Even if
some minimum agreement can be reached on what constitutes
a socialist programme, that does not solve the basic problem.
How much can these objectives be secured within the framework
of existing capitalism, and how much do they require a wider
economic transformation? Is the aim to socialise capitalism – or
outright socialisation?

In fact, the Labour Party, born from the trade union movement and British non-conformism, was never likely to attempt
the socialist transformation of society. Trade unions were more
like professional associations or guilds of working men promoting
their interests within the existing order than instruments with
which to transform capitalism. Labour was a reformist party
aiming to socialise British capitalism and to alleviate the condition of the working class rather than build a socialist Britain.
The economy might need to be more scientifically organised
but nobody doubted the underlying fecundity of capitalism.
The object was to secure for the worker the product of his hand
and brain, and to buttress his security within a wider structure
of welfare. There seemed to be nothing essentially complex
about running an industrial economy; the urgent priority was
distributing its bounty more fairly.

The early socialists were also sure of the historical inevitability
of their success. It was not just that the working class were more
numerous, so that their votes outnumbered those of capitalists;
capitalism was a fundamentally irrational and wasteful process.
As the natural world had succumbed to the march of scientific

rationalism so must the human world – with socialism succeed-
ing capitalism. Planning and public ownership were expressions
of rationality in economic affairs. British free-market capitalism
was therefore doomed.

This utopianism also discouraged socialists in general from
thinking too much about democracy. The object was equality;
the means was planning; and the management of the economy
would be driven by scientific principles – Keynesian or Marxist.
Pure Marxists thought that after the revolution the state would
wither away, and certainly British socialists never gave the issue
much thought. Social justice required redistribution and public
ownership; control of the House of Commons would permit the
prosecution of both. Democracy or reforming the structure of the
state never ranked high on the socialist wish list. Neither Shaw
nor Keynes nor even Bevan ever doubted that the state would
do their bidding.

Yet this gap is perhaps the single most important cause of
the British left's undoing. Not only did it leave in place the old
constitutional structure, it disabled the left's internal organisation,
thinking and, more importantly, its capacity when in government
to achieve its goals.

The problems began with Labour's own constitution. Informed
by the idea of a socialist labour movement that does not need to
pay attention to bourgeois conceptions of one person-one vote, it
was disfigured by the trade union block vote. Its attempts while in
government to establish social partnership were properly regarded
with suspicion by business, which felt itself – not unreasonably –
to be an unequal partner with a government that regarded itself
as the political wing of the trade union movement. This, until
the recent extension of the franchise at the 1993 Labour Party
conference, championed by the then Labour leader John Smith,
seriously delegitimised the Labour Party's claim to govern in the
wider public interest.

Making a priority of redistribution and accepting a crude
economism, whether in the shape of demand management or
of nationalisation, never allowed the party to attack the social
and political roots of British capitalism – and thus its short-term

hostility to investment. It was typical, for example, that Labour should nationalise the Bank of England in 1946 to gain control of monetary policy yet leave in place its governing court. The nationalised Bank remained the voice of the financial interest in British government – paradoxically strengthened in its lobbying role by public ownership.

The welfare state was launched as the incorporation of a new form of social citizenship in a Britain where political citizenship had never been explicitly encoded in a written constitution. T.H. Marshall might have hailed the welfare state as the establishment of social rights to counter the polarising effects of capitalism, but the Beveridge blueprint of collective social insurance was a qualified and temporary advance. It was enacted in a society still ruled by the gentlemanly ideal of exclusion – even if it was out of reach for many – and where the political institutions exercised a discretionary sovereignty of the rulers over the ruled that negated any positive conception of citizenship. So from the beginning the welfare state was not embraced by the entire political class, but seen as something that a conservative state had created at its discretion, for sound reasons, without cutting across the principles upon which that state was founded. Indeed Beveridge made it plain that he saw the very concentration of power the state conferred as an advantage: it allowed a top down imposition of welfare.[15]

Rising prosperity was bound to make a growing proportion of the electorate attempt to express themselves like the gentleman class; to try to attend similar schools, live similar lifestyles and, of course, adopt the same disdainful attitude to those beneath them. Without either constitutional protection or the commitment of the political class, the welfare state would be vulnerable once the political circumstances of its creation had passed away. Britain had once produced the Poor Laws, in which the able-bodied poor had been stigmatised by confinement in workhouses; it had also operated the means-tested benefits of the 1930s. It was more than capable of reverting to type once the coalition supporting the reformed structure weakened.

The privileges given to trade unions were based in legislation and court judgements before the First World War which conceded that collective bargaining was above the common law; they were not achieved through concessions to working-class values or any conviction of the merits of trade unions and working-class representation. British employers still considered themselves sovereign stewards of their shareholders' assets, and saw no reason to concede participation or consultation with their workers unless forced to do so; trade unions, in the main, saw their role as confronting the power of organised capital rather than helping in its management. Collective bargaining was thus a trial of adversarial strength in which wages and better working conditions were won without changing any of the fundamental corporate structures in which people worked. There was no reason, once the trade unions lost their influence with the demise of British corporatism, for the state and employers to do anything other than withdraw the privileges the unions had enjoyed and rebalance this adversarial relationship in capital's favour.

The argument that the post-war reforms were vulnerable applied with even greater force to the nationalised industries. In the British system, which lacks any institutional expression of the public interest, it was impossible to have a model of a nationalised industry that was independent of the all-sovereign Parliament – which meant that the nationalised industries became part of the public bureaucracy directly responsible to the sponsoring minister. The state had little capacity to develop a tradition of public enterprise, because the objectives of the industries were political – variously supporting employment, investment, regional policy or prices and incomes policies. The conservative state guaranteed the ultimate failure of public ownership.

This did not prevent Tony Crosland, in the 1950s, from declaring that the welfare state, full employment and nationalisation had in effect achieved the socialist blueprint. Britain, he thought, was no longer a capitalist society. Yet even as he wrote, British corporatism was being crippled by the lack of any space in which the state could operate between the impotence of non-binding voluntarism and the rigidity of statutory intervention – as we will see when we examine the sad history of attempts to regulate industrial relations. Indeed, compared with the European corporatist model it is not clear that the British variant ever warranted the name. A succession of broken incomes policies with a reluctant business establishment looking on does not make corporatism; it constitutes failure.

The failure to tackle the structure of the British state grievously damaged the Labour Party's own agenda and worse still, it left untouched all the crucibles in which the Conservative reaction developed. British capitalism, *pace* Crosland, proved to be very much alive, from the City of London to the House of Lords, the public schools to the great landed estates. All were left intact as breeding grounds for the Conservative renaissance. And when it came, Mrs Thatcher found that every constitutional building block she required to establish her dominance had been left in place.

The Labour Party did not have the intellectual tools to fight back. Its vanguard socialists insisted that its problems lay in compromising with capitalism – a view that was hardly helpful given the lack of alternatives, but which retained immense political and rhetorical appeal. At the same time Labour reformists were in disarray, with the promises offered by Marshall and Crosland in ruins. The welfare state had not adapted to the changing position of women; it had engendered a culture in which rights were asserted with little accompanying sense of obligation; its spending implied a growing tax burden; and mass provision of homogenised education, housing, pensions and health failed to meet working-class demands for a degree of customisation and sensitivity to individual needs.

The unions were incapable of transcending their adversarial role and so any viable form of British Keynesian corporatism seemed impossible. There was no tradition around which ideas like workers' participation could take root; the unions and business were equally opposed to them. Meanwhile the tools of Keynesian economics were crumbling, as higher inflation and unemployment accompanied each economic cycle. The British economy was not responding to scientific intervention at either the macro or micro level, and new international forces were compelling change.

By the end of the 1970s there was a wider crisis in the idea of socialism as a scientific creed, and the capacity of science to improve the world. As Tony Giddens argues, the early-twentieth-century faith in the march of progress in the natural and human worlds was failing. The planned economies of Eastern Europe and the Soviet Union collapsed, and even in the less developed world it was increasingly clear that state-led development was inefficient and wasteful. As ideological competition in the Third World gave way to a new interest in markets and privatisation, even socialist impossibilists found themselves beleaguered. At home and abroad the message was the same. Twentieth-century socialism had failed. The people themselves were moving on. Mrs Thatcher's radical marketisation of Britain was met by a barrage of criticism, but there was no alternative model in sight.

Decline, fall and renewal?

1979, for all these reasons, was a crucial year. It was the moment when conservative England reclaimed its institutions and traditions from the attempt to bend them to a social democratic cause. Labour's weaknesses had made the 1974–9 government a dismal affair, even though it was battling against mountainous odds, and tensions over the nature of the socialist project finally led to the defection of over thirty MPs to the newly-formed Social Democratic Party in 1981.

But Labour's inadequacies were only part of the story. Of equal importance was the willingness of a growing number of natural Conservative sympathisers to sign up for the cause and in so doing to consolidate the hegemonic position of the Conservative Party. More and more businessmen, officials and opinion-formers began to line up behind Mrs Thatcher and her programme. This was partly because the credit boom gave it the illusion of success; but also because the language of free markets, sound money and individual choice had a profound resonance. Mrs Thatcher was speaking for a set of values that had existed long before the post-war consensus.

Sound money and limits on public spending implied no more

than a return to the orthodoxies of the 'Treasury view' that Keynes had mocked in the 1930s, while the promotion of competition, free trade and low taxation drew on a tradition that reached back to the eighteenth century. *The Economist*, for example, was as assiduous as the free-market think tanks in reaffirming the purpose for which it had been founded in the early 1840s; to fight vehemently for free trade.

Moreover, the teachings of neo-liberal economics, with the emphasis that the general good can only result from the free interplay of supply and demand, now seemed to be in harmony with the thinking of a straight-talking politician. And if one stream of economics, Keynesianism, contested the direction of policy on interest rates, taxation, spending, borrowing and the exchange rate, it broadly accepted that at the so-called micro level Mrs Thatcher's convictions were not misplaced. Resources were best allocated where there was more competition; government regulation did stand in the way of market forces; and trade unions did force up the price of labour. Keynesians might jib at the consequences of an overvalued exchange rate, for example, but they were not minded to attack moves to reduce trade union power or roll back the tide of nationalisation. For a determined ideologue the path to change was open – and history was on her side.

But something deeper was also at work. The British state had not been designed actively to intervene in economic management at either the national or local level. The Civil Service tradition that officials should not engage in private sector activity remained strong and, unlike France or Germany, Britain had made no systematic attempt to train a class of officials competent in commerce and finance. The accent was still placed on administration rather than intervention; on high policy rather than commercial strategy.

So the state had no apparatus for making British industrial policies work and its efforts were undermined by a latent value system always ready to return to an earlier relationship between state, society and economy. Once Keynesianism had been discredited, Mrs Thatcher's job was more to disinter *laissez-faire* than to reinvent it. The England of Adam Smith, John Stuart Mill and

Herbert Spencer had been submerged by the rise of Keynes, the welfare state and the attempt at government direction of the economy, but it had not been extinguished.

Once uncovered, these foundations supported fifteen years of building Conservative hegemony. But the theory was to prove a poor master and the results disappointing. Indeed, by the middle of the 1990s Mrs Thatcher's bargain was looking more Faustian than Hayekian. Mephistopheles, in the person of economic underperformance and social fragmentation, would collect in full from her party. Although her programme had enriched some individuals vastly, it had not produced any generalised good for the party, economy or wider society.

In this respect the early socialist critics of the degenerate and exploitative character of unalloyed British capitalism had been right. If the social democratic settlement of the post-war years had not delivered the economic growth enjoyed by other industrial powers, it had at least reined in the worst impulses of British short-termism, along with its violent economic cycles and structural unemployment. In doing so, it had maintained social order and, paradoxically, preserved the institutions of Conservative England better than Conservative England was able to do when given its head – an irony lost on Mr Major when he mourns the lost world of the 1950s. The stable communities of that era were not produced by flexible labour markets, a minimal welfare state and the sanctification of the market principle.

Mrs Thatcher's radicalism was in this respect regressive, taking British social cohesion for granted while recreating the conditions that in the early part of the century had endangered the very social order she purported to admire. The Conservatives she dismissed as wets had saved Conservative England. Core conservative values such as good parenting, dedication to community, deference and home-ownership are threatened by a whirlwind of casualisation of work and uncertainty – let alone the impact of the accompanying social changes on church, court, monarchy and the military.

Yet the clock cannot be put back – nor should it be. The post-war settlement may have stopped the rot, but it did not solve the basic British problem. Keynesian economics as practised in the UK had limits. Industrial policy was not a success; incomes policies were an ignominious failure. The welfare state was creaking at the seams, unable to meet the new demands placed upon it. Productivity growth was poor. It is true that income inequality narrowed and wealth became more equitably distributed and that, compared with what went before and what was to follow, the period can appear like a Golden Age. But even within its own terms it was unsustainable.

If Britain cannot go back, to continue on the present path offers little but increased social polarisation, political authoritarianism and economic weakness. The aim of the chapters ahead is to unravel what has gone wrong and why; to show what the true economic problems actually are; to demonstrate how closely tied they are to social and political institutions and forces; and to attempt to map a way forward. It is a first stab at an alternative future, and nothing more – but it is rooted in a conviction that there are other values apart from conservatism and New Right economics that merit and deserve expression. And so we begin where we must, with the story of the rise of British finance, its ideology and international connections.

3. Finance Unbound

Ideas travel ever faster; economies are ever more interdependent. The Renaissance and Reformation were a common European experience, as were colonies and empire as Europe expanded abroad. In the twentieth century the depression of the 1930s, the rise of Keynesian economics and the long post-war boom were shared by all industrialised countries. It was never likely that Mrs Thatcher and the rise of the New Right would be an isolated British phenomenon. Nor were they.

Over the 1980s the march of the pro-marketeers and anti-statists circled the globe. Their ideas both reflected and gave added impetus to the new direction in which the international economy was moving. By the 1990s they had helped to create the beginnings of a truly internationalised market. Capital can now flow freely within the EU and between Europe, Japan and North America. The flows have grown exponentially. In 1992, for example, the stock of international bank assets was more than double the volume of world trade; thirty years earlier they were only fractionally more than 10 per cent of world trade.[1] Trading in currencies takes place twenty-four hours a day. Multinationals have global production and distribution networks. The stock of inward investment as a proportion of the developed countries' national output has nearly doubled in twenty years, and now stands at more than 10 per cent of GDP.[2] Private capital and private corporations have never before so influenced the world economy.[3] Capitalism as a system has no competitors.

Yet the dark side of this internationalisation of production and exchange is rising unemployment throughout the industrialised West, and particularly in the EU. Unemployment has increased six times since the first oil shock of 1973, when it stood at around 2 per cent of the labour force, to today's 12 per cent. Although the US has created more jobs it too has been hit by the whirlwind blowing through the industrialised countries' labour markets. The counterpart of this job creation has been that the real wage for its manual workers has scarcely risen for twenty years, while for the bottom 10 per cent real wages have fallen by a third. As a result the gap between the rich and poor in the US has widened dramatically.

Some of the features of the British economy – high unemployment, the growth of inequality, the attempt to reduce the role of the state through privatisation and spending cuts, the containment of the welfare state, the sharp increase in imports, the falling proportion of manufacturing output – can be said to be general trends throughout the industrialised West. What happened and is still happening in Britain is a special case, certainly; but without the recent evolution of the world economy and the ideas that rationalised it, the particularly hair-raising switchback ride taken by the British economy would not have been so dramatic.

For without free capital movements, the growth of investment by multinationals and the development of what the leading Japanese commentator Kenichi Ohmae portrays as a 'borderless world' it is improbable that the Thatcher consumer boom would have lasted so long or been so vigorous, or that so much foreign capital could have been drawn into the country so easily and thus allowed the balance of payments deficit to become so large. In the borderless world Britain could borrow in order to consume rather than produce because the capital was there – in the form of international bank loans, investment in British stocks and shares and multinationals stepping up the pace of their investment in the UK. During the late 1980s, for example, inward direct investment was running at 12 per cent of all British domestic capital formation – more than twice the rate in the early 1980s.[4] English-speaking, low-wage Britain with its access to European Community markets was well-placed to receive a disproportionately large slice of the cake.

Thus was born the notion, much favoured on the far right of the Conservative Party, that Britain should and could follow a 'Hong Kong' style of economic development. The Conservative programme that had started as a means of attacking collectivism, reducing taxes and lowering inflation began to develop into a messianic *laissez-faire* philosophy, seeing Britain's future as a low-cost, deregulated producer in a free-market world with low social overheads and a minimalist welfare state. More than that, because international lenders and investors demanded stable prices the government felt even more compelled to justify its own rhetoric, and set about making Britain look as much like the low inflation, *laissez-faire* paradise as it could.

Not only did the world of the late Cold War make Thatcherite economics possible, it also seemed to be a place in which the only sensible choices were right-wing: you had to deregulate, to lower taxes, to attract inward investment, to reduce inflation at any cost. Conservatism was not only hegemonic in Britain; it seemed to be the only game in town anywhere – and before its triumphant advance the Labour Party grew progressively less confident, its intellectual challenge more muted. Perhaps social democracy really was dead – and parties of the left would everywhere have to accommodate themselves to the same realities.

The international economy since the 1970s

In 1970 oil was cheap, capital markets were still predominantly national ones, exchange rates were pegged to the dollar at semi-fixed rates and unemployment was low. By 1980 oil was dear, the relaxation of exchange and capital controls had internationalised the key capital markets, exchange rates floated freely (the European exchange rate mechanism was only 15 months old) and unemployment had quadrupled. Forces had been released that shook the Western industrial order to its foundations – and their impact is still intensifying.

By the early 1970s the US capacity to anchor the dollar's value in gold at the centre of an international, fixed-exchange-rate system had come to an end; the Vietnam War, Lyndon Johnson's 'Great Society' programme, the structural nature of the US trade deficit with Europe and Japan and the rise in US consumption all contributed to that end. From 1972 onwards the dollar would float in value against other currencies, and the first link in the chain that would create a global capital market had been established.

But it was the consequences of the Arab-Israeli War and the decision by the oil producers to quadruple the price of oil that gave the capital markets their next impetus. Oil, after all, is an industrialised economy's lifeblood: very little can function without it. When the price increased fourfold between 1973 and 1974, and then doubled again in 1979, it meant that virtually the entire capital stock of the industrialised world became less profitable. Its factories, machines and vehicles were dependent upon cheap oil but oil was now dear. Industries everywhere had to restructure as their real profits fell; necessarily real wages had to fall to restore their real profits. And real wages fall only when unemployment rises.

While firms in every part of the world were struggling to restore their profits, the oil shock also offered a dramatic opportunity for the international financial system. There was suddenly a whole new geography of haves and have-nots, depending on whether they were oil exporters or importers. For some oil importers, of course, with strong international accounts and economies, the shock could be quickly absorbed but for others it brought a structural trade deficit that needed correcting by lower growth. Or by borrowing. The international banking system, most of it based in London, had already developed markets in which dollars could be borrowed and lent outside the US free of US regulatory and tax requirements. These were known as Euro-dollar markets because the dollars were traded in Europe without being repatriated to the US. But the new wealth of the oil exporters gave the system a further impetus. The oil exporters now had dollar receipts far in excess of their immediate requirements, and their dollar deposits in the international banks piled up. What could be simpler than relending them to those countries and companies that were suddenly in debt?

The recycling of the petro-dollars by the international banking system was one of the main novelties of the 1970s, leading, among other things, directly to the Third World debt crisis. It also had consequences for the way the system of floating exchange rates worked and therefore for the wider international financial system. For as the volume of dollars held by international investors, central

banks, commercial banks and multinationals exploded so the price
of dollars in terms of other currencies fell; in other words, the
dollar devalued, actively encouraged by the US policy of 'benign
neglect'. As expectations grew that the dollar would continue to
fall, dollar-holders wanted to hold alternative currencies – and
floating exchange rates made it much easier to do so. International
payments flows and stocks of currency could be traded rather than
exchanged into domestic currencies; London offered the markets
in which the currency could be bought and sold freely; and the
floating-exchange-rate system simply allowed demand and supply
to determine the price. In the old national markets, government
rationed the volume of currency through exchange and internal
financial controls; in the Euro-markets, no such controls existed.

This then brings in a third element to the story – the growing
impossibility of maintaining capital controls in such a volatile
environment. German, British, Japanese, French and Swiss banks
found that international investors wanted to hold deposits denomi-
nated in their domestic currencies because they did not want their
international buying power solely in the form of depreciating dollars. Now they could buy the currency they wanted to hold in the
international foreign exchange markets; and then keep it 'offshore'
– typically in the London branches of the banks' international networks.

Alongside the Euro-dollar, markets developed in Euro-marks,
Euro-yen and even Euro-sterling. The marks, for example, might
have come from an exporter earning them from export sales to
Germany – but instead of changing the marks into his or her
currency of origin, they were left on deposit with an international
bank. With the dollar falling, such marks would be worth more
and more in dollar terms the longer they were kept on deposit.
The exporter gained by betting that marks would rise in value in
relation to dollars, any international investor who subsequently
bought the marks gained from diversifying out of dollars, and the
bank gained from charging fees together with interest-rate margins
for all the transactions.

Such was the demand for Euro-marks that the interest rate
on them was slightly higher than on marks held in Germany.

Attracted by this, domestic savers began to find ways of evading controls and depositing their own money where it could attract higher interest. After all, they were the same marks on deposit with the same banks but by redefining them and depositing them in offshore branches, they could earn more money for no extra risk. International banks were desperate for the deposits and so depositor and bank alike connived at bending the law. The same process was at work everywhere in the world. Exchange controls became less effective, and governments responded by easing the controls.

Countries began to find that the rules of monetary policy were changing as well. Two IMF economists, Mundell and Fleming, had developed a theorem in the 1960s showing that countries could not simultaneously abandon exchange and capital controls, set their interest rates as they chose and fix their exchange rate. They could do two of these things but not all three together. As the Mundell-Fleming conditions took hold, the world found itself leaving Keynesian economics behind.

Mundell and Fleming showed that a country could fix its own exchange rate and choose to have low or high interest rates only if it imposed capital controls – for the exchange controls would prevent money pouring in or out of the country and changing the chosen interest rate or exchange rate. If it abandoned exchange controls it could only fix *either* the exchange rate *or* the interest rate.

What Mundell and Fleming were saying is that once capital and exchange controls go, governments lose control of one of the two key instruments of monetary policy. On the one hand, if they lower interest rates to get the domestic economy moving, then with free movement of capital the consequence may be a flight of money abroad and the depreciation of the currency. Without exchange controls, lowering interest rates can become self-defeating, forcing interest rates to go back up to keep in check the inflationary consequences of any devaluation. The most famous example of such self-defeating reflation was France in the early 1980s, but all Western countries have found that without capital controls they risk capital flight and an imposed hike in interest rates.

On the other hand, if a government wants to peg the exchange rate, then with free movement of capital it loses control of interest rates because the first line of defence against speculative flows of capital that might force a change in the announced exchange rate is the level of interest – which can be raised or lowered to encourage or prevent the capital flows. Capital controls are essential if a government wants to retain both levers of monetary policy.

This partially explains the rise in unemployment during the 1970s. The Arab démarche over oil prices triggered inflation and reduced profits. To contain inflation as exchange controls progressively lost their effectiveness, policymakers were obliged to jack up interest rates to minimise the risk of an inflationary currency depreciation while firms reacted by trying to restore profits. Faced with this double adjustment the level of unemployment had to rise to force real wages down.

This was the environment into which the Thatcher government pitched itself and while the Prime Minister only dimly understood the new rules she quickly saw that the world had changed in ways that decisively favoured her project. The lady, as she famously opined, was not for turning – a statement she made, safe in the knowledge that the world economy was pushing all states in the direction in which she wanted to travel.

The financial dam breaks

The growth of the new capital markets meant that exchange controls in Britain had been under severe strain throughout the 1970s. London's role as an international banking centre made policing of the controls difficult in any case, and the growing realisation that North Sea oil could transform Britain's economy began to give sterling the status of a 'petro-currency'. After the 1976 IMF crisis the pound joined the cherished ranks of currencies favoured as alternatives to the dollar – and exchange controls, which had been introduced to stop the pound from falling, were now perversely helping it to rise by restricting the supply of sterling that could be freely bought.

Although the British economy was outranked by Germany, France and Japan the legacy of empire meant that the market in sterling as an international currency ranked second only to the dollar. Given the size of London's sterling markets it was an obvious bolthole for dollar holders – but they were held back in part by the capital controls and partly by fears that they would lose out from the devaluation that always threatened Britain's inflationary economy. North Sea oil would change that. Already the outgoing Labour government had been reluctantly forced into a partial relaxation of exchange controls because the promise of oil riches pushing sterling higher was hurting the manufacturing sector's trading prospects. Even so the pound continued to rise.

The advent of a Conservative government and the imminence of North Sea oil flowing on shore (now worth twice as much after the second oil shock) triggered even more international enthusiasm for the pound. Abolishing exchange controls, it was argued, would accomplish simultaneously a number of objectives. It would increase the supply of pounds and so stop the exchange rate from rising to the point where it spelt disaster for British industry; it would boost the position of London as an international financial centre by making sterling unconditionally available to support international lending and investment; and it would help British investors build up a stock of foreign assets which would strengthen Britain when the oil ran out. For a Conservative government pledged to rolling back the state and for which the City was an important constituency, the argument was overwhelming – and Chancellor Geoffrey Howe acted promptly. Controls vanished in October 1979.

Yet throughout 1980 and 1981 sterling soared to new and extraordinary heights – more than 50 per cent higher in real terms than it had stood just two years earlier. Given floating exchange rates, the hunger to diversify out of dollars, the breadth of the sterling markets and the arrival of oil, any British government would have had difficulty stemming the pound's rise. Perversely the abolition of controls had the effect of stimulating demand by allowing an avalanche of buyers to hold the currency.

Exchange controls were also the first line of defence in a

system of direct controls over bank lending and deposit-taking that were designed to limit the growth of credit. Once exchange controls had disappeared the City lobbied hard for credit controls to be abolished too. If sterling could be moved freely offshore, ran the argument, British and foreign banks would be able to use their offshore subsidiaries to lend to the British public. It did not matter to home buyers or entrepreneurs whether their borrowed pounds had originated from sterling deposits made in Luxembourg or Macclesfield; what mattered was that there was money to borrow. The boom in credit began.

The same argument was used as with exchange controls. If industry or consumers felt that there was an activity that was worthwhile enough to make them want to borrow to finance it, why should the state stop them? Industry would be prevented from undertaking investment projects; and consumers from spending their money in ways they are uniquely qualified to decide upon. Controls were preventing investment and spending decisions from taking place that would otherwise have occurred and thus damaging economic efficiency. Better to allow the price of money, the interest rate, to regulate the supply and demand for credit.

But of course interest rates are a rather poor guide for banks to the riskiness of their loans. Ten years earlier, under Edward Heath, controls over the banks' balance sheets had been lifted, resulting in an orgy of lending, a property boom and the secondary banking crisis, and interest rates had been useless at warning of the impending disaster. First, London and County Securities suffered a run on deposits when depositors feared for the viability of the bank, but in a domino effect the panic ran through almost all the country's secondary banks including legendary names like Slater Walker, and even touched the clearing banks. Only a financial lifeboat, organised by the Bank of England to ferry deposits to the troubled banks, saved the system. The Bank of England then insisted that there should be no Department of Trade inquiry, which might have led to reregulation.[5] It had learned nothing.

For what seemed like prudent lending when interest rates were low and property values rising could quickly turn into profligacy when interest rates rose – but no individual bank making an individual lending decision was in a position to judge whether the results of lending by the whole banking system had gone too far. There is, as Bank of England official Eric Davis argues, a chronic bias in any competitive banking system for lending to oscillate violently. In the upswing of the business cycle all that any one bank knows is that if it gives up the chance of lending, a competitor will step in and it will lose immediately profitable business; but in the downswing it fears that it is the only lender and therefore much more at risk. Banking competition leads to a lowering of standards of risk assessment, increased lending and then an excessive reaction with standards of risk raised too high.

This time round, ministers and their advisers assured themselves, it would be different. If the market could set interest rates freely, and the government controlled the supply of money tightly, then excessive lending would force interest rates up – choking off any credit boom before it got started. Markets had self-regulating tendencies which could be relied upon to deliver the goods as long as they were not tampered with, and whatever the short-term drawbacks this had to be the direction in which to move. British 'collectivism', complete with all its rules and regulations, had to be systematically scrapped.

Eight months after exchange controls were abolished, the government duly abandoned the 'corset' which set targets for the growth of bank deposits and thus the amounts which banks could lend. Under the old system if the targets were exceeded, the Bank of England was responsible for collecting and sterilising the excess deposits, charging progressively higher penalties. Although the details were technically complex the idea was blindingly simple; if the banks had not got the money to lend, then they could not lend it.

And two months later, in August 1980, another financial control – that of the 'reserve requirements' – was lifted. This, despite the jargon, was another essentially simple idea. Under its rules the banks had to keep a fixed proportion of their deposits in cash or its equivalent. But the ultimate provider of cash *is* the Bank of England, so the rule in effect gave the central Bank leverage over every bank's balance sheet. If a bank lacked cash to meet its legal requirements under the rule, it had to ask the Bank of England for the money, offering collateral in exchange (Treasury bills or government bonds) as a kind of IOU. But as a penalty the Bank would only accept their IOUs in exchange for much less cash than the IOUs were worth in the marketplace. Because banks did not want to pay what was effectively a hefty fine, they were careful to keep control of their lending and their cash, so biasing them towards caution. Despite intense lobbying against them, both reserve requirements and the 'corset' had worked well during the mid 1970s as constraints on bank lending and had allowed interest rates to be lower than they otherwise would have been without stimulating excessive credit growth. Although there was much talk of the controls being evaded, even the Bank of England was later to conclude that the amount of evasion was comparatively trivial. But such considerations were not in keeping with the mood of the late 1970s or the ideological aims of the government. Suddenly the banks were free not only to lend as much as they liked, but to finance it how they pleased.

By the end of 1980 the Conservatives had taken the key steps that would so unbalance the economy for the next decade and a half. Scrapping exchange controls, allowing the pound to float to new heights and creating the conditions for the credit boom created the imbalance between production and consumption that still plagues the British economy today. The high pound decimated the country's production base, while the credit boom would drive consumption to ever higher levels. By the mid 1990s consumption would represent some 65 per cent of national output, and still Britain's capital stock relative to demand was smaller than that of its chief competitors. The economy was to be vandalised by the financial sector in the name of market freedoms.

There is no alternative!

The Conservative government decided early on that its overriding priority was low inflation – and the means to that end was control

of the money supply by limiting government borrowing and setting appropriate interest and exchange rates. The precise weight
applied to the chosen policy levers changed as the years and the
theory wore on, but the consistency of intent was remarkable.

Although inflation picked up from around 4 per cent in the
mid 1980s to over 10 per cent in 1990, the average inflation rate
over the ten years from 1983 to 1993 was just over 5 per cent – a
significant improvement on the previous twenty-five years during
which it had averaged 9 per cent, and much closer to the average
of the industrialised countries. Single-mindedness of purpose was
beginning to yield results.

Low inflation was seen as the 'supply-side' reform to cap
them all. Apart from improving the functioning of the market
economy (by making price signals less distorted by volatile and
unpredictable changes in the overall price level) low inflation was
important because it would stop savers being robbed of their
efforts. Indeed, some of the messianic fervour that consecutive
chancellors brought to their task was the sense that inflation was
the ultimate sign of economic degeneracy; the battle was less an
economic than a moral one. A famous *Times* leader of the early
1980s linked Keynesian economics, homosexuality and treachery
to one's country as part of the same pattern. A revitalised British
capitalism, having thrown off the dead-weight of socialism, should
simply never inflate the value of its money.

But behind that conviction lay the long-standing dominance
of the values of finance – of *rentiers* who live off the income
others produce – over the values of production. The concern was
less to promote the interests of production, which would flourish
if the promised land of low inflation and low interest rates could
be reached, than to set the framework that would – in the words
of endless Treasury statements – 'bear down upon inflation'. All
the majesty of Conservative hegemony in the unreformed state
was deployed to increase the role of markets, disengage the state
and fight for price stability. It was the apotheosis of rentierdom.

The genuine gains of low inflation were bought at terrible
cost, from the growing dilapidation of the public infrastructure
to the erosion of the country's productive base. The attempt to

contain monetary and credit growth in a deregulated banking
system without exchange controls led to a decade of high real
interest rates and a level for sterling in relation to other currencies that fluctuated from fantastically excessive levels in the early
1980s to never less than significant overvaluation for the rest of
the decade – at least if the levels of the 1960s and 1970s are used
as a benchmark. Before this onslaught, investment in productive
industry wilted while credit-driven consumer spending climbed
to ever higher levels, bringing in its wake a flurry of investment
in consumer services and property, all dependent upon spending
that could never be sustained. Britain had become the laboratory
for an extraordinary experiment in economic theory – and with a
dominant party running a centralised state, there was no escape.

The period began with declarations of slavish belief in the
notion that there was a systematic relationship between the
rate of growth of some measure of the money supply and
the subsequent inflation rate. This identity could only hold if a
number of impossible assumptions were made about the nature
of a market economy, in particular that it actually stood at or was
tending to a perfect state of economic grace – but such belief was
the badge of the New Right. Economists call this a competitive
equilibrium – a condition where every market in the economy has
simultaneously arrived at a point of balance: it depends on the idea
that as producers and consumers in a free market will undertake no
act against their economic self-interest, so the market must always
tend to an unimprovable equilibrium. Because the economy is in
this state of grace, all the government can do by permitting the
money supply to expand above some target consistent with that
state, is to push up prices. On this piece of theology a great nation's
economic policy was based.

So how was the money supply to be controlled? The ultimate
responsibility for money, reasoned the theorists, lies with the
state – because money is legal tender. And what dictates above
all else the amount of legal tender the state issues is the level of
its borrowing. As long as it sticks to borrowing from the nation's
pool of savings by offering savers its longterm debt there would be
no need to print money; but if it strays from that sacred injunction

and issues legal tender to finance its deficit (in other words printed money) the money supply would grow and inflation would result.[6] Thus the first task was to eliminate government borrowing; and while that was going on, to set interest rates at a level that could attract sufficient savings to finance the deficit. The process would necessarily be gradual – but eventually inflation would be eliminated.

This 'monetarist' philosophy neatly dovetailed with the long-standing prejudices of the Conservative right, because it provided a heaven-sent justification for the crusade against collectivism in all its forms. The best way to lower public borrowing, of course, was to reduce public expenditure rather than raise taxes, which were felt already to be too high; and reducing public expenditure would entail shedding the responsibilities that the state had undertaken in the fruitless attempt to make Keynesianism work, along with endlessly expensive social contracts with trade unions. Low inflation and the attack against the red menace became intertwined.

So in the spring of 1980 the Medium Term Financial Strategy (MTFS) was unveiled – the concrete policy targets that put numbers on the strategy. Public spending as a proportion of national output was to fall progressively in the years ahead, thus lowering public borrowing; and as borrowing fell the growth of a particular measure of money supply, M3 (the total lendable deposits of the banking system, but excluding building societies), was to fall in tandem – and with it the projected inflation rate. The performance of the economy was to be improved by tackling its other 'supply-side' deficiencies. Overmighty trade unions were to be cut down to size and managers encouraged by lower taxes to work harder. Competition and market forces would energise the economy as the government grimly struggled to meet the terms of the MTFS.

The intellectual deficiencies of this approach were numerous. The alleged linkage between public spending, public borrowing, money supply, interest rates and inflation was tenuous to say the least, with all kinds of qualifications required at each link in the chain; and the basic assumption that private sector activity in an unregulated market would tend to improve the economy was

unreal. Indeed, throughout the decade interest rates remained
high in real terms, and money supply broached the government's
targets without any predictable effect on inflation, and government borrowing fell. It became ever more clear how idealistic
the theory and policy were.

Already Britain's place in the international monetary order was
driving the pound too high; the impact of domestic monetarism
encouraged it to rise still further. The government felt it had to do
more than just set interest rates to finance its deficit; it had to pitch
them high enough to deter borrowers from demanding bank loans,
and so inflating the money supply. In the autumn of 1979 bank base
rates soared. International speculators not only diversified into a
widely traded petro-currency; they could get 17 per cent interest
as well.

The results were catastrophic. Facing super-competitive imports and priced out of export markets by a fantastically expensive
pound, manufacturing production fell by 14 per cent in 1980 and
1981 and profits dropped by a third. National output (GDP) fell
cumulatively by nearly 5 per cent and by 1983 there were 2 million
fewer people with jobs than in 1979.

But although interest rates were to come down, the concern to
hold back credit demand and make sure government borrowing
was financed wholly from the nation's savings kept them well
above inflation – so that in real terms they remained much higher
than at any time since the war. The 1981 budget raised taxes by
some 2 per cent of GDP in an attempt to control borrowing (and
thus the growth of the money supply) in the middle of a recession,
signalling decisively the change in economic priorities; but the
growth of the money supply stubbornly failed to slow down as
the monetarists had expected. On the other hand, the recession did
not become more prolonged, as the Keynesians warned. In fact the
economy picked up and the inflation rate remained relatively sub-
dued despite the excessive growth of money supply – confounding
everybody.

What was happening was, in truth, very simple. The high
exchange rate and the associated growth in unemployment were
together depressing inflation through their twin impact on import

prices and wage increases – even though the money supply was growing rapidly. For at the same time financial deregulation was propelling a dramatic increase in credit-financed consumer spending. In the previous three decades, governments had aimed to manage the level of demand in the economy through changes in taxes, public spending and borrowing – the policy that the Thatcherites deplored, arguing that it produced ever higher inflation and unemployment because it enlarged the power of the state. Although such management of demand by the government was now officially eschewed, financial deregulation was producing the same result. In the old days governments had incurred public debt to finance their stimulation of the economy; now, private consumers and businesses were doing the same with private debt. In effect the government, by deregulating finance, had privatised an enormous reflation.

Over the 1980s private debt levels doubled, so that by 1990 households held £114 of debt, up from £57 in 1980, for every £100 of disposable income; both the fastest growth rate and highest absolute level of debt of any western industrialised country. Most of the lending was for buying houses and flats, and the stock of mortgage debt increased sixfold from £52 billion in 1980 to £294 billion in 1990. House prices more than doubled over the same period.[7]

Banks and building societies were inadvertently taking over the role of managing demand. Lending against house purchases seemed a cast-iron risk, and together with the sale of insurance policies – notably endowment policies to finance mortgage repayments – the business quickly earned a reputation as an apparently bottomless source of commission income, fees and bank charges. From 1979 to 1990 there was no year when bank and building society lending did not grow by at least 15 per cent, reaching a peak of 24 per cent in 1988.

This could not have happened without the banks campaigning for further deregulation to exploit the fact that the monetary corset and reserve requirements had gone. Hire purchase controls on consumer credit were scrapped. Banks were allowed to enter the mortgage market in 1981; building societies were allowed to compete for longer-term deposits in the London money markets; neither were asked to check how their borrowers used mortgage loans, so that increasingly the loans allegedly for home purchase were used for consumption purposes. This was the phenomenon of 'equity withdrawal' – in effect, people were eating their own seed-corn. And as property prices rose, lenders became more and more confident in their lending – advancing ever higher proportions of the value of homes at ever greater multiples of the borrowers' income.

Borrowers for their part became more confident about taking on such debt. Wages for those in work outpaced the rise in prices, which were depressed by the same high pound that was making British producers' trading prospects so difficult. With real incomes rising, borrowing followed suit and gradually house prices began to increase. Occupants of houses felt wealthy, able to borrow and spend in their own right. And around the whole activity a mini-industry of financial services was being constructed, which took on workers and allowed the number employed to start rising as early as 1983.

There was a self-reinforcing circle – well described by Professor Duncan Maclennan in his report for the Joseph Rowntree Foundation. As employment rose, there was more spending and borrowing power – and consumers began to learn that the Conservatives meant business when they talked about tax reductions. This created yet more false confidence about taking on extra debts, and gave yet another impetus to the rise in house prices.

The growth in consumer spending was slow at first, rising by about 1 per cent in 1982, but its growth averaged 3.3 per cent in the next three years to climax at 6.3 per cent in each of the three years straddling the 1987 election.[8] Yet the growth within that total was heavily skewed towards consumer services – everything from dry cleaning to private schools – where growth averaged 6.4 per cent a year over the 1980s. And on the back of this growth new firms and industries – from luxury chocolate importers to designer lingerie – prospered.

That all of this had its origins in the abolition of exchange and banking controls in 1979 and 1980, which in turn had been triggered by Britain's particular role in the international financial system, was beside the point. For entrepreneurs in the bustle of the marketplace the experience was that people were spending; and they invested in the expectation that they would go on doing so.

As the upturn swept to its climax, some two million houses were bought and sold in 1988 – each requiring new kitchens, bathrooms, curtains and carpets; each transaction required estate agents, banks, building societies, insurance companies, lawyers and architects, thus generating a new round of income, employment and spending. The boom was feeding on itself.

The government boasted that private business investment was reaching new peaks, and so it was; but it was only in 1988 that manufacturing investment recovered to its 1979 level. While manufacturing investment represented some 5 per cent of GDP at the peak of the boom, investment in services and construction climbed to 12 per cent of GDP – predicated upon levels of consumption growth and property price inflation that could not continue. Rising house prices and rising spending had defied the fact of high interest rates for a decade; and the correction when it came would surely be painful.

The government itself was wrestling with the inconsistencies of its theory. Its aim was to produce low inflation by controlling the money supply, but inflation between 1983 and 1988 averaged 4.7 per cent while the growth of broad money supply averaged 14.7 per cent. If the theory had been true, inflation should have been in double figures: instead it seemed low and stable.

For a non-monetarist it was no mystery at all. The economy had never been in the state of grace represented by competitive equilibrium, so no systematic relationship between money growth and inflation was ever likely to be provable. The chief influences keeping inflation down were unemployment and the high exchange rate. But this meant that the balance of payments became a kind of disinflationary safety-valve, with demand leaking abroad to buy cheap imports, which doubled over the decade. At the same time exports increased by 40 per cent – less than half the rate of imports – so that the visible trade deficit mushroomed.

The first grim milestone was passed in 1983 when Britain became a net importer of manufactured goods for the first time since the Industrial Revolution, but the process continued remorselessly so that in 1989 the visible trade deficit – excluding oil – climbed to £26 billion, close to 5 per cent of GDP. Yet as the evidence mounted that success in lowering inflation had little to do with monetary targets the government persisted in believing that the cause of low inflation was monetary stability. In fact, the chain of causation runs from economic strength to low inflation to price stability – but the government, fixated on financial variables and free market economics, believed that the chain ran the opposite way.

The world beyond the UK was increasingly unbelieving, and so in an attempt to give its ideas more intellectual credibility the government switched horses in the second half of the decade, moving away from trying to control the money supply to fixing targets for the exchange rate. If the money supply seemed a poor anchor for monetary policy, then at least the exchange rate was more explicit. Other European countries had tied their exchange rate to the mark in the European exchange rate mechanism, and if they were to hold the rate then their inflation could be no higher than Germany's – famous for its commitment to price stability. France was in the process of dramatically lowering its inflation rate, and the Thatcherites sat up and noticed. Chancellor Lawson may have been rebuffed by Mrs Thatcher in his attempt to join the system in 1985 but for five years he and his successor, John Major, either explicitly or tacitly used a strong exchange rate as a yardstick for how tight or loose monetary conditions were – and to 'bear down upon inflation'.

As we have seen, by trying to control the exchange rate the government necessarily (given that anyone could move capital into or out of the UK at will) surrendered control of interest rates. In the first phase of shadowing the mark at DM3, interest rates were driven down too low to stop the pound from rising above its 'shadow rate', helping the boom to reach its climax – and the famous fall-out between the Chancellor and the Prime Minister over the merits of 'trying to buck the market' was to lead to Lawson's resignation.

Interest rates were then ratcheted higher as the government at last recognised that it was presiding over a credit boom.

Sterling, which had been allowed to depreciate from the absurd levels it had reached in 1980 to a still overvalued but lower level in 1986, began to strengthen again under the new policy direction. The squeeze on manufacturing was relentless. Although profits as a share of national output rose remarkably, the distribution of profitability was skewed, as John Muellbauer and Anthony Murphy have shown; the more a sector was exposed to international competition, the less profitable it was – and the lower its rate of investment. The capital stock of manufacturing as a whole barely rose across the decade, outstripped by the rise in the capital stock of financial services, dwellings and hotels. Britain finished the 1980s with shopping malls, banks and houses aplenty but its manufacturing base static.

A decade of attempts to control the money supply and produce monetary stability was in danger of collapsing in near farce – and the Treasury saw ERM membership as the best solution. When Britain finally joined in the autumn of 1990, in a last attempt to find a credible monetary anchor, control of interest rates was lost completely. Real interest rates (as measured by mortgage rate less retail price inflation) climbed to nearly 10 per cent, as German interest rates rose to contain the inflationary consequences of reunion. The great surge in lending and borrowing that had characterised the 1980s came juddering to a halt – and a second severe recession began.

The processes that had fuelled the nine-year boom were thrown into reverse. Burdened by debt and shaken by unemployment and wage cuts in the new deregulated labour market, buyers withdrew from the property market. Lenders took fright. Property prices fell, exposing banks and building societies to unprecedented levels of bad debt – and they drew in their horns. Turnover in the housing market halved and equity withdrawal collapsed. Consumption stagnated.

The financial and consumer services industries had swollen too much and now retrenched, adding further to the downward spiral as they laid off workers. The government's tax revenues fell and its spending on income support to offset the recession ballooned; the public sector, in surplus in 1990, went into the biggest underlying deficit in peacetime history. And all the while real interest rates, with Britain's exchange rate pegged to the mark inside the ERM, remained at a stifling 5 to 6 per cent.

Finally a wave of speculation sprang the trap, and Britain was forced out of the ERM. The devaluation and lower interest rates that the economic establishment had confidently predicted would provoke a fresh round of inflation instead proved the trigger of recovery, while inflation remained low. Purely by chance and against all its instincts and efforts, the government found itself presiding over a successful devaluation – at the bottom of a recession and compelled by its own finances to increase taxes.

For the Conservative government re-elected in 1992 found that the mushrooming budget deficit required drastic attention. Stripping out all capital expenditure and receipts, the public sector's current deficit had plunged into the red to the tune of 6 per cent of GDP. Chancellors Lamont and Clarke together imposed £17 billion of tax increases in the two budgets of 1993 (to be phased in over three years), which were regarded as the minimum necessary to rectify the situation. Public spending was cut dramatically, involving a further 17 per cent drop in public capital investment that was already the lowest as a proportion of GDP since the war.

Burdened by tax increases, and with the debts of the 1980s still hanging over their heads, it is obvious that consumers cannot drive the recovery onward. Indeed, with consumption at a post-war high and its counterpart, savings, at the lowest level in the international league table, consumers are not in any position to do so. Britain has to look to production, investment and exports to capitalise upon the gains from devaluation – the sectors that have been left so weak by the fifteen-year experiment.

The reckoning

Among the industrialised countries only the growth of manufacturing output in France, Greece and Norway was worse than
Britain's during the 1980s. At the peak of the 1980s boom, in 1989,
manufacturing output had grown no more than 1.2 per cent per
year from the peak of the previous cycle. Manufacturing investment as a proportion of national output had continually *fallen* over
the decade – intensifying a trend discernible since 1960. Since then
Britain has suffered the largest fall of manufacturing employment
of any industrialised country, and the switchback ride of the 1980s
intensified the rate of job loss. Yet as the defenders of the Thatcher
and Major years argue, manufacturing productivity in Britain has
risen significantly faster than in the years beforehand.[9] But this
rise did not translate into investment and output growth. Why?

The answer lies in the dominance of financial values over British
corporate life and economic policy. The overvalued exchange rate
damaged industrial competitiveness, but in the Treasury/Bank of
England scheme of things that took second place to the contribution a high exchange rate could make towards price stability.
High real interest rates, designed to contain the avalanche of credit
unleashed by financial deregulation, were always judged in terms
of their impact upon inflation and never upon the internal rates
of return that firms set for their investment projects. The policy
priorities were always firmly financial; there were targets for the
money supply, for the exchange rate, for the reduction of public
borrowing, for the percentage share of public spending of national
output and latterly for the inflation rate. These were the ancient
totems of the British state speaking in the new economic language
of monetarist economics. Targets for employment or for growth
were never mentioned. They were to be left to the market.

But if manufacturing output growth was depressed, it was
argued that Britain's export performance had improved. The
British share of the industrialised countries' manufactured exports
was stabilising and even rising; something was improving.

However, as Kirsty Hughes and others have shown, the improvement has to be seen in a world context. If the newly

industrialised Asian and Latin American countries' exports are included in the computation, then Britain's performance was as indifferent as its position in the manufacturing output league table suggests. What was happening was that the UK was specialising in fewer sectors – such as chemicals and aerospace – while giving up ground in others like textiles and mechanical engineering. In high-growth sectors there was virtually no British representation, while in areas like consumer electronics and cars the turnaround was wholly due to inward direct investment, notably from Japan, which itself implied rising imports of Japanese-made parts. Although exports were rising, imports were rising even faster. Between 1979 and 1989 exports rose by 18.7 per cent, Kirsty Hughes calculates; but imports rose by 56.5 per cent. And while total production in the economy fell by 3.8 per cent over this period, British producers' production fell even further – by 9.6 per cent. The 1980s were not a success story for indigenous British producers.[10]

As a result, the country is in an unsustainable position. It is running a chronic trade deficit, financed increasingly by bank lending. Between 1990 and 1993 the cumulative current account deficit was just under £50 billion, yet at the same time inward direct investment flows were more than offset by British companies investing overseas. British pension funds and insurance companies have invested £87 billion abroad. The balance has been made up by British banks cumulatively borrowing over £90 billion.[11] Britain may have assets overseas amounting to some 30 per cent of GDP, but it also has short-term liabilities to foreigners equivalent to 30 per cent of GDP – the highest in its peace-time history.[12]

This cannot continue – and in any case makes the UK highly sensitive to changes in interest rates abroad and the willingness of foreign institutions to continue to build up short-term deposits in Britain. The larger their holding of British debt becomes, the more powerful their veto over the autonomy of British economic policy. If they were all to withdraw their money simultaneously the exchange rate would fall and interest rates rise sharply, generating unwanted inflation and a slow-down in economic activity. The country therefore needs to move towards balance on its trading account.

This places a particularly heavy responsibility on the already weakened manufacturing sector. As the Select Committee on Trade and Industry reported, every 1 per cent fall in manufacturing exports must be compensated for by more than a 2.5 per cent rise in exports of services. Although Britain's service sector is held up as the industry of the future, world trade is still predominantly in manufactures. To achieve balance on the UK's international accounts by the year 2000, while economic growth averaged 2.5 per cent a year, would require Britain's financial sector to absorb the entire current international financial activity of New York and Tokyo.[12] Since this is plainly impossible, manufacturing exports simply have to play an enlarged role.

As a result the economy and state now face a series of strategic dilemmas. There has to be economic growth to lower unemployment and improve the government's fiscal position but, if the current relationships hold, any significant economic growth would suck in imports so greedily that the balance of payments deficit would explode superimposed upon Britain's already heavy short-term borrowings. Because this is unsustainable, the financial markets would demand a policy change and interest rates would rise and the exchange rate would fall. Consumers would be squeezed savagely as their wages bought less, for the scale of the necessary adjustment is staggering.

If economic growth were to average just 3 per cent over the next five years, the government's budget deficit would fall towards near balance by 1998 or 1999, as long as public spending grew at less than half the rate of the economy as the government currently projects. But the growth of consumption, on current form, would imply such high import growth that the total balance of payments current account deficit – visible and invisible trade – would climb to between 4 and 5 per cent of GDP even after allowing for the improvement in 1994 following devaluation in 1992.[13] The difficulty is compounded because the City has reclaimed its ancient freedom to invest overseas which, as we have seen, has meant a cumulative outflow of £87 billion between 1990 and 1993. The consequence of such growth in these conditions would be unfinanceable, and long before the deficit climbed so high the exchange rate would have fallen and the growth in the economy checked by a tightening of economic policy.

To put it another way, if Britain's shrunken manufacturing base were able to support export growth of 5.5 per cent, this would prevent the current account deficit from becoming unsustainably large, but the most the wider economy can grow is by 1.5 to 2 per cent.[14] This would imply unemployment staying above 2.5 million, with the economy unable to offer any prospects for the one-in-four adult men who are economically inactive. But it would also imply, as social security expenditure rises to relieve poverty, that the government's current budget deficit would stay at around 4.5 per cent of GDP. There would have to be tax increases to correct the imbalances, which would slow growth down even further.

The terrible paradox is that modest growth is almost too much for Britain to bear. The economy is trapped by its own weaknesses. As Tony Thirlwall and many others have observed, economies that experience strong GDP growth depend upon a strong growth in their manufacturing output and exports – otherwise they find themselves in Britain's present situation. The position is worsened by the use of international borrowing to finance consumption and not investment, so that the adjustment, when it comes, will be more severe. The City's power to set policy is matched by its capacity to borrow to hide the consequences – but that cannot continue for ever.

Manufacturing output cannot rise without investment, R & D and innovation. One of the key free-market propositions is that growth and investment are determined 'naturally' by technical change and population growth, and that the best governments can do is not 'artificially' interfere with these processes. To lift investment above its 'natural' rate by government action is to reduplicate existing factories, offices and machines, lower the profit rate and overheat the economy. The best policy is just to improve 'natural' market efficiency. But, as John Wells argues, this neglects the statistical fact that across countries and time the higher the growth rate, the higher the investment rate especially in plant and equipment. Moreover, government action from raising skill levels to redesigning systems of finance has succeeded in raising investment levels and the rate of growth of productivity – as the experience of Japan and East Asia highlights dramatically. It is possible, via government institution-building, to improve the trajectory of growth, investment and export performance – whatever the free-market purists claim.

Over the 1980s and 90s this insight has been neglected. British investment in human capital, in the physical infrastructure and in industries which can trade internationally has languished, focusing instead on the service sector. Business R & D is the lowest of the major industrialised countries while the registration of new patents has continued to fall.[15] The country's competitive sinews have wasted even as the strategic options facing the nation have become more challenging.

What is now required is a national effort to organise a sustained increase in investment, but the economic institutions and state structures are no more ready to respond to such a call than they ever were. The dominance of financial values and targets, the tolerance of ever rising consumption as a proportion of GDP, and the indifference to investment and employment are deep-seated. The Conservative Party simply gave the old beast its head – with familiar results.

But even as it caved in to the City's age-old lobby for financial freedom, it had to listen to another lobby from industry that wanted to regain the right to manage – or more plainly to break the power of the trade unions. Monetary discipline would produce price stability and financial freedom would ensure the productive use of savings, the third prong of the free-market attack was to secure freedom from the unions in order to secure higher productivity. To achieve this the awesome power of the state was brought to bear, just as it had been used to free the City. But as the consequences of *laissez-faire* in finance had been perverse, so the deregulation of the British labour market brought precious little benefit and an awful lot of pain.

4. The Revolution Founders

At the heart of the attempted Conservative revolution was the belief that capitalism works, if it is left to its own devices. There are imperfections, certainly, in the operation of markets but there are greater gains in liberating capitalist endeavour than in trying to regulate and manage it. In fact, forcing capitalism to act in ways it does not 'naturally' choose can only be self-defeating. This was the central credo.

With the disciplining of the state's spending and borrowing activities and the deregulation of the City, a campaign was launched to revitalise the capitalist spirit. It was taken as read that any capitalist institution, having developed freely in a market place, must in essence be sound and fit. If productivity was low or efficiency poor, the problem could not lie with the free enterprise basis of British capitalism; rather it must lie with externally imposed constraints on its operation. And in 1979 those constraints seemed self-evident. They were trade unions and their malevolent influence on wages and productivity levels. Attacking the institutions of collective bargaining – especially in the public sector and the nationalised industries – was seen as the absolute priority of Conservative policy. In some respects it was even more important than bringing down inflation or rolling back the state. Trade unions caused inflation by pressing for unjustified wage rises; trade unions obstructed management from introducing new technology and raising productivity; they caused high taxation by insisting on unreasonable wages in the public sector; they locked Britain into the cycle of inflation, lost competitiveness, poor productivity, devaluation, low growth and yet more inflation. And to give real political edge to the Conservative case, it had been the National Union of Mineworkers that had brought down the Conservative government in 1974. Unions were not just the *economic* enemies of successful capitalism – they were over-mighty subjects challenging the structures that sustained Conservative hegemony.[1]

Nor, in the late 1970s did such a view seem out of touch with reality. British trade unions, founded and defined in corporate opposition to capital, were never organised to do other than champion a very narrow conception of working-class interest. Indeed, the first unions had come into being as giant co-operative voluntary trusts to protect the unskilled labourer from black-legging; and the later craft unions were modelled on professional associations and guilds, whose job was to manage access to jobs so as to protect the wages of those already in them. The craft unions and the big general unions had members in various industries, so with no industry-wide unions (such as developed in mainland Europe) it was never easy to protect the system of industry and national pay-bargaining, established after the war, from the determination of individual firms and plants to take back control.

The confrontation between capital and labour was institutionalised in an annual wage round, in which the relative muscle of employers and the particular combination of unions with whom they bargained would determine the outcome in terms of higher wages or better conditions. It was none of the unions' business or interest to solve employers' problems for them by exercising wage restraint, participating in decision-making or sharing in profits. That would only compromise the interests of organised labour, represented, by the 1970s, by some 350,000 shop stewards in local workplaces, a growing number of whom ran guerrilla warfare against employers in waves of unofficial strikes.

Nor were British employers notably ready to challenge this working-class self-definition; it was in part the anxiety of British companies to retain their autonomy of decision-making and their readiness to exploit any opportunities to keep the labour market as deregulated as possible that had provoked the unions' attitude in the first place. Companies also wanted to bargain through the antagonistic confrontation of rival interests, with collective industry agreements rarely doing more than setting minimum wage rates. The class enemy was kept at arm's length and if cheap labour ever did become available, employers would not be tangled up in co-operative structures and therefore were free to

take advantage of it. Company law laid down that managers' prime
responsibility was to their shareholders and the maximisation of
profits; to share profits or decisions with unions in the interests
of better industrial relations was anathema, inhibiting managerial
options and freedoms.

In this way the efforts of successive governments to reform
the structure of trade unions and of wage bargaining proved
unsuccessful – foundering on the implacable opposition of trade
unions to the extension of state power into their own terri-
tory, companies' opposition to joint decision-making and the
weak structures of collective bargaining through which attempts
at incomes policies had to work. The Donovan Commission,
reporting to the Labour government in 1968, conceded that shop
steward power and unofficial strikes were ruining industrial relations, but shied away from making collective agreements legally
binding or demanding statutory cooling-off periods before strikes
and compulsory ballots. It was not for the state to intervene in
essentially private arrangements between voluntary agents over
the terms of employment; instead, the best the Commission could
recommend was to encourage the recognition of unions and to
create an enabling body that would advise on industrial relations
– the Commission for Industrial Relations.

Harold Wilson and Barbara Castle's efforts to harden up the
proposals in the famous white paper, *In Place Of Strife* – empowering
the government to impose settlements and strike ballots as it saw
fit – were bitterly opposed by the TUC and an important section
of Labour MPs. The state should not weaken unions in their
battle with capital. A mild strengthening of the TUC's powers
to intervene in disputes was advocated as a compromise and the
Prime Minister and his Secretary of State for Employment had to
withdraw their legislation because it would almost certainly have
failed.

In a sense, of course, the unions' opposition was justified. Since
the power of the British state is untrammelled by any constitutional
check or balance, the unions would have had no redress against the
Secretary of State's discretionary powers, which in Conservative
hands would be used more aggressively than by Mrs Castle. Nor

could sympathetic Labour governments and their employment ministers always be relied on; general elections led to unexpected changes. Moreover, unions had a privileged status in Britain, with the 1906 Trade Disputes Act excusing them from being sued by employers for damages caused by their withdrawal of labour – a naked attempt by the Liberals at the turn of the century to buy the working-class vote, which the Conservatives never dared repeal. To surrender that privilege so that incomes policies could work – the subtext of *In Place Of Strife* – while dividends, executive salaries and prices were rising faster than wages, was an inconceivable concession in the 1960s. Trade-union-sponsored Labour MPs so isolated Mr Wilson that his position as prime minister was briefly under threat and the proposals were consigned to oblivion, and with them the credibility of the Labour government.[2]

So the problem remained. The unions could not be sued if they went on strike, official or unofficial; yet the power of the shop stewards was spreading and hardening, so that the numbers of strikes went up year after year. Wage inflation began to look endemic. The malign effect of restrictive practices was increasing, so that productivity growth in Britain was lagging behind that of other industrialised countries – and all this was sanctioned by talk of working-class solidarity (and for some extremists, the fight for a socialist future based on workers' councils or soviets).

But union members' willingness to take strike action was based as much on a desire to protect their jobs and secure their relative status in the wages pecking order, as it was to a belief in any class war. In this respect unions were more like professional associations and the old guilds than the shock troops of the working class. The establishment of closed shops and managing the terms and conditions of employment, were old-fashioned restraints on trade by a group of workers attempting to protect their individual privileges and wages.

It was to fall to Mrs Thatcher to turn the political reality behind the unions' strength to her own advantage, but not before Edward Heath, her predecessor, had attempted once more to bring the unions under the scope of the law with the Industrial Relations Act. Although this was bitterly criticised at the time, exemplifying the socialist case that the state and private property interests in a capitalist society must always ally against organised labour, in fact Mr Heath's strategy and objectives were fundamentally different from those of Mrs Thatcher. While her aim was to remove the problem of union power by attacking the source of its strength and so to fragment the labour market into powerless, atomised units, Mr Heath's objective was to create a union movement that could be a European-style social partner, capable of delivering on national wage agreements and adapting to technological change. Unions would be required to register with a registrar of trade unions and employees' associations and collective wage bargains would be legal contracts enforceable in law through an industrial relations court. This could impose strike ballots, fines for unfair industrial practices and conciliation procedures but it could also be used by unions to force employers to recognise and bargain with them. The closed shop was not banned; rather it could be implemented if the employer agreed or if a majority of employees voted for it. The source of union power was not attacked but codified and legalised. In the 1990s such an initiative would be seen as enlightened and progressive; not in the 1970s.

Massive union resistance – the TUC insisted that no union sign on with the registrar – and the failure of some early test cases to prevent strikes brought the Act into disrepute. When Mr Heath lost the 1974 as election as his incomes policy collapsed around him under the twin shock of the oil price increase and the second miners' strike of the decade, it was the Labour Party's turn once again to attempt to manage the British labour market.

The response of the third Wilson administration was three-pronged. The Industrial Relations Act was abolished, and in its place came an Employment Protection Act which enshrined free collective bargaining as the centrepiece of British labour law, with improved protection against dismissal and more access by unions to information about companies' circumstances. The unions were to be coaxed into becoming social partners and to drop their purely oppositional role in two ways; a new incomes policy was presented as a social contract in which unions won concessions over their employment rights and social security entitlements in return for moderate wage settlements – and the Bullock Committee was set up to explore industrial democracy and co-decision making.

The majority report of the committee in 1977 recommended that workers and shareholders should have equal representation on the boards of directors of all companies employing 2,000 or more people. The problem was that the CBI minority on the committee dissented and, as with the TUC's refusal to register with the registrar of unions in the early 1970s, they simply refused to discuss the matter further. In vain might the committee plead that co-decision making and the enfranchisement of trade unions allowed for stable industrial relations in Germany and Sweden; in British terms it meant allowing unruly trade unions into the gilded world of the board room, qualifying managerial autonomy and setting other objectives beside the maximisation of the shareholders' interests. Workers simply could not be trusted to behave moderately or to have access to commercially confidential information.

The CBI's opposition was as understandable as the TUC's suspicion of Heath's reforms. German and Swedish corporate law and wage-bargaining structures were embedded in an institutional network of support, underpinned by a value system of co-operative behaviour, which did not exist in Britain then any more than it does now. Longterm financial relationships allowed workers and management time to reap the rewards from working together, but this was only one part of an institutional structure that locked together to produce more collaborative practices and outcomes. By contrast the companies bargaining with trade unions in Britain were increasingly owned by institutional shareholders who required high short-term returns.

Above all, British notions of sovereign and autonomous action for shareholders as much as for workers are borrowed from the Westminster model of the state; the democracy in British corporate law is the democracy of owners, who vote at a parliament of annual shareholders on which directors will be the custodians of their interests. They are lords of what they own, in the same way that the majority party of the House of Commons acts as a sovereign legislator. Dialogue and participation are not the British way at the level of the state and trying to encourage them at company level without any buttressing structures or cultural support was doomed to failure. Mr Callaghan consigned the Bullock Report to history.

But in so doing he wrote the last chapter in the history of British corporatism. For, as the social contract collapsed in the so-called 'winter of discontent', during which public sector unions used their power to insist on double-figure percentage wage claims to match the inflation rate, all possible solutions to the labour market problem seemed to have been explored and to have failed. Unions could not become social partners because industry could not accept them as such; but using the law to referee and enforce conciliation, while accepting that unions legitimately had effective control of the labour market, had also failed. Two incomes policies (Heath's and Callaghan's) had collapsed after less than three years; and the unions' capacity to fend off state initiatives to contain their power seemed infinite.

The consensus of mainstream economic and political opinion remained that the British disease originated in arrangements at the workplace. Defenders of corporatism might insist that the right-wing arguments that union power alone caused poor productivity were unreasonable, as both fast-growing Italy and the USA lost more working days to strikes than Britain – but they argued in vain. The new wave of neo-liberals claimed that unofficial strike action was only an indicator of a more profound problem – the veto that unions exercised over working practices and the push they gave to inflationary wage settlements. Britain might not top the international league table of strike action, but that was only because too many employers, frightened of union power, gave way to excessive wage claims and sanctioned overmanning because they knew they were afraid of a strike. There was only one way forward, the right argued; to tackle the unions head-on. And in 1979 there was a politician who was willing to do just that.

Enter Mrs Thatcher

Mrs Thatcher's union reforms were crucial to her larger aim of revitalising British capitalism. Unlike any of her post-war predecessors her objective was not to make unions 'responsible' or to find some way of transforming collective bargaining so that better trade-offs could be achieved between inflation, growth and unemployment. Rather she wanted to abolish collective bargaining altogether, along with all its baggage – Keynesian economics, industrial policy, state intervention, incomes policies and even aspects of the welfare state. She would proceed cautiously, recognising that every attempt to attack trade unions in the twentieth century had been beaten back – but her direction from the beginning was unmistakable.

In this she was aided not only by her visceral conviction that British corporatism had had its day and that trade unions were malevolent but also by the revival and representation of classical economics' description of how a capitalist economy should be managed. Her own prejudices were the spur; popular disaffection with trade unions gave her a political base; and New Right economics provided the compass for a ruthless campaign against trade union power which, fifteen years later, has transformed the British labour market.

Inflation, claimed Mrs Thatcher's new theorists, did not originate in the bargain between employers and employees over wages; as a monetary phenomenon, it depended on the way the government organised the supply of money. Professor Milton Friedman and his followers in Britain purported to demonstrate that there was a systematic relationship between the growth of the money supply and the inflation rate – and the ultimate source of money was the state. After all, the government owned the Royal Mint, not the trade unions – and once too much money was chasing the same amount of goods (because the printing press did nothing to boost production), inflation resulted.[3]

Mrs Thatcher did not need incomes policies – she needed to control the quantity of money in circulation; from notes and coins to the deposits in the banks and building societies with which individuals and businesses could settle their bills.[4] If trade unions settled for wage increases that were above the rate of growth of the money supply, they would soon find that there was not enough money around to warrant the wage increase – and they would lose jobs. But that was their look-out. The government would play fair by announcing in advance its targets for money supply growth, so that unions had the chance to bargain responsibly; if they did not they would have to face the consequences.

This was, and remains, a highly contentious theory of inflation. While it is true that inflation is a monetary phenomenon, that merely begs the question of the chain of causation; the rise in the money supply can just as easily be induced by structural economic weaknesses in pay bargaining, or by the failure of the real economy to deliver the kind of real wage increases expected by employees – hence money wage settlements that outstrip the economy's capacity to deliver them, resulting in inflation. In other words the increase in the money supply is at the end of the chain rather than at the beginning, and if a government attempts to control it without addressing the other structural weaknesses it is doing no more than tackling symptoms.

Yet this could not be admitted because monetarism was part of a wider body of free-market thought that did not concede such possibilities; instead the market would deal with everything. It argued that employers must only pay wages equal to the market value of what workers produced; that the wage paid to the extra worker should exactly equal the value of what the extra worker produced. If unions insisted on higher wages and there was no compensating rise in the price level because the money stock was not growing, then employers were faced with a cruel choice; either they gave up their business or accepted that they could continue trading but earn lower profits than they should. Equally if unions insisted that they control manning levels or, say, the speed of an assembly line rather than allowing managers to do it, then again the wage bill would be higher than that of overseas competitors with no such constraint; profits and ultimately investment would be lower.

Stable, non-inflationary money supply growth and wages equalling the economic value of output were two of the three elements needed to produce full employment. The last was that the unemployed actually looked for work, accepting a job where the wage reflected the supply and demand for labour. In this scenario firms' wage costs would exactly reflect the condition of the labour market, and if job-seeking workers bid down wages this would imply higher profits, investment and output. Ultimately firms would soak up all the unemployed until wages exactly reflected the value of output, which would now be higher – and all the time prices would be stable because the money supply was under control.

Full employment was not to be generated by government pump priming and incomes policies – the typical responses of post-war corporatism; rather it would be achieved by 'freeing-up' the labour market. There was no need to integrate unions into company decision-making; creating work was about improving the efficiency of market signals, not gumming them up with messy committees and phoney compromises.

The New Right economists' undilutedly classical arguments about boosting 'labour market flexibility' and 'controlling the money supply' in truth spoke to longstanding Tory prejudices; here was theoretical justification for tackling social security scroungers, bashing trade unions and cutting taxes and government spending. They were a godsend, especially now that the public's tolerance for trade unions and the terms of the post-war settlement were weakening.

Although individual unionists were anxious to protect their own jobs, unofficial strike action, of course, – especially in the public sector – also impacted upon them as members of society. Reports in the media of private sector disputes emphasised lost output and exports, and rarely explored the underlying reasons for strikes – the speeding up of production lines or challenging of old working practices. Unions were portrayed as greedy and stupid vehicles of militant shop steward power, solely responsible for running down the country. The caricature had sufficient truth to sustain the Conservatives' political position; and by talking about the need for protecting individual rights in secret ballots and crossing picket lines, Mrs Thatcher was able to tap an important reservoir of working-class support. Union privileges were to be emasculated with the connivance of a significant number of union members.

By 1993 nine major pieces of legislation had been enacted, all but one under Mrs Thatcher's premiership, which transformed British industrial relations. In 1979 there were 5 million members of closed shops; by 1993 the closed shop had been outlawed. Union membership in 1979 stood at 13.3 million; by 1993 it had shrunk to under 9 million, with only 31 per cent of employed workers belonging to a union – the lowest level since 1946.[5] Close to three-quarters of the workforce were paid under collective bargaining arrangements in 1979 but by 1993 these applied to well under half of it and pay was now linked to profits in nearly 50 per cent of all companies.

Meanwhile, the trade unions' wider powers were systematically reduced in a series of acts, each building on the last. Secondary picketing was banned. Ballots before strike action became mandatory. Individuals not wishing to abide by majority union decisions could violate them freely, without any fear of disciplinary action. Unions could be sued for damages if they went on strike without fulfilling the statutory procedures. Companies were under no obligation to recognise unions, and if they chose to undermine collective bargaining agreements with individual contracts they were free to do so.

At the same time qualifications for unemployment benefit and income support were made stiffer, while the benefit levels themselves, indexed to the growth of prices rather than wages, became less and less attractive – falling by more than a quarter in real terms over fifteen years. The so-called 'replacement ratio', expressing unemployment benefit as a percentage of average earnings for male workers, fell from 16.3 per cent in 1979 to 12.4 per cent in 1992 for single workers, and from 26.2 per cent to 20.1 per cent for married men.[6] To encourage 'active' job search by the unemployed, all claimants had to be interviewed every six months about their efforts to find a job while unemployed workers were forced to join 'job clubs', where the Department of Employment offered free advice and monitored their efforts to find work, without which benefit payments would not be paid.

Although the tide of legislation was cumulatively devastating to the unions, a more old-fashioned phenomenon was undercutting their power in the early part of the decade – unemployment. Monetarism, with its impact on the exchange rate and real interest rates, squeezed output sharply; unemployment rose from 4 per cent of the labour force in 1979 to over 11 per cent in 1986 even though the official claimant count under-estimated the rate of job loss. Non-employment, those claiming benefit but unavailable for work, climbed steadily from 4 per cent to 11 per cent.

From the middle of the decade, as the legislation began to bite, employers took advantage of the new buyer's market for labour to launch a savage campaign of union derecognition. Between 1984 and 1990 unions were derecognised in 9 per cent of workplaces[7] – a remarkable proportion for a six-year period, and easily the most aggressive assault on British unions this century. The number of workplaces that recognised unions fell from 52 to 40 per cent, with the number of employees in such workplaces dropping from 58 to 43 per cent of the total. Derecognition accounted for three-quarters of the fall.

Nor was it easy to organise unions in the growing service industries, which had a large number of scattered sites (hotels, catering and so on) and in which part-time work prevailed. In exchange for giving any union the privilege of sole recognition employers typically insisted that they were free to organise work at the establishment as they saw fit.

This opened the way to the scrapping of industry-wide collective bargaining arrangements; by 1993 all such private sector structures had been wound up or their coverage greatly reduced, and only a handful of public sector arrangements remained. Wage bargaining was left to individual firms, who tended to delegate decisions down to plant level. Here, it was argued, wages could be more closely linked to productivity increases. Britain now has over 30,000 sites where wages are set unilaterally.[8] Far from destroying capitalism, as the left thought in the 1970s, plant level bargaining – once the unions' legal protections had been weakened – was seen as a way of revitalising it. Left arguments were stood on their head.

Public sector unions, a particular *bête noire* of the Conservatives, were singled out for special treatment; part of the purpose of the privatisation programme was to weaken their recruitment base, access to government funds and leverage over the political process. Steel-workers were defeated in a long strike in 1980, the forerunner of the battle with the miners; and the privatisation of British Steel and British Telecom struck an important blow at these bastions of well-paid, skilled and organised workers. In the local authorities tight financial controls and the demand that authorities contract out as much of their work as possible struck at the power base of white-collar unions.

The miners' strike of 1984–85 was perhaps the seminal act in this drama of labour decline; the union whose solidarity and industrial importance had made it seem invincible was beaten savagely. By building up coal stocks and outlawing secondary picketing the government had some key strategic advantages over its opponent, but even so it required all of Mrs Thatcher's single-mindedness, above all in nurturing the Nottingham miners who worked through the strike, to win the victory she required. The miners returned to work having gained nothing and lost almost everything except their dignity. The example was enough to persuade Rupert Murdoch that the print unions of Fleet Street could be broken in the same way. They were, in 1986 at a new union-free fortress in Wapping – itself an area that had once been a stronghold of the vanished dockers of the Port of London.

Fifteen years after the Conservatives' election the scope of labour reform exceeded even the wildest dreams of the New Right in the 1970s. There was no regulation of working time; no legally-protected conditions for labour hired under fixed term contracts; no minimum wage legislation; minimal employment protection; and employees had no legal right to representation at the workplace. The OECD, compiling a composite index of these measures, could, by the summer of 1994, rank Britain at zero – the lowest, apart from the US, in the industrialised world.[9] With the lack of legislation there was no obligation on employers to treat their workers other than as disposable commodities, or even to pay them fairly. A new world of free and flexible labour markets had been constructed, just as the free market textbooks demanded – but the results were to be strangely disappointing.

The results

Some neo-liberals like Liverpool University's Patrick Minford say that unemployment can now fall to under 1 million without inflation accelerating above an acceptable low level.[10] All that is required, he argues, is the low interest rates that the new, low-inflationary climate justifies; growth will resume and the full benefit of the 1980s reforms will manifest itself.

But Mrs Thatcher herself was arguing in 1988 – as were many of her economic mentors – that the reforms had *already* worked. So to be asked, seven years later, to wait a little more time for the real benefits to show themselves is more akin to the rationalisations of a millenarian cult than of economists observing the real world. One more year, or one more half-decade, we are told, and the magic will work; we only need to redouble our efforts and attack the vestigial elements of union power, collective bargaining and statutory protection of the individual at work.

But neither at the macro level, improving the performance of the economy by reducing inflation and increasing growth, nor at the micro level, improving the degree to which unemployment falls if wages fall, can the reforms be shown to have met the promise of their sponsors. Far from requiring a little more time and one more heave, it looks increasingly as though the programme itself was misguided – driven by a theory with an incomplete and highly partisan view of how the labour market functions and what pressures the wage bargain reflects.

The same is true for the much trumpeted improvement in wage inflation, with average earnings growth falling to some 3.5 per cent in 1993 and rising only fractionally in 1994; the best result for a generation and apparently the effect of the new flexible labour market. Nearly all computer models of the economy would have predicted this result based on pre-1979 data and relationships. A rise in unemployment to nearly 3 million, together with price inflation averaging less than 2 per cent, as it did in 1993, would have led to a collapse in wage growth even in the miserable world of the 1970s. For the reforms to have made a really measurable impact, the growth of earnings would have had to be lower still. 'Wages', as the Bank of England commented in 1994, 'are still strikingly unresponsive to changes in unemployment.'[11]

Research by David Blanchflower and Richard Freeman shows the extent to which this principal aim of the reforms – to make real wages more responsive to changes in unemployment – has failed. The original idea was that if the demand for labour fell, and if wages – the price of labour – could be made to fall too, then employers could afford to hire more people at the lower wage level, thereby reducing unemployment. But for men this simply has not happened. Unemployed males are as likely to stay unemployed as they ever were – indeed, the rate at which men are finding work has actually slowed down; and real wages show little sensitivity to the male unemployment figures. More men have moved from being unemployed to being self-employed – but self-employment for unskilled males in Britain means little more than using the enterprise allowance scheme to enjoy higher levels of benefit while attempting to start a so-called small business. These are not 'businesses' in the orthodox sense of the term but represent the unemployed trying to sell their labour in a casual labour market as mini-companies, sustaining themselves with state support while it lasts, and then returning to unemployment when the support expires.

Blanchflower and Freeman do find that women's employment has been more responsive to real wage changes but, as they implicitly acknowledge, it is difficult to work out whether that was because the demand for female workers was rising anyway. During the 1980s the credit boom and the growth of consumption caused an explosion in service-sector industries, such as hotels, catering and retailing, which demand a lot of female labour. This explains at least some of the rise in female employment – although women's willingness, and often necessity, to accept part-time work with flexible hours may also be a reason why they find jobs more easily.

There is also some evidence that the mark-up unions can achieve for their members over non-union labour has shrunk.[12] One researcher estimates that the union dividend has fallen from 8.8 to 6.2 per cent over the 1980s and that unions now represent 10 per cent less of the workforce than they did. As a result the most optimistic assessment is that real wages in Britain fourteen years after the reform programme began were a mere 0.5 to 1 per cent lower than they otherwise would have been.[13] This means that unemployment can fall by up to a quarter of a million without inflation picking up or the balance of payments deficit increasing; a gain, certainly, but this is hardly an earth-shattering result.

But what about strikes and productivity, ask the New Right and their apologists? Strike action in Britain has not been so low since the 1930s and productivity growth in manufacturing has jumped over the 1980s, growing at more than 4 per cent a year. From the docks, where the unions' resistance to containerisation was broken, to the printing works where new technology has at last been introduced, the labour market reforms have allowed managers to manage and breakthroughs in technology to be applied to the workplace. The failure of the 1994 rail strike was the last gasp of an old order.

It is true that strikes per worker in Britain fell more rapidly than in other countries during the 1980s – partly because of the drop in unionisation and partly because of the rise in unemployment. But the effect of strikes is overemphasised. Even in the 1970s' heyday of strike activity Britain lost fewer working days per 1,000 workers than Canada, Italy or the USA and by the second half of the 1970s the level of strike activity was already falling away, converging towards the average for industrialised countries.[14] Even then strikes were concentrated in a few industries. Between 1971 and 1973, 83 per cent of employees were not engaged in strike action.[15] It was always the coalmines, car plants and docks that experienced most trouble; industries with very particular adjustment problems or long histories of difficult industrial relations. Certainly the weakening of trade unions has allowed sharp jumps in productivity in all three industries but this alone is not the solution to the British economic crisis.

For while it was probably true that strikes were a desperate sign of power in the workplace, and this inhibited the improvement of old techniques, this is only one of many reasons for poor British labour productivity. Now that the inhibition has been lifted, and productivity has risen markedly, it has still not been accompanied by a notable increase in investment or output. Between 1979 and 1993, for example, there were only two years – 1988 and 1989 – in which manufacturing investment climbed above its 1979 level. Manufacturing output in 1993 was only 5 per cent above 1979, with little prospect – given the impoverished capital stock – of the level rising significantly in the years ahead.

Estimates of the age and size of UK capital stock – the machines, buildings and techniques that allow labour to be more or less productive – show that it is both older and smaller than that of any of its major competitors. For example, a recent investigation by Mary O'Mahoney and Karin Wagner of the National Institute for Economic and Social Research found that in 1989 German manufacturing had at its disposal about 30 per cent more machinery per worker-hour than British manufacturing – up from a 15 per cent advantage in 1970. Using extensive statistical tests, O'Mahoney and Wagner conclude that differences in physical capital are the most important factor in determining differential productivity growth, but that skills are also significant, and Germany had twice as many skilled workers as Britain. In other words, any explanation of British performance that does not incorporate poor investment is plainly inadequate; the blame can no longer be pinned wholly on trade unions.

The heart of the problem is that the labour market cannot be visualised as a market like any other, with unions blocking prices from doing their proper job of equalising the supply and demand for labour. Human beings are not tradeable commodities. As Nobel-prize-winning Professor Robert Solow argues, the theoretical categories that might apply to analysing trade in chocolate bars, fish or computers cannot be extended to labour because we have to confront the issues of fairness, morale and human motivation that permeate human action. Orthodox classical theory completely misinterprets these forces, instead imposing a simple economism that can only explain part of the story.

The key free market assumption is that work is a 'disutility' and leisure a 'utility', and the wage reflects what is necessary to persuade individual workers to forego the leisure they prize and undertake the work they hate. The wage any individual employer can afford to pay reflects the productivity of labour, given the plant's existing stock of machines and planned level of output. The rational worker will only give up living on social security to go to work if the wage is high or the social security payment low; and the rational employer will only be able to employ him or her if no trade union bids up the economic wage. Work is supposed to be a commodity like any other and obey exactly the same rules.

But are these assumptions correct? What if work is not a disutility? What if it is rational for workers to expect and seek rewards from work other than wages? What if productivity varies with levels of demand and investment that are independent of the wage bargain, so that wages alone cannot determine hiring prospects? What if workers are valuable to the employer even though an outside applicant might accept lower wages, because they have knowledge and particular skills that make their replacement costly? What if the firm itself is mobilised by a culture and sense of mission that means it is anxious to keep its existing workforce together? What if it is irrational for the unemployed to bid down wages? What, in short, if work and people are not commodities? Then the New Right case collapses.

And it must, for the bounded rationality assumed by the New Right does not exist in practice. Work is not a 'disutility', even for those whose wages and conditions are poor, for the rhythm of work gives life meaning. The achievement of new tasks, the acquisition of skills and the social intercourse that is part and parcel of the work experience is not something human beings want to avoid; they want and need it. Above all, work offers a sense of place in a hierarchy of social relations, both within the organisation and beyond it, and men and women are, after all, social beings. Inevitably some work is demeaning and poorly paid, but the same need is there. Those who work belong; those who do not are excluded. Work, in short, is a utility.

Workers make a series of calculations that are much broader than simply the calculus of wage maximisation and the trading off of leisure against work. The employers' calculus is more complex so that, for example, the apparently rational idea of laying off an old worker and replacing him with a younger, cheaper recruit may have knock-on effects in terms of morale inside the company, making the act self-defeating. The so-called 'insiders' who have skills, whose worth is known to the employer and who are members of a cohesive team, are more valuable than 'outsiders' – and it is virtually impossible for outsiders simply to price themselves into work given the value of the insiders.[16] It may even be worthwhile paying a wage higher than the local labour market demands, in order to create a sense of loyalty and commitment in the workforce out of which grows productivity and stability – the so-called 'efficiency wage'. None of this is captured by orthodox free market theory.

In particular, as Robert Frank argues powerfully in *Choosing the Right Pond*, some workers gain an advantage from being paid below their actual worth because they are compensated by being comparatively high up the firm's pecking order. Top staff in estate agencies and car dealerships rarely get paid what they are worth to their firms, but they enjoy status in the informal social hierarchy at work which makes up for this. At the same time an employer may not pay the going rate to keep a valued employee who has been poached by a competitor, because he knows that if he does he will have to raise the entire salary scale for the rest of his staff.

Paradoxically some employees may be paid more than they are worth, justifying their overpayment by their inferior status because hierarchies demand that somebody be at the bottom.

Internal wage scales are much more egalitarian than economic theory predicts, says Frank, and they are increasingly egalitarian the more the firm has to organise its workforce as a team. The army is more egalitarian than a factory which in turn is more egalitarian than an estate agency, but all are more egalitarian than the theory of competitive markets suggests they should be. Social and psychological theory tells us that people work for motives other than money; observation of pay scales proves the point.

As soon as you drop the prism of free market economics and look at what happens in the labour market, you discover that the laws of supply and demand do not fulfil the predictions of the neo-liberals. For example, Harvard's Professor Truman Bewlay conducted 183 interviews with businessmen and women during the 1992 recession in Connecticut to see why firms were not implementing more pay freezes and wage cuts – and why they were not hiring the unemployed at lower wages. The answers were instructive.

Bewlay found that firms did not lay off workers unless they were compelled to, because of the demoralising impact on the workforce. They did not hire the unemployed at lower rates because a 'two-tier pay system would cause internal pay inequities which would be resented by new employees and hurt their morale'. Moreover the unemployed had huge problems obtaining work, even if they were well qualified and flexible over wages. Employers worried about hiring overqualified applicants, because again it would upset the existing structure of pay and skills inside the firm – and when conditions improved the overqualified applicant would be likely to quit for a more suitable job. Only those employers who accepted high turnover rates – like temporary employment agencies – were prepared to accept overqualified candidates.

Bewlay's findings support the argument made by Robert Solow in his Berkeley lectures in 1989 – the labour market really is different. It is a social as much as an economic institution, and needs to be analysed as such. For example, using game theory he argues that it is perfectly rational for unemployed workers not to seek to bid down wages to get jobs because once they are employed they will want to enjoy good money – and all they achieve by being ready to work for rock-bottom wages is a brutish world of low reward for everybody. If firms refrain, as Bewlay and Frank show, from chasing wages down because of their concerns about internal pay parities and morale, then neither party to the wage bargain has much incentive to lower wages. Small wonder that Mrs Thatcher's labour market reforms should have had so little effect.

This debate prompted the British economists David Blanch-flower and Andrew Oswald to examine the data in twelve countries about the actual relation between wages and unemployment – and what they have discovered is another major challenge to the free market account of the labour market. Free market theory would predict that low wages would be correlated with low local unemployment; and high wages with high local unemployment.

Blanchflower and Oswald have found precisely the opposite relationship. The higher the wages, the lower the local unemployment – and the lower the wages, the higher the local unemployment. As they say, this is not a conclusion that can be squared with free market text-book theories of how a competitive labour market should work.

None of the links in the chain of causations imagined by the text-books works in practice. Somebody with precisely the same skills will earn more in a city or region with high employment than somebody with the same skills in an area of high unemployment. Whether in trade union-dominated Germany, the deregulated USA or the police state of South Korea there was no measurable competitive effect: the unemployed in the adjacent area of high unemployment did not bid down the wages of those in work in areas of low unemployment. There was no tendency – as the market theorists would predict – to equivalence of wages or employment whatsoever.

The way to visualise the labour market, say Blanchfower and Oswald, is not as the interaction of the supply and demand for labour. Rather there is an employed labour force and a stock of unemployed who have little or no impact in determining the price of labour in any labour market that exists in the real world.

The more the labour market is organised as a market in a commodity like any other, the more destructive the results. Blanchflower and Oswald have no simple explanation for this, but all the theories they advance are united by citing some form of human agreement that raises the value of work above the minimum or 'market-clearing' level.

It may be that when times are hard, workers who have jobs put in more effort, thus warranting a higher wage than the market alone might suggest – the efficiency wage effect again; it might be that employers choose to reward their existing labour force highly because they have skills, and monitoring the performance of new workers is expensive. But these are human bargains in which morale, motivation and productivity have been achieved independently of the market in jobs, and so they underline Solow's point – labour is a social institution.

More important still, the key to making the labour market efficient is to respect peoples' desire for fairness. In Switzerland, says Solow, local workforces react to economic downturns by sharing out the short-time work and parcelling out wage reductions equally – but only on the premise that they will be reversed when times improve. This is not the result of an atomised deregulated labour market; it is organised around legally binding consultative relations, with unions sitting on boards and with a good deal of trust all round.

Far from this, New Right economic policies attempt to turn labour into a commodity – not only in the way wages and conditions are set, but the way labour is managed in the workplace. The resistance by Conservative governments to all European initiatives at improving workplace consultation under the so-called 'social chapter' is symptomatic of a deepseated predisposition by British companies to treat their workers simply as factors of production. 'Britain is approaching a position', writes Neil Millward, 'where few employees have any mechanism through which they can contribute to the operation of their workplace in a broader context than that of their own job.[17] The presumption is simply that workers will do what they are told, and have no rights of redress, or even channels through which they can make suggestions of better working practices. They are meant to be impotent, and it is assumed that they have nothing to contribute to workplace organisation.'

The new economism towards work is personified in the obsessive linkage of pay with performance, in the belief that only the prospect of higher pay will produce higher productivity. In fact, as the Institute of Manpower Studies found, performance-related pay tends to lower morale, weaken worker commitment and lead to higher turnover rates. In a survey of over a thousand workers in three organisations the Institute showed that success was dependent upon the degree to which workers trusted those upon whose judgement their performance pay depended; the more they had been involved in the design of schemes and the more they trusted their superiors, the better the performance. Thus the paradox that although the origins of performance-related pay lie in viewing labour as a commodity, success in the implementation of the schemes lies in the degree to which labour is *not* regarded as a commodity and is fully involved in the work process. Where there is trust, involvement and a commitment to fairness the schemes work; where only economic values rule, the schemes fail.

These are insights that the neo-liberals have neglected at their peril. Insider power exists whether there are trade unions or not. To reduce insider power we do not need to emasculate trade unions but to empower outsiders and make them more attractive and employable compared with insiders; and at the same time we need to prevent industries breaking down into mini-social hierarchies competing with each other to maintain the internal logic of each hierarchy's wage scale. What we should avoid is the situation where a pace-setting firm increases wages for a given skill by some percentage justified by that firm's productivity, and that wage then becomes the going rate for that skill across the whole industry, and for other wages to be talked up to preserve the internal wage scales and relative positions in each firm's hierarchy. If this happens, average wages will always grow faster than the growth in average productivity, because the less efficient firms will have to pay the same rate as the most efficient.

Disastrously, this is precisely the situation that has been created by the supposedly rational reforms of the 1980s. The savage cuts in public spending on training, together with companies' own cutbacks, have made skilled workers more and more valuable. In the face of skill shortages good firms have had to pay to keep skilled insiders; insiders have gained more and more 'economic rent' from having scarce skills. The collapse of collective bargaining arrangements and trade unions, and the creation of many small isolated bargaining units have produced a dizzying *smörgasbord* of petty fiefdoms, all anxious to preserve their pay relativities. Earnings growth therefore fluctuates wildly with the business cycle.

The New Right reforms have made insiders perhaps even more powerful than they were. Average wage settlements are still running above the level of average productivity. The level of employment stubbornly refuses to respond to lower wages. Communication at work has been reduced. Labour has been turned into a commodity, but the trade-off between growth and inflation has only been marginally improved. It is difficult to imagine a greater failure.

The thirty, thirty, forty society

Not all insiders have had their position strengthened. Although employers may still prefer to retain valued and skilled insiders, they are tougher about the conditions on which they are prepared to employ unskilled workers at the bottom of the hierarchy. The impact of sustained high unemployment, the abolition of wages councils, the weakness of employment regulation and the growth of contracting-out have combined to expose growing numbers of unskilled workers to naked employer power. Wages can now be lowered summarily; workers fired, then rehired at lower wages or not at all; hours and the working week extended – and all this can happen at will.

The trend has many different guises, varying from firms who dismiss people only to rehire them as 'self-employed' workers without defined terms and conditions, pension rights or even personal insurance, to firms that cut the pay of long-serving workers by as much as a third despite longevity of service.[18]

Firms employing low-wage employees in some service industries like cleaning or hotels are more likely to be offenders in this regard than firms in high-value-added sectors like computer software or publishing – although even here the practice is spreading.

Society is dividing before our eyes, opening up new social fissures in the working population.[19] The first 30 per cent are the *disadvantaged*. These include the more than 4 million men who are out of work, including those who do not receive unemployment benefit or have not looked for work, within official definitions, and so do not count as officially unemployed. It also includes unemployed women and women married to economically inactive men who are unable to take work because the loss of their husband's income support would more than offset any wage they might earn. Altogether some 28 per cent of the adult working population are either unemployed or economically inactive. Add another 1 per cent who are occupied on government schemes to alleviate unemployment, and the proportion of the population living at the edge is close to 30 per cent; and this excludes those who can only find scraps of part-time work, typically on terms offering no protection or benefits, and who are paid half or less of the average wage. This 30 per cent, with their children poorly fed, their families under stress and without access to amenities like gardens, are the absolutely disadvantaged.

The second 30 per cent are made up of the *marginalised* and the *insecure*. This category is not so much defined by income as by its relation to the labour market. This is not the world of full-time jobs with employment protection and benefits such as pensions and paid holidays. Instead people in this category work at jobs that are insecure, poorly protected and carry few benefits. This category more than any other is at the receiving end of the changes blowing through Britain's offices and factories; it includes the growing army of part-timers and casual workers. There are now more than 5 million people working part-time, of whom over 80 per cent are women. Two million work for 16 hours or less a week, and have no formal employment protection; for example, they have no right to appeal against unfair dismissal and no right to statutory redundancy payments – and as 70 per cent of all new part-time jobs are for 16 hours or less, the workforce as a whole is growing progressively less protected. Although many women say they prefer to work part-time because it suits their family responsibilities, more than three-quarters are defined as low-paid – earning two-thirds or less of the average.[20]

Yet to describe all part-time workers as insecure is plainly unreasonable. Many come from two-income households. More than 15 per cent have held their job for more than five years. Although their wages, employment rights and social entitlements may be minimal, this 15 per cent will not feel particularly insecure and so they are excluded from the calculation.

On the other hand the numbers of self-employed nearly doubled to 11.6 per cent of the labour force during the 1980s – people who have only their own resources standing between them and the fluctuations of the marketplace. The growth in their numbers was driven in part by the 'enterprise culture', but some was the result of firms exploiting their new power and 'contracting out' work that used to be done in house in order to avoid all social overheads, forcing employees to take out individual contracts.

Around half of the self-employed work part-time, so they should not be double counted. However I have assumed that those who have been self-employed for less than two years should be regarded as marginalised or insecure. Those who have maintained their self-employed status for longer are assumed to be in this condition voluntarily and to be prospering. On the other hand I have categorised temporary work, which is wholly dependent upon fluctuations in demand, as insecure for obvious reasons; this is the most brutish corner of the labour market. Together these two groups constitute more than 3 per cent of the labour force.

The rest of the category is made up of those in full-time work whose terms and conditions have been weakened by the decline of trade unions and the weakening of employment law. Employment on fixed-term contracts increasingly defines many middle-class jobs – from university lecturers to television journalists – while the abolition of the closed shop has exposed once-safe working-class preserves like printing to casual employment. One of the best ways of measuring the size of this category – insecure but full-time work – is that 3.5 million people have held full-time jobs for less than two years, and therefore have not qualified for any employment protection. I also add here the near million full-time employees who earn less than 50 per cent of average wages. They may hold full-time jobs, but they are poor. Altogether just under 30 per cent of the labour force, by these definitions, are insecure and marginalised.

The last category is that of the *privileged* – the just over 40 per cent whose market power has increased since 1979. These are the full-time employees and the self-employed who have held their jobs for over two years – many of whom are the insiders described earlier – and the part-timers who have held their jobs for more than five years. Full-time employees are the category who have benefited from the 50 per cent increase in share ownership or share option schemes between 1984 and 1990, and the more than doubling of profit-sharing arrangements.[21] The 31 per cent of the workforce still represented by trade unions generally fall into this category.

This group too has its splits between rich and poor. Thirty-five per cent of full-time employees, for example, earn less than 80 per cent of the median wage.[22] Nevertheless the secure income defines them as relatively advantaged even if their living standards are low. But with the numbers of full-time jobs shrinking year by year, the shadow of the new labour market is lengthening over the privileged. After all if in 1975 some 55 per cent of the adult population held full-time, tenured jobs, and in 1993 the proportion fell to some 35 per cent, this fact is likely to enter popular consciousness. The 40-hour week, full-time job is set to become the preserve of a minority.

It is this segmentation of the labour market that is sculpting the new and ugly shape of British society. The polarisation of the advantaged and the disadvantaged has done little to check average earnings growth or lower the real wage; while the new 30 per cent of nomads move more and more between unemployment, self-employment and insecure work. Two-thirds of all new jobs offered the unemployed are part-time or temporary: and only 10 per cent of the insecure 30 per cent move to full-time employment. Instead 50 to 60 per cent return to unemployment.[23] It is in this section of the labour market that the reforms have worked to bid down wages and conditions.[24]

The fact that more than half the people in Britain who are eligible to work are living either on poverty incomes or in conditions of permanent stress and insecurity has had dreadful effects on the wider society. It has become harder and harder for men and women in these circumstances to hold their marriages together, let alone parent their children adequately, as the hours of work in which a decent wage can be earned grow longer and longer. Britain has the highest divorce rate and the most deregulated labour market in Europe, and these two facts are closely related.

The widely noticed decline in the number of marriageable men who can support a family, which means that the task of child-rearing and family-building has fallen to single women is not an act of God; it is because men, especially unskilled men, can expect little but to work for very low wages or to live off income support and the black economy. Nor can insiders look at their plight with equanimity. The impact of inequality and insecurity is pervasive, affecting everything from the vitality of the housing market to the growth of social security spending – and ultimately the growth prospects of the entire economy.

Beside these severe economic and social costs must be ranked the loss of civil liberties and the qualification of democratic principles entailed in the Conservative governments' version of trade union reform. The right of a majority, after a secret ballot, to require acquiescence in agreed decisions, should be a sacrosanct democratic principle – but not for British trade unions. Here the government has enshrined a higher principle: the right of the individual to work or to reach an individual arrangement with his or her employer so that majority decisions need not bind them. The right of free association has been curtailed by laws outlawing secondary picketing and sympathetic action. Important freedoms and a long-respected conception of democracy have been sacrificed – but for what?

By the mid 1990s it had become clear that while Britain had acquired all the worst traits of the deregulated US labour market it had achieved few of the benefits of that system. Instead it had European levels of unemployment, with none of the compensations in terms of higher levels of social welfare or of security at work. The Thatcherite programme had been imposed at a colossal social cost and had weakened democracy with few discernible gains. Bad theory and visceral prejudice had not after all proved a good guide to policy; the wrong objective had been selected and implemented in the wrong way. There were other reasons why British capitalism wasn't working – and the disease had grown worse during the period when Mrs Thatcher was putting the axe to the root of organised labour. Other roots tapped deeper springs, and were untouched by reform.

5. Proud Finance

The basic actor in a market economy is the firm. It brings material, money and labour together to produce goods and services. It is the firm that supervises the process of adding value – from buying in raw materials to organising the marketing and distribution of the final product. It is the firm that puts new techniques and ideas to practical use; and it is the firm that harnesses human capital to the best advantage. The vitality of a capitalist economy depends upon the vitality of its firms.

But firms do not emerge perfectly formed from the body of capitalism. Their legal structures and their aims necessarily reflect and reinforce a business culture and institutional structure and these in turn relate to the wider culture of the political and economic élite. The firm is not only at the heart of the economy; it is at the heart of society. It is where people work and define their lives; it delivers wages, occupation and status. It is corporate citizen, economic actor and social institution.

New Right economics admits none of this. Instead firms are considered to be the Darwinian creatures of the economic textbooks, buying cheap and selling dear. However they are financed, whatever their relations with workers, suppliers or customers, they simply have to bow to the superior logic of the market as it overrides culture and institutions. In the same way that an automatic and impersonal process of natural selection determines the rise and fall of species, so competition ensures the survival of the fittest economically, the weaker firms losing out.

But while competition may be Darwinian, there is nothing 'natural' about the institutional, social, legal and cultural context in which it takes place. In fact firms have hugely differing constitutions in different capitalist economies. As a result they change production, investment and profit plans in different ways to the same price signals from markets. At moments of crisis their readiness to restructure and refocus their businesses can be immensely different. The rate of innovation and speed of diffusion of new techniques also vary enormously. The relationship with workforces is different, ranging from the authoritarian to the collaborative. Their capacity to increase productivity is different.

Yet if this is the reality, it was one that Thatcherite economists and politicians could not see. In their theory, such a world could not exist. Economic underperformance, and disappointment about the vitality of firms, had to be caused by distortions of the market – trade unions, taxation, inflation or high levels of public expenditure. Just as the left argues that the capitalist firms must necessarily be labour-exploiting, so the right insist upon the primacy of market imperatives. Both claims are altogether too primitive.

Above all, it is the nature of the financial system in which ownership is located that is central to the character of any given economy's firms. This is what dictates the cost of capital and commercial priorities; it is the driving, mobilising part of the economy. And financial systems are themselves part of a still wider system of political and social relationships. If an economy's firms are not functioning as they should, defects in the financial system will be involved one way or another.

The counter-revolutionaries of 1979 inherited a financial system whose proclivities were intensely hostile to production and innovation – yet they looked the other way. The wave of deregulation, releasing the financial system from the few restraining influences upon it, was always likely to make the system worse.

The story of British capitalism is at heart the peculiar history of the destructive relationship between British finance and industry. Our financial institutions and the ideology of perfect competition and free markets have deep and interlinked roots.

The rise of British finance

The British Industrial Revolution was unique. It was an act of apparent spontaneous combustion that seemed to owe nothing to

deliberate state action or consciously-designed social and economic institutions. It happened without a well-developed banking and
financial system. Markets and private endeavour seemed, without
premeditation, to create a new and revolutionary productive system.

The results were spectacular. In the early part of the seventeenth century Britain was a state inferior to Spain, France,
Holland and Austria in terms of population, wealth and political power; but by the middle of the eighteenth century it
was contesting European supremacy with France; and during
the nineteenth century it emerged as the pre-eminent European
and global power. The agricultural and industrial revolutions that
spearheaded this rise to global domination may have originated in
a unique set of circumstances – ranging from being an island and
therefore spared the worst destructive effects of European wars, to
being the first to industrialise – but they appeared to generations of
political economists to owe everything to markets and the minimal
state.

In fact the state played a larger role in British economic
development than those who explained the British phenomenon
acknowledged either at the time or later – protecting the domestic market; guaranteeing traffic in British vessels; developing the
London banking system through government deposits; issuing
government stock, and underwriting loans and using the power
of public procurement to develop key industries – but even so it
was hardly as proactive as its counterparts in Germany, Japan,
or today's Asian tigers. British industrialisation was sufficiently
market-led for the free-market explanation to correspond to some
version of reality.

The state did not have to direct capital to industry; it did not
have to train and educate the workforce; it did not consciously
foster industrialisation. Nor did it have to create industrial banks
and a financial system that would support investment and national
development. Britain had coal and water in abundance as sources of
power; it had a rich market, a large pool of skilled workers, sympathetic laws and a business-friendly legislature; it had a culture
that favoured the practical, trial-and-error experimentation that

produced a clutch of new innovations.

In the view of some historians industrialisation also happened accidentally within a wider system geared to the development of trade, commerce and finance rather than industry. Cain and Hopkins in their two-volume book on British imperialism stress the vitality of the commercial and financial wing of British capitalism and the British élite's lack of interest in industry right from the beginning. Their central thesis is that successful British capitalists, politicians and officials have always been driven by the social goal of becoming gentlemen, apeing the lifestyle of the English aristocrat and aiming to have the same kind of effortless, invisible income. The English aristocrat lived on rents from his land; and with only a finite amount of land available, the rising bourgeoisie latched on to interest, dividends and profits from finance and commerce as the best alternative to rolling acres as a gentlemanly way of making a living.

This gentlemanly ideal is difficult to define – that is part of its mystique – but there is no doubting its motivating power for generations of Englishmen. A gentleman does not try too hard; is understated in his approach to life; celebrates sport, games and pleasure; he is fair-minded; he has good manners; is in relaxed control of his time; has independent means; is steady under fire. A gentleman's word is his bond; he does not lie; takes pride in being practical; distrusts foreigners; is public spirited; and above all keeps his distance from those below him. The gentleman is a human island, simultaneously aware of the nuances of rank while recognising the importance of integrity and reputation in his relationship with his peers. The civilisation fostered by such values is extraordinarily favourable to finance, commerce and administration – but not to industry.

London has played a key part in this social configuration. The country's chief port and commercial centre was also near the Court and Westminster Parliament: the successful City merchant or banker could expect his money to buy a place in society quickly. From the late-seventeenth century a unique political, social and economic constellation has held together, and it remains the foundation of contemporary Conservatism. Court, land and finance –

extending outwards to the military – have become the apex of the social and political pyramid and the focus of economic endeavour.

For, as Cain and Hopkin argue, the purpose of Empire was as much the generation of invisible, gentlemanly sources of income as international aggrandisement; British financial interests were at least as important in South America as they were in India in the late-nineteenth century, and driven by the same motive.

Britain's commercial and financial interests were cosmopolitan, searching for the highest rates of return to bond-holders and merchants. From the establishment of the great trading companies in the seventeenth century to foreign wars in South Africa or China the purpose was the same; to open up channels of exchange, merchanting and finance. And when the British founded a colony, the gentlemanly ideal haunted the minds of the colonialists. The plantations in Virginia and the West Indies; the great farms in Kenya; the rituals of the Indian Raj – all were united by the same ethos. The gentlemanly life could be lived abroad, often more fully than at home.

Industrialisation was a byproduct of this effort, not central to it. During the late-seventeenth and eighteenth centuries English landowners deployed new farming techniques to boost agricultural productivity, and with them came the enclosure of the medieval open-field system into privately owned fields and farms where the new techniques could be freely practised. The state was happy to legislate to encourage enclosure, and there was little concern for the condition of the poor as they were thrown off the land and began to drift in to the neighbouring towns to find work in the burgeoning factories, workshops and networks of craft-based, cottage industries. At first, the rise in productivity and output was less the result of applied science, and more the consequence of breaking down the processes involved in making already established products and allocating one task each to individual workmen, women and children.

Adam Smith captured the spirit of this primitive industrial revolution by dubbing it the Division of Labour. In his famous example of the pin factory he argues that breaking down the task of making a pin and allowing each workman to specialise in a particular part of the process greatly increases the overall output. A man might make no more than a few pins a day when working by himself; but by joining a factory of ten men where each specialises, daily production could climb to 48,000 pins and the output attributable to each individual shoot up to 4,800.

Industry was thus literally manufacture – production by hand – in factories where the division of labour had taken hold, specialising in production by machines whose origins lay in trial-and-error experimentation; it was accelerated or improved craft production rather than applied engineering. Innovation originated from amateurish efforts at improving techniques, with individual factory owners – an Arkwright, Hargreaves or Watt – stumbling upon improved processes.

Industry in late-eighteenth-century Birmingham or Sheffield corresponded pretty closely to Smith's picture; networks of small and medium-sized firms each specialising in one component of the production process as labour was divided and redivided. The economic historian Maxine Berg describes how in the Birmingham metal industries a myriad of firms devoted themselves to one step of the production process – either stamping, piercing, spinning, brazing or annealing. There were over eighty different steps in the button-making industry, with a button mould turner, for example, casting moulds in blanks supplied by others and then selling the turned moulds to button manufacturers – but not producing buttons himself.[1]

Local knowledge and information was central to the success of this operation, and often – as in Birmingham's jewellery centre, Nottingham's lace or Sheffield's cutlery districts – the small companies were all close to each other. These complex networks of firms dividing and subdividing, all connected by the same production chain, were the forerunners of the British industrial districts cited in Marshall's *Industry And Trade*; early exemplars of the 'industrial clustering' that we see today in successful industrial economies from Italy to the Guangdong province of China.

There was no public effort to design and build financial institutions that supplied equity, loan and working capital; instead they were generated by individual proprietors and their networks of contacts. The typical firm was family-owned and if extra capital was required it was provided by investors known to the family – Arkwright, for example, obtained his first funds from the local publican. Once the initial equity had been raised, new investment and working capital had to be generated internally by profits; but these were substantial – Arkwright achieved returns of 100 per cent when he introduced the water frame system for spinning cotton.[2] Local banks rarely did more than offer cash advances against invoices (discounting bills), in effect recycling money from businesses in temporary financial surplus, who deposited cash with the bank, to those in temporary deficit. Yet while British banking was very sophisticated for its time, beside the scale of financial mobilisation that fuelled later industrial take-offs its contribution was negligible.

The profits from the early cluster of inventions between 1760 and 1800 were staggering, but unless they had been high the rate of investment could not have been sustained. High tariff walls supported high domestic prices and profits, while the Navigation Acts, restricting imports to trade carried in British ships, limited foreign competition and helped to support profits. The division of labour itself, together with simple mechanisation also lowered the costs per unit of production dramatically; but the urgent necessity to make profits also forced the workshops to hire labour on increasingly abominable terms.

In the early phases of industrialisation, where the cottage industries relied on skilled workers, there is some evidence that artisan labour in small industrial firms, such as the Birmingham metal factories described by G.C. Allen and Asa Briggs, had harmonious industrial relations with working masters treating their skilled workers well. But as the machine age matured in the early-nineteenth century and the size of factories grew larger, with tasks reduced to simple and repetitive functions, the relationship between worker and boss became one of confrontation and exploitation. The overwhelming necessity was for cheap labour – and women and children supplied it. This was the commoditisation of work that Marx described.

In the textile industry conditions were particularly bad. The lack of financial institutions capable of offering finance over the whole business cycle or of financing new waves of investment forced individual firms to generate profits as quickly as possible; and that in turn forced them to minimise wage costs whilst retaining the right to expand and contract the labour force at will. Smith, Malthus and Ricardo all described correctly how starvation and death regulated the supply of labour and so prevented wages from falling below subsistence levels – but that was the price paid for minimal state regulation and non-existent financial institutions.

There was no need for new universities, schools or systems of apprenticeship; no call for the training of skilled managers; nor any need to mobilise large amounts of capital. Profits were so high that companies could finance themselves without recourse to external finance; and the state did not have to sponsor any of it. It could concentrate on what it had always done; husbanding its resources and sticking to the canons of sound finance.

The nineteenth century

As industrialisation took off, the domestic market exploded and export markets in the colonies offered additional assured prices and profits for goods like iron, steel, ships and textiles – the staples of the British economy throughout the nineteenth century. The London financial system could continue to be as international and trade-oriented as ever; industry in the great northern river valleys and estuaries was growing independently.

This early British industrialisation had some of the features noted in subsequent phases of industrialisation in other countries. The owners of enterprise were committed and dedicated, if necessarily inhumanly ruthless about their workforces. And while London finance retained its international orientation, for a brief period in the middle of the century local banks began to extend their lending operations and became a little less disengaged from the companies they financed. There were dense clusters of sometimes competing and sometimes collaborating firms. New techniques were quickly diffused around the companies, often by word of mouth.

But what was notably different from later experiences elsewhere was that the state was not involved and that the urge of the financial system remained distant from large-scale industrial lending. As industrialisation deepened it became apparent that the primitive systems of local finance were insufficient to finance increasingly large and risky investments; and that the response was to look to the same spontaneous market solutions that had apparently created industrial success during the previous century. The financial structures in the British regions were to find themselves sucked into the London market-based system – and adopted the same arms-length relationship with industry.

Herein lies the importance of the Cain/Hopkins description of gentlemanly capitalism. Industrialisation was welcome. At its zenith in the 1850s, the country's inventiveness was proudly celebrated at the Crystal Palace Exhibition; and there was pride in the British constitution that had fostered this growth. But it had not happened by deliberate choice or conscious political effort. Indeed the social mores of gentlemanliness remained firmly in place. The kind of economic activity the élite acclaimed was not industrial; it was financial, commercial or mercantile. Thus when industry began to be apprehensive about growing competition from the US and Germany in the latter part of the nineteenth century, there was an energetic public debate about the kinds of institutional reform and state initiative needed to meet the challenge – but it fell upon deaf ears.

Attempts had been made to launch industrial banks to meet the new financial needs of companies, but none took root. The General Credit and Finance Company of London, for example, copying the French industrial bank or *crédit mobilier*, survived three prosperous years after its launch in 1863 before succumbing to liquidity problems following the near-collapse of the famous discount house, Overend Gurney. In their absence the hotchpotch of local banks did their best, but there was never any real departure from the practice of offering short-term trade credits. The seminal moment was in 1878 with the collapse of both the West of England

and South Wales District Bank and the City of Glasgow Bank.

The Scottish institution was a classic Victorian regional/city bank, closely involved in the financing of its local industry – Glasgow shipbuilding. It was not especially well-run, but even though its lending tended to be short term it was trying to be as supportive of its customers as its German peers. It knew its clients and the soundness of their business plans well; it took their deposits and lent to them. But its liquidity depended upon its clients' capacity to maintain loan repayments, and when recession struck in the late 1870s the bank was faced by a double problem; its industrial customers needed more cash to tide them over their difficulties, but at the same time they were defaulting on their existing loan commitments. The bank was solvent, but not liquid. It had managed to ride out similar difficulties in the past, but the sheer scale of the lending needed to support even trade and commercial credits in the new world of steamship manufacture made it more heavily committed to one industry than ever before – and it needed to be able to gain access to cash deposits quickly in order to keep trading.

As numerous banks have found before and since, this access is precisely what the British market cannot provide. No single private lender will put his or her money at risk to save the bank, because the risk/reward ratio is unfavourable. There is no reward if things go right; but there is the real risk of losing all your money if things go wrong. Once a bank starts to go down, it becomes locked into a vicious circle of decline.

The City of Glasgow Bank turned to the Bank of England and asked it to supply cash against the security of the loans made to Glasgow shipbuilders. In Germany the Reichsbank had developed a system under which it would supply cash against industrial loans as long as other intermediaries also offered to do so; but in Britain the Bank of England, as a private bank run by City merchants and bankers, was under no such public obligation. It had to make a judgement in its own commercial interest and in terms of its own defined objectives – and they were to keep both its own reserves and those of the banking system stable, supporting price stability and the international value of sterling. Moreover there

were questionmarks about the Scottish bank's management. But
instead of engaging with the problem in the service of Glasgow
and its industry, the Bank of England refused the request. The
bank's business, in its view, was to keep at least an arm's length
from its customers.

'A point had been reached', writes William Kennedy, 'where
the entire system had to be reorganised to withstand the greater
risk of steadily enlarging industrial requirements or the system had
to withdraw from longterm industrial involvement. The system
withdrew. After 1878, no longer would banks become willingly
involved in the longterm financing of industry.'[3]

Local banks everywhere understood the message, underlined
by the collapse of the West of England and South Wales District
Bank. The involvement with industrial clients had in any case
been regarded as unsound banking practice and was kept to a
minimum; now it could also mean disaster. Banks must confine
themselves to short-term financing, discounting bills and invoices
and offering overdrafts as long as they were collateralised against
property assets. Equally they must have as large a deposit-taking
base as possible to minimise the danger of a run on the bank
through a bunching of local requests for cash.

The merger wave that followed reached a peak in the late
1880s and early 1890s, and by the First World War the hundreds
of banks, with an average of eleven branches each, which had
existed in 1875, had been merged into a handful with about 150
branches each. The big five banks – Lloyds, Midland, Barclays,
Westminster and National & Provincial – accounted for 80 per cent
of deposits in 1914. Their disengagement from industry proceeded
apace, so that they held no industrial securities at all – with most
of their assets held in cash or invested with the London discount
market.[4] They confined their support for industry to discounting
commercial bills and acceptances.

If industry was to gain the financial support it needed for
increasingly expensive and complex investment, it would have
to find groups of investors willing to club together and buy
shares and bonds issued by individual firms – in a sense a larger
version of the personalised system of raising money through

family networks. In the 1870s firms like Chadwick, Adamson and Collier[5] acted as intermediaries offering share issues to 5,000 or so wealthy subscribers, and finding buyers and sellers of the shares they issued within their own client bases; but by the end of the century the market had to be broadened and the first of the infamous share promoters – men like Harry Lawson and Ernst Terah Hooley – were putting together groups of speculators to back the first companies whose shares would trade on the Stock Exchange.[5]

Whether it was the first British car companies, Humber and Daimler, struggling to pay the huge dividends imposed upon them by Lawson and his friends which inhibited their production plans, or the failure of Brush and Crompton, the two largest electrical engineering firms, to raise money and exploit the 1880s' electrical boom, the story was familiar. The early financing of Mond and Brunner, who laid the foundations of what was to become ICI, was done by bank overdrafts using the firm's assets as collateral and with loans from Solvay in Belgium. Banks would not lend; stock market finance was prohibitively expensive and subject to waves of enthusiasm and pessimism; and so technical opportunity after opportunity was never fully exploited – leaving German and US producers the chance to forge ahead, their products pouring into the UK. Dr Herbert Levinstein, son of the founder of one of the most successful Victorian dye-stuffs firm and a prominent chemist, wrote: 'The application of knowledge requires finance and the capacity on the part of those who control finance to judge the value of a scientific discovery. The main cost of industrial research is not in the laboratory but in the application to the large scale . . . Who in England was going to find money for this? In Germany the banks would and did find it. We in England suffered and have always suffered from a lack of "educated" money.'[6] It was a sentiment that would be echoed throughout the twentieth century.

The structure of British finance was thus a major, perhaps the key factor, in explaining Britain's comparative inability to exploit the wave of new inventions of the late-nineteenth century – electricity, the internal combustion engine, chemicals and the rest. It is true that between 1885 and 1907 the number of domestic manufacturing companies quoted on the stock market increased ten-fold, but typically the dividend commitments nearly bankrupted many of those which floated, while there were many more who could not get any external finance at all – with deleterious effects on investment and output. Indeed, Kennedy calculates that had Britain been as successful in exploiting the technology of the second wave of industrial revolution at the turn of the century as it had been with the technology of the first wave of coal and steam, then in 1913 income per capita would have been at least 50 per cent higher than it was. Instead of entering the twentieth century lagging behind the US and Germany, Britain could have retained her leadership.

But London's interest was firmly international. Home companies in 1913 accounted for only 17 per cent of all outstanding securities traded on the London stock market while foreign issues, ranging from Indian and American railway bonds to overseas government bonds, accounted for 49 per cent and British government and railway bonds accounted for the balance. It was these assets, the City judged, that offered the best return for the least risk; and the Rolls-Royces, Monds and Humbers had to do better – or not get any support at all. Company shares remained the Cinderellas of the stock market, Lord Revelstoke of Barings famously remarking in 1911, when asked to finance a coal products company: 'I confess that personally I have a horror of all industrial companies, and that I should not think of placing my hard-earned gains in such a venture.'

By the First World War, a pattern was firmly established: a national banking system disengaged from production; a risk-averse London stock market focused on international investment; equity finance made available only on the most onerous terms, heaping large dividend demands on British producers; a Bank of England concerned to preserve price stability and the international value of sterling; and an industrial base losing ground to foreign manufacturers with higher productivity – and having to respond by bidding down wages to maximise retained profits, the only reliable and cheap form of finance.

'It is not, I believe, too sweeping a judgement to say that in the nineteenth century the City stood in complete indifference to domestic industry,' writes Geoffrey Ingham, who describes in his important book *Capitalism Divided* how the Bank of England together with the City and Treasury began to form an axis which has survived to this day promoting financial values above those of industry.[7] Cain and Hopkin carry the argument even further, showing how foreign and imperial policy was shaped by the needs of the City. The Boer War was fought to prevent the Transvaal's gold reserves, then 25 per cent of the world total, falling via the Boers into the hands of their German backers and so permitting the Reichsbank to challenge the supremacy of the Bank of England. The invasion of Egypt in 1878 was intended to enforce Egypt's interest payments on British bonds. The City, and its social values, was the dominant element in the rise of the Empire and the development of the British economy. Industrialisation was never the central project.

By the last quarter of the century the fact that London's financial system was organised as a market independent of the state, with strong international leanings, was beginning to have powerful influences on the power balance within the British state. The Treasury had to borrow from these independent markets and pursue the policies that they preferred if it was to get the best terms; and together with the Bank of England, it presented a common front to government, asserting the need for balanced budgets, maintaining the gold reserves and promoting free trade. Gladstonian budgetary policies and the Liberal commitment to free trade neatly dovetailed with the Bank of England's interest in promoting the City of London as the stable centre of world finance. 'Free trade and sound money are really two sides of the same coin,' commented Robert Chalmers, Permanent Secretary to the Treasury at the turn of the century.[8]

The Treasury and Bank became the guardians of a financial orthodoxy, trusting in the minimum state and the self-adjusting market system, that lasted from the late 1870s through to the early 1930s and then re-emerged in the 1980s.

The system in the twentieth century

The British are very good at finance and commerce. For over three hundred years London has sustained its position as a pre-eminent world financial centre, ranking with Amsterdam as the centre of international finance in the 1690s and now sharing that distinction with New York and Tokyo – a rare example in world history of continued success in one branch of economic activity. The historian Bill Rubinstein argues that, even at its height between 1815 and 1870, Britain was predominantly a commercial rather than an industrial society; and that the middle classes of industrial Yorkshire and Lancashire never succeeded in challenging the hegemony of the middle classes in London and the Home Counties. The incomes from London-based commerce were the richest throughout the nineteenth century, and even if those from the industrial areas rose relatively quicker in the first two-thirds of the century, they later fell.

Rather than berate the British élite for their concentration on finance and commerce, Rubinstein celebrates it. The gentlemanly ideal, fostered by the public schools and the class system, has in his view given the British a superb comparative advantage in their chosen areas of economic endeavour. Trustworthiness and an anxiety to maximise immediate financial returns in order to sustain gentlemanly lifestyles are potent weapons in establishing a financial centre and reassuring depositers that their money is safe, while using those deposits to maximum effect. Equally, he says, detractors of the role of the City and finance in British life neglect to remember the fact that Britain remained unbeaten in two world wars; and that on both occasions output rose faster than in Germany. The industrial sector was stronger than its British critics allow.

Here Rubinstein over-reaches himself. It is true that there have been periods during the twentieth century when British industry has recovered some of the *élan* of early industrialisation – but those were the periods in which the City and financial interests have been controlled and regulated, and when industrial rather than financial objectives have been the principal targets of policy.

These were also times when the very survival of the state was at stake. In peacetime, when the financial system and its maxims have reasserted themselves, British industry has continued to lose ground; with the experiences of the pre-1914 electricity, chemical and car industries, as described by Kennedy, reproducing themselves many times over.

The period from 1931 to 1951 is the most instructive, for over these two decades British industry underwent a remarkable transformation. The old staples of cotton, coal and iron and steel, still dominant sectors in the early 1930s, were supplanted by chemicals, electronics, aerospace and cars. Yet this required twenty years of cheap money; important reforms in the financial system; the first purposeful government and banking intervention since the industrial revolution; and a sustained effort to boost industrial profits through imperial preference and permission to create industrial cartels – the antithesis of the free market orthodoxies of the previous century. Gentlemanly interests were subordinated to those of production; the north was given equal preference to the south; and during the Second World War there was unprecedented direction of capital and state encouragement of investment.

The turning point was the international financial crisis of 1931 which not only saw Britain's dramatic departure from the Gold Standard but also the quieter, and no less effective publication of the deliberations of the Committee on Finance and Industry. The first event inaugurated a period in which sterling was priced to give the export industries an advantage, its value secondary to the prime objective of maintaining the bank rate at 2 per cent. In other words, cheap money for industry for once became more important than the interest payments to southern financiers. And the second ventilated a new preoccupation with the welfare of industry over that of finance which, although it did not produce any of the thoroughgoing reforms that the Committee recommended, at least gave intellectual support to a series of direct interventions in the operation of the financial system and qualified its anti-industrial proclivities. In one key paragraph the committee had this to say:

British companies in the iron and steel, electrical and other industries must meet in the gate their great American and German competitors who are generally financially powerful and closely supported by banking and financial groups, with whom they have continuous relationships. British industry, without similar support, will undoubtedly be at a disadvantage. But such effective support cannot be obtained merely for a particular occasion. It can only be the result of intimate co-operation over years during which the financial interests get an insight into the problems and the requirements of the industry in question.[9]

The Committee sought to rectify the problems that had emerged since the 1870s. It wanted to see a revival of 1–5 year loans; a resurgence in the supply of long-dated industrial capital; and in particular it felt that small to medium-sized firms were poorly served by the City, identifying the so-called 'Macmillan gap'. It called for the Bank of England to be more keenly aware of the consequences of longterm interest rates on industrial investment. In short it examined the City and found it wanting.

Given the scale of the problem, the response was feeble – but it was at least a response. The Bank of England set up the Bankers' Industrial Development Corporation to finance industrial reconstruction schemes, and the shipbuilding, cotton and steel industries were aided by its intervention – with steel and cotton benefiting in particular from the Lancashire Steel and Cotton Corporations; Bank of England-sponsored vehicles for bank financing of industrial reorganisation.

In one famous example the Bank of England chivvied the Midland Bank into nursing the Royal Mail group of companies back into financial health – a group which accounted for 15 per cent of Britain's merchant shipping fleet. Midland found itself developing an almost German-style industrial banking relationship, being involved for five years between 1931 and 1936 in detailed negotiations over business strategy and plans. It also backed Austin, and Lloyds took an aggressively interventionist

stance towards Rover. All the banks found themselves involved
in refinancing and restructuring the steel industry.

But although the involvement was impressive, it was very
much by *force majeure* – resulting from a combination of Bank of
England pressure, a change in the intellectual climate and above
all the extreme difficulties of British industry. Steven Holliday,
for example, shows how the banks were so reluctant to become
involved in the steel industry that as soon as their assets were
secure they tended to withdraw from managerial decision-making
as quickly as they could and return to short-term, arms-length
financing. Duncan Ross acknowledges that although the banks
did become more involved in industry, it was largely because
of immediate circumstances. The results were beneficial; but the
relationship did not endure.

The watchwords of the time were rationalisation and reorganisation. If banks were pulled willy-nilly into a closer involvement
with industry, so firms themselves were concentrating behind
tariff walls to boost profits and investment. From soap and mar-
garine to chemicals and cable-making the government permitted
a degree of industrial concentration it had hitherto attempted to
obstruct, while in areas as disparate as sugar beet, milk and coal
production it set up marketing boards whose aim was to secure
orderly demand for orderly production.

Above all there was the priority attached to cheap money,
which together with the drying up of government bonds led to
a collapse in interest rates. Bank rate may have been only 2 per
cent but with government borrowing falling, Treasury Bill rates
fell to 0.5 per cent, a step in the direction of what Keynes came
to call the 'euthanasia of the rentier'. The international demand
for British loans fell dramatically, removing another prop to
high interest rates. Gentlemanly capitalism, its values and its
institutions had never experienced such an assault in the previous
hundred and fifty years.

The war saw the process intensifying, with British scientists
once more capturing the inventiveness of the industrial revolution, but now, for the first time, finding strong government
and financial support. Nuclear fission, computers, antibiotics,

jet engines, radar, magnetron valves, artificial rubber, nylon –
the list of innovations was endless. At the same time production
in the key sectors necessary to the war effort increased hugely.
The machine tool industry, woefully neglected by the City, saw
its output increase five times between 1935 and 1942, while aerospace and chemical output jumped sharply. The steel industry was
overhauled and modernised while agricultural productivity, again
supported by government grants, exploded, stimulating a sharp
increase in the output of chemical fertilisers.

Gentlemanly capitalism was in retreat, and the British were
rediscovering some of the engineering and productive fecundity
of their forefathers. The clearing banks were simply told to resume
the type of lending they had discontinued in the 1880s. Overseas
investment was impossible. Shareholders' dividend requirements
were secondary to those of production. The results were dramatic.

In this respect critics like Corelli Barnett who argue about
the productive shortcomings of the British economy have missed
the point. What was remarkable about the British economy in
the 1930s and 1940s was not the extent to which it was held
back by a welfare-oriented, romantic, do-gooding élite – but
the immense productive and scientific progress it was able to
make given its starting point. It outproduced Germany during
the Second World War and narrowed the gap with the US – a
remarkable achievement. Barnett's critique, as David Edgerton
argues, is placed neither in a historical nor a properly international context. It is basically a right-wing, anti-welfare polemic
– one of the reasons it was taken up so enthusiastically by the
New Right.

Barnett, argues Edgerton, is too uncritical of Germany. German
aircraft factories suffered from restrictive practices, and Barnett's
figures showing that their productivity exceeded the British are
suspect. Indeed Britain entered the war with the biggest European
aircraft industry and succeeded in sustaining higher output than
Germany right up to Speer's reorganisation in 1944. Moreover,
comparisons by weight, Barnett's chosen indices, are irrelevant;
the true comparison is with the fighting capacities of comparable
planes and the technology they embodied – and here the British

were at least the equal of, if not better than the Germans. As for Germany's commitment to technology, the horse remained fundamental to its fighting strength while the British army was totally mechanised. Barnett is traducing history to cover his attack on liberals in general and the Labour Party in particular.

For while Labour was committed to creating a welfare state and ensuring social justice – hardly surprising given the treatment of the working class over the preceding hundred years – it was also committed to industrial modernisation, science and technology. After the war the Labour government tried to maintain the wartime system, but under increasing strain. Nationalisation and economic planning were to be peacetime instruments reproducing wartime direction of production, and physical financial controls were aimed at keeping interest rates low and reconciling Britain's overseas and domestic commitments. Large resources were directed to the scientific establishment created during the war.

By 1950 the results of this twenty-year interlude favouring production over finance were plain to see. Britain had a strong aerospace industry and a flourishing chemical industry, and was represented across the range of high technology manufacture – a partial recovery of the position that had been eroding since the 1870s. It was an unsung new wave of industrial revolution.

But there were already signs of future crisis. Nationalisation, while it was a way of offering external finance to key industrial sectors, was already showing its inability to challenge the deeper industrial/financial system; that would have required more wholesale reform of the City, which was not forthcoming. Although the Bank of England was nationalised in 1946 the government did no more than keep in place those controls needed to protect cheap money – and made no effort to establish institutions that might channel credit to industry as the clearing banks had been forced to during the war.

Instead, the Treasury regained control of economic and financial policy, and the City began to chafe under the continuation of wartime financial controls. Producers, benefiting from low interest rates, wanted more money at these rates but, as Sidney Pollard shows, they saw the very rationing that permitted cheap money as the obstacle to them having more. Against this powerful coalition there was little chance of increasing economic planning and ambitious ideas of sustaining planning in peacetime soon disintegrated. Old verities were reasserting themselves – and as the incoming Conservative government in the early 1950s celebrated its bonfire of controls, the City of London could heave a sigh of relief. The patterns established in the centuries before 1931 could gradually be reintroduced.

As the 1950s wore on the Treasury and Bank of England worked closely together to re-establish London's former role. E.H.H. Green, for example, cites a Bank of England paper in late 1957 which acknowledged that if the Treasury wanted to run the economy at full employment without causing excessive build-up of credit and inflation, then it would need to extend controls over the banking system to supplement interest-rate policy – but given the international role of the City, this would 'prejudice the standing and operations overseas of British banks'. Production and employment, in other words, must take second place to the role of the City. In the hearings of the Radcliffe Committee, the Treasury and Bank co-ordinated their presentations to resist any retention of controls over the financial system.

The clearing banks could once more absent themselves from British industrial investment. Shareholders could return to their historic mission of searching for the highest returns. The great merchant banks could again look for the best returns from the international arena and even if capital controls restrained their appetite, the Euro-dollar market was soon to provide juicy pickings. British companies, with their shifting shareholder base and weak support from their banks, would be forced to finance their operations from retained profits – and displace risk on to their workforces. The government would remain only weakly committed to scientific and technological support, focusing on defence and military requirements. The juggernaut with its roots deep in British economic, political and social history could again resume its destructive advance.

6. Tomorrow's Money Today

The key to the British financial system is to understand it as a *system*. The financial talking-points of the last fifteen years – merger booms, support to small businesses and the boom and bust cycle of British credit – have been discussed as though they were isolated problems, capable of being analysed and corrected one by one. Yet each of them is a manifestation of the way the entire system has evolved over centuries and now operates as an inter-related structure. It could hardly be otherwise, but one of the more remarkable aspects of British debate is how little analysis is made in these systemic terms.

The overriding property of the system is its desire for liquidity – in other words, the ability to be able to reverse a lending or invest-ment decision and return to the *status quo ante* of holding cash. It is the desire for liquidity that animates the dominant stock market, allowing investors in company equity, company bonds and gov-ernment debt to sell their ownership title so readily to others – and to get back into cash. The clearing banks strongly prefer lending short-term because they are haunted by the desire for liquidity – nor, except briefly in the 1870s and 1930s, have they ever behaved differently. They want to be able to have their advances repaid quickly. And it is because the Bank of England respects this desire for liquidity that it chooses to supply the banking system with cash in the way that it does – and to ensure that the City works as a series of related markets in which financial assets of any type are readily tradeable for cash.

All financial systems must, of course, have this capacity, for ready access to cash is the fulcrum upon which finance turns. Depositors must be certain that they can withdraw their cash on demand or else they will be unwilling to deposit their money; and wealth-holders supplying risk and loan capital to large companies and governments will be more ready to do so if, when they need to regain their investment as cash, they can do so by selling their own-ership titles to other wealth-holders. The stock market's capacity to offer liquidity is one of its key functions – and the reason why all capitalist economies possess such a market.

But what is so distinctive about Britain is that liquidity has become a fetish and that attempts to counteract this desire for instant gratification have been so minimal. For while the capac-ity to provide liquidity is evidence of financial soundness, it also demonstrates lack of commitment. The more liquid a financial asset, the less committed the owner must be to the longterm health of the underlying investment. If the going gets tough or conditions change the investor has already made provision for his or her escape: sell the financial asset, withdraw the short-term loan, rather than share the risk of restructuring and of managing any crisis. There is a permanent bias in the British system to lack of commitment – and from this all else flows.

As we have seen, the industrial revolution was made possible because local industry was able to obtain financial commitment from entrepreneurs and their individual networks of investors – and from suppliers and customers who offered credit. But as the nineteenth century progressed these local and committed networks were subsumed into the capital, with its overwhelming desire for quick returns. For London, as the centre of a world financial sys-tem, rapid money was essential to allow it to earn the highest rate of return by quickly recycling funds to the most profitable market when opportunities arose. But for domestic industry this was a disastrous tendency.

The stock market and clearing bank system are the poles around which a very particular financial culture turns. The capital markets have earned a deserved reputation for innovation in clever financial instruments and a willingness to trade in them – but by the same token the system fails the corporate sector, affecting companies negatively at all stages of their life cycle.

The system is deeply inhibiting to anything but short-term risk. Its effects can be seen from the lowest level of capitalist endeavour to the highest and most complex. It could be the proprietors of a small firm having to surrender their house as collateral to the bank in order to secure working capital, and then having to pay fees in advance as well as a large mark-up in the rate of interest they have to pay on any loan. It could be an individual innovator securing the support of a venture capitalist, and then being forced to prepare the company too early for flotation on the stock market in order to repay the venture capitalist's original investment – and to raise prices and profits to ensure the success of the share issue. This may be good for the venture capitalist, but bad for the individual company's longer-term prospects. Investment and the careful building-up of market share have to be foregone for the immediate aim of boosting profitability.

The system forces larger companies to pay high and steadily growing dividends to a shifting cast of large shareholders, mindful of securing their loyalty against the approach of a predator – whose aim will be to repay the borrowings needed for the takeover by again raising prices and foregoing market share. There is a strong incentive to be 'risk averse' in drawing up investment strategies, because at moments of crisis shareholders retain the right to sell their equity rather than put up fresh risk capital – and are more likely to exercise that right than support the beleaguered company. As a result companies themselves place a premium on stable cash flow, high security and high returns. Technical innovation and building market share take second place to financial imperatives.

The disengagement of the banks, their obsession with short-term lending and their unwillingness to support companies in trouble, puts an additional pressure on companies to rely on retained profits as a source of finance – and obliges them to sanction only investment projects with a high rate of return. The banks' instinct to bale out rather than to finance restructuring is encouraged by the short term nature of their lending.

Defenders of the banks, such as Forrest Capie and Michael Collins[1] emphasise the reluctance of industrial customers to borrow as much as the banks' unwillingness to lend – and say that it is difficult to believe that if there were profitable investment opportunities lenders would not have entered the market to supply the necessary funds. From before the First World War, Capie and Collins argue, it has been impossible, with investment finance, to disentangle lack of demand from lack of supply. Although they acknowledge a degree of institutional sclerosis they cannot believe that banks, as profit-seeking firms, would have turned away profitable opportunities for so many generations – and say that critics ignore the value of a financial system that was not prone to collapse, as the German and American systems did after the First World War.

The trouble with such an approach is that it refuses to see how finance operates as a *system*, or how it interacts with the state and the labour market. The fact that neither the banks nor the stock market were major providers of finance before 1900 does not mean there was no problem with the financial system. The absence of a fire brigade does not prove the non-existence of fire. In Britain, the necessity of financing investment from retained earnings forced wages down and fostered brutal exploitation at work, and the formation of British trade unions and working-class attitudes to management was closely linked to this searing experience in the early factory age.

Likewise, the development of a market-based financial system was actively encouraged by both the Bank of England and the Treasury for important reasons of their own. The Bank of England's prestige and importance was enhanced by London's role as an international financial centre at the heart of the Gold Standard, and it saw every reason to encourage the clearing banks to remain at a prudent distance from British industry, keeping the bulk of their assets in cash. In this way the Bank would be absolved from expensive interventions to bail out overstretched banks.

The Treasury, growing into its role as the pre-eminent institution of British government, found it useful to have the spokesmen of powerful, independent financial markets insisting on budgetary probity – they reinforced its own position as the arbiter of sound money and tight budgets. The Treasury and the Bank were part of Britain's unique state structure which put the levers of power into gentlemanly capitalists – and they had no wish to let them go. The state and British culture played their part in constructing the financial system – and in turn had their own character developed and shaped by it.

The way the banks conceived of profit is not as neutral and technical as Capie and Collins would have us believe. By enabling British wealth-holders to shop around the world for the highest rate of return, the financial system sets the highest benchmark possible for domestic firms: in the 1990s as much as the 1890s. A market's conception of an acceptable rate of return is not independent of its social and institutional framework; it is determined by it. Industrialists' ideas about the profits they must earn are framed by the demands they know that finance capital will make. These demands will affect the size of dividend pay-outs and the speed at which firms have to repay loans.

As Harvard's Professor Michael Porter says, it is impossible to argue about individual bits of a financial system.[2] They are all 'symptoms of a larger problem: the operation of the entire capital system'. He explains, for example, that the American system as a whole 'creates a divergence of interests among shareholders, corporations and their managers that impedes the flow of capital to those corporate investments that offer the greatest pay-offs'. His strictures apply equally to Britain.

The system at work – British finance and the motor industry

It is at moments of crisis that the system's proclivities as a *system* are most exposed – and the subtle but vital relationship between finance, the labour market and the state is seen. Robert Reich compares how the British banking system responded to British Leyland's financial crisis in the mid-1970s to the way the Japanese banks reacted to an equally grave crisis in a key Japanese manufacturing company – Toyo Kogyo, maker of Mazda cars.[3] The different attitudes to financial commitment and willingness to sustain illiquidity, the contrasts in the capacity to shape helpful managerial strategies and win the collaboration of workers' organisations, and the final consequences for government policy are marked – as are the results. BL is a fraction of its former size, the group has been dismembered and passed into foreign ownership. Toyo Kogyo flourished, even though it has again encountered problems during the most recent recession. It is still a potent force in world car manufacture; BL has disappeared.

British Leyland had mounting financial problems ever since its creation by the forced merger of older British car firms in 1968, but it was the 1973 oil shock that delivered the *coup de grâce* – raising its production and debt-servicing costs while sales fell dramatically. Staying afloat demanded an expensive investment programme; but in July 1974 the four major British banks simply refused to supply the required $1.2 billion, arguing that with the stock of debt effectively equal to the value of the company's equity such lending would be imprudent – echoing the banks' standard line since the twin bank failures of 1878.

With losses mounting the company failed to raise the money from the Stock Exchange. Shares plummeted downwards, with investors already exercising their right to sell. The financial system's preference for disengagement, liquidity and lack of commitment left BL with no option but to turn to the government; which became the investor of last resort. Since BL had a third of the UK car market, produced over a million cars and employed around 200,000 people, the government could hardly refuse – at least not in the 1970s.

The National Enterprise Board – the instrument created by the government to support strategic investment – was used to feed in successive doses of equity capital, supposedly the basis of a new investment programme. The funds were used not to finance new model launches and the introduction of robot production to the factories, but to fund first wage increases to buy industrial peace, and after 1977 to finance waves of redundancies. BL's famously bad labour relations continued; shop stewards resisted attempts to democratise the way the company was run fearing it would dilute their power and workers' freedom to strike for higher wages. A tradition of purely oppositional working-class culture, concerned only with conditions on the shop floor and old memories of resistance to exploitation, together with the bewildering multiplicity of trade unions in the plants, could not be overcome in a few years.

By 1982, eight years after the first signs of crisis, BL's production had been halved and the first new models were launched. Jaguar

was privatised, ultimately to be bought by Ford, while the rest
of the group was sold to British Aerospace. Renamed Rover, the
company had developed an alliance with Honda, using its engines
– the critically important and 'clever' part of car manufacture –
and borrowing heavily on its production techniques to increase
productivity. But its market share in Britain was now below 15
per cent, and it had only a small share of export markets. Viability
demanded an enormous investment programme to establish a solid
market share and BAe itself, operating under the same restrictive
bank covenants, could not raise the working capital to support
Rover's expansion. Nor could BAe find British equity investors
prepared to support Rover as an independent car company, albeit
strategically dependent upon the Japanese. In 1994 Rover was sold
to BMW, the change of ownership formally confirming what was
commercially obvious; the company could not survive as an independent force in a British financial and industrial environment. The
mass production British–owned car industry is no more.

The Japanese response to the same problems could hardly have
been more different. Mazda's difficulties were also prompted by
the oil price rise that followed the Yom Kippur War, and were
compounded by its investment in a rotary engine that was a heavy
user of petrol. Output of three-quarters of a million vehicles a year
meant it was a smaller producer than BL, with a smaller market
share; worse, its debt was four times the value of shareholders'
funds. In Britain the company would have been either nationalised
or allowed to go bankrupt, even in the twilight years of corporatism.

Instead of refusing to help, the Sumitomo Bank stepped in.
Unlike British banks, Sumitomo had a sophisticated information
system that had already picked up the company's financial difficulties and pre-planned a response; and unlike the British banks
it owned 11 per cent of Toyo Kogyo's shares – so that as a
shareholder it had a vested interest in the outcome. While the
British banks knew of BL's investment plans only days before the
formal request for help was made, Sumitomo had been working
on a turnaround plan for Mazda for months beforehand.

In return for substantial financial support, Sumitomo installed

its own management team which began a programme of massive
cost saving while investing in a new model range with convention-
al, piston-driven engines. Tsutomu Murai, the bank's managing
director, joined Toyo Kogyo as executive vice-president – token
of a willingness to commit financial and managerial resources to
a customer that is unthinkable in Britain, despite the major banks'
television rhetoric of avuncular support for creativity. 'For now,'
said Murai, 'we're an army of occupation. Active intervention is
unavoidable.'

The cost-cutting that took place was typical for a company in
trouble, but the way the pain was distributed is instructive. While
directors took pay cuts, managers had their salaries frozen – and the
sacrifice asked of production workers was merely to accept wage
increases below the going rate. Shareholders were asked to accept
dividend cuts. There was a freeze on new hiring and 10,000 job
losses – but here again the approach was distinctive.

Toyo Kogyo tried to avoid compulsory redundancies, retraining half of the production workers as car salesmen in the
Mazda network and allowing the balance to take early retirement.
Mazda had a weak distribution network which needed expanding,
and using its own car workers to man it was a novel way of solving
two problems at once. At the same time Sumitomo was trying to
find financial support, while the company reorganised its production and designed new cars.

Total debt was some $1.5 billion in 1974, but rather than
reduce its loans Sumitomo actually increased them by a quarter
so that its share stood at 16 per cent of the total – even though
the debt to equity ratio was four times worse than in BL's case,
which had prompted British banks to refuse the company a further
penny. When the smaller of the sixty banks who had lent to Toyo
Kogyo threatened to withdraw, Sumitomo twisted their arms to
ensure that no-one pulled out – and behind them the Ministry of
Finance was making sure that the longterm investment banks –
the Industrial Bank of Japan and Long-term Credit Bank – were
pumping new finance into the business. For the critical first rounds
of equity finance Sumitomo turned to the members of the *kigyo
shudan* – the unique Japanese system of industrial companies linked

by cross-shareholdings and finance – of which Toyo Kogyo was a member. They stumped up the initial new equity.

The first new models appeared in 1977 – five years before BL managed to produce the Mini Metro – and with new production techniques the rate of productivity had more than doubled by 1980, with Toyo Kogyo producing 43 cars per worker compared with 19 per worker when the crisis broke. Ford were invited to take up a 25 per cent stake, which was quickly waved through by the Ministry of International Trade and Industry – and by 1980 the debt to equity ratio was down to two to one.

Additional help came from Hiroshima, the company's home city. Business leaders clubbed together, forming an association aimed at promoting Mazda car sales in the region – and the regional government enacted tougher environmental legislation with the byproduct of making rotary engines more attractive and nearly doubling Mazda's market share.

By 1983 Mazda's production had climbed to 1.2 million cars, some two-thirds more than in 1973–74; over the same period British Leyland's production had halved. As Reich comments, all companies in trouble must respond in part by shrinking their operations and in part by shifting the focus of the business and trying to expand from that new base – but in Britain the bias had been towards shrinkage with little innovation, while in Japan the bias had been towards shifting focus and expansion, with some initial shrinkage as the platform for change. In terms of output, investment, employment and productivity, the differences could hardly have been more stark. And in financial terms, the loans that Sumitomo made in 1974 which seemed unsafe had by the early 1980s secured the future of the company – and in turn all of Sumitomo's financial involvement.

Some of the disparity in performance was connected with events in the wider economy; the years between 1974 and 1982 saw exceptionally low growth in Britain, constraining car sales – and the 40 per cent appreciation in the real value of sterling with the arrival of North Sea oil damaged all British manufacturing, making imports cheaper and exports dearer. It became more attractive to own a Mercedes, or a Mazda for that matter, than a British car. With

Ford's equity stake, Mazda was well equipped to take advantage of the upturn in the US economy as the Reagan boom took hold in the early 1980s.

But such events are not gifts of God. The Japanese had planned the US connection, while the British government actively welcomed the appreciation of sterling as an aid in the fight against inflation. This was seen as of greater importance than production and investment – which were supposed to follow on naturally from more stable prices. The priorities of British institutions were woven into their fabric, and their responses to one company's crisis were reproduced again and again at the level of state policy.

Sumitomo was both a committed banker and owner. It was actively involved in providing managerial assistance to Toyo Kogyo, reassuring itself that the corporate strategy would finally allow it to recover its debts and permit further loans to be made. It made sure that it knew the key information and that the recovery strategy was on track.

Through the networks of city, regional and national government the bank was able to marshal further support that helped buttress its position, with the informal network of companies of which Toyo Kogyo was part offering vital risk capital at the critical moment. Commitment; information; strategic intervention; a public framework of support; reliance on supplier, customer and business networks; longterm debt; and partnership with the workforce. All these features enabled Mazda's turnaround – and all these were conspicuous by their absence in Britain.

Not only was the very fact of public support for British Leyland controversial, hotly contested by the Conservatives in opposition and later in government as offending the basic principles of free market economics – the company could find no institutional framework to parallel its Japanese counterpart. The National Enterprise Board was a poor substitute, accepting uncritically the company's requests for cash and BL's own evaluation of its strategy because it did not have the managerial or technical capacity to do otherwise. Neither did anyone else. The British simply could not match Sumitomo's rescue effort; there was a lack of *institutional competence*.

The British banks and shareholders alike were anxious to keep their distance and their liquidity; and if central government didn't choose to help out there was no network of regional or autonomous local government to which the company could turn. It was on its own.

And while labour was compliant and co-operative in Japan, the unions were confrontational and hostile in Britain. Management could only offer unsustainable wage increases to buy peace; the security and welfare that comes from the shared knowledge that intelligent strategies are being put into place were not available. There were no clearly articulated longterm goals. The unions responded with suspicion and wildcat strikes, resisting new technologies. Yet their reaction has to be linked with the financial context in which British Leyland found itself. Without Japanese-style institutional and financial support, the burden of adjustment was bound to be shouldered principally by the workforce; and the unions knew that only through worker solidarity could their interests be preserved. The system interlocks, forcing both partners into a stance from which neither ultimately profits.

In his assessment of the determinants of corporate success, Professor John Kay insists that the chief requirement is a legal and financial architecture that allows companies to develop bonds of trust and co-operation with the various stakeholders in the company – from workers to owners. But that capacity is not allowed to develop in Britain because of its peculiar financial institutions. Their desire for instantly available cash and indifference to the longterm stem from the organisation of London as a series of inter-related financial markets – the root of the system's destructive tendencies.

The Bank of England and the banking system

The City is constructed around a series of markets whose guardian and midwife is the Bank of England. Both the stock market, where company shares can be bought and sold, and the money markets, where banks and other financial institutions can lend each other spare cash, are unusually wide and deep. More than 3,000 companies are quoted on the stock exchange where the daily turnover in UK stocks averages £2.5 billion.[4] Turnover in government bonds exceeds £6 billion a day.[5] On the London derivative exchanges three-quarters of a million contracts are bought and sold daily.[6] Annual turnover of domestic and foreign equities together exceeds any other financial centre except New York.[7] The financial sector's share of the value added in the economy is 20 per cent[8] – four times higher than the US and twice as high as Switzerland. For a medium-sized economy these are staggering numbers.

London's financial markets are a kind of vast pyramid in which the size of each individual market helps other markets grow, so that markets beget markets. The key relationship is the one between the domestic and international markets, whose size, breadth and liquidity support each other. The massive turnover in the foreign exchange markets, sterling included, helps turnover in the domestic money markets, for example; that supports turnover in the market for government bonds, which in turn supports the turnover in the markets for foreign bonds, or Euro-bonds. The depth of the Euro-bond market is assured by the turnover in the foreign exchange markets, because currency is needed to buy different bonds; and so it goes on in an apparently never-ending circle, in which liquidity and marketability beget more liquidity and marketability.

This churning sea of money has attracted over 500 foreign banks to London – and this critical mass of buyers and sellers in the various markets further deepens the markets' liquidity. London has become the centre of the new 'derivatives' markets. These are not financial assets like shares or bonds, which have a claim on real assets and income flows; they are financial instruments dreamed up by bankers and brokers whose function is to allow the holder to bet on what the price of real financial assets will be in the future. These are the hedges in future exchange rates, options on the level of the stock market, contracts in interest rates in six and twelve months' time and so on. For a price, almost any buying or selling order in the future value of any financial asset can be accommodated, with the banks insuring their positions in one derivative market by covering themselves in the spot market of the financial asset concerned. But in order to do that you need many markets in which offsetting covering positions can be taken.

It is this dense inter-relationship between markets that allows London to keep its premier place in the world financial order, despite the weakness of the British economy. The depth and vigour of the markets becomes a self-fulfilling prophecy – a kind of confidence trick. It is because there are so many institutions buying and selling, depositing and borrowing from each other that there is the confidence to launch new financial products.

The Bank of England is no innocent bystander in the development of the financial system; it is the main actor. The Bank's overwhelming objective is to sustain London's position as an international financial centre – and its history, internal organisation, culture and recruitment policy all reinforce that mission. Although it was nationalised by the Labour government in 1946 it has never felt any need to qualify its basic credo that the promotion of the City of London's financial markets is synonymous with the public interest. All central banks are concerned about the viability of their financial system, and the Bank of England prides itself that while individual banks have encountered problems there has never been a general banking collapse in its entire history. The emphasis on liquidity, breadth of financial markets and solvency seems amply justified – especially as it has brought Britain international financial power, increasingly important foreign earnings and hundreds of thousands of jobs in the financial sector.

The Bank is uniquely dominated, for a national central bank, by the concerns of the financial institutions for which it is responsible. While the US central bank is located in Washington and not in the main financial centre of New York, and the Bundesbank is on the outskirts of Frankfurt, the Bank of England is located symbolically in the heart of London's financial district. It is within a short walk of all the key financial institutions – something vitally important to the way it views itself and conducts its business.

The governing body of the Bank is the Court, with an inbuilt majority of members whose interest in the promotion of the City mirrors that of the Bank's own officials. Of eighteen directors, six

are Bank officials running the key departments, including the Governor and Deputy Governor; and another six are drawn from City
institutions. Six industrialists complete the membership (with the
government refusing to renominate a trade unionist in 1994 when a
position became vacant). Of the non-Bank members of the Court,
five run companies which are important contributors to the Conservative Party. The Governor of the Bank of England, who in the
post-war period has always been drawn from a merchant or clearing bank, is now Eddie George – a career Bank of England official.
In short the governing body is constructed so as to legitimise the
Bank's role as defender-in-chief of the institutions of gentlemanly
capitalism; there can never be enough outside members, even if
they were so minded, to challenge that role – nor is the Court
organised to permit that kind of intervention. Like the monarchy,
its role is to 'dignify' the Bank's constitution.

It is thus a public body in name, but its overweening objective
is to further – as it would say – the smooth running of a financial
system whose sense of the public interest is extremely tenuous. The
more liquid and broad the markets the better. When it needs to,
the Bank looks for theories that justify its instinctive institutional
preoccupation – and there is no better tool than classical economics.

The Bank believes that the stock market is an effective way
of raising money for companies – as classical economics predicts.
It believes that takeovers are a good means of keeping companies
efficient. It distrusts arguments that the financial institutions are
not serving the wider economy well, arguing that in a free market
any demand by companies for different kinds of financial support
would naturally appear, supplied by profit-seeking financial institutions. It regards low inflation and financial stability as the prime
sources of growth. These are cardinal verses in the classical economists' bible.

But the Bank's formal job is not to run the City's markets;
it is to act as the government's banker and the instrument of
its financial policies, raising money day by day so that the government can pay its bills and also managing the state's foreign
exchange reserves and its currency policy. It is a matter of pride
that it gets the keenest terms for the government IOUs it issues,

ranging from Treasury Bills to longterm government bonds – and it has structured London's financial markets so that they serve its own role of being an efficient banker to the government while placing the least onerous burden on the financial system. With the publication of the Quarterly Inflation Report independently commenting on the government's capacity to meet its inflation target, and the minutes of the Governor's monthly monetary meeting with the Chancellor, the Bank has become a high profile adviser on interest-rate strategy.

The core of any financial system is money; and legal tender can only be supplied by the government of the day. Thus how the Bank chooses the terms on which it issues notes and coins to the banking system and manages the day to day financing requirements of the government and its longer-term borrowing is the fulcrum upon which the financial system turns. The emphasis the clearing banks place on maintaining their liquidity is thus substantially supported by the readiness with which the Bank makes that liquidity available.

The British system turns on an unspoken but explicit deal between the Bank and the financial markets, which is the first of many impulses driving the system's short-termism. The Bank wants to run the government's finances with maximum flexibility so that, borrowing an analogy from an individual person's finances, whether it wants to run an overdraft with the financial markets, or take out a longterm mortgage, the markets guarantee to meet the Bank's demands. Whether the Bank offers Treasury Bills or Government Bonds, the market will buy them. In return the Bank will supply legal tender on demand to the system whenever it is short of liquidity. This bargain is similar in other financial systems; what is distinctive about Britain is that the central Bank has chosen to execute the bargain through a system of markets.

The discount houses are the designated intermediaries between the financial institutions and the Bank; they assemble the necessary cash from the banks and buy whatever amount of short-term Treasury Bills and government IOUs the Bank is offering to finance the government's needs. But they also perform a similar function for the banks, so that those banks who need cash to square their books overnight can turn to the discount houses, who can go to the Bank of England if they cannot find the cash from the markets on the keenest terms. In the morning the markets and banks supply the discount houses with the cash they need; in the afternoon they can look to the same houses for cash back. Again what is noticeable is the lack of formal administrative mechanisms – and the reliance on markets.

The system is dynamised by the movements of interest rates on the varying maturities of the financial IOUs (Bills, Certificates of Deposit, etc.) over the day as demand and supply ebbs and flows. The fluctuations in the capital value of the underlying financial assets may be minute, but because the volume of the financial assets runs into billions they still produce useful profits. The value of the monthly turnover of Treasury Bills handled by the discount houses alone is some £20 billion – and the interest rates on these bills are the benchmark for all the bank bills and certificates of deposit that financial institutions issue to each other to raise money, and which are then traded in the London money market. The daily turnover runs into tens of billions; it is so large it is not even measured. When the Bank wants to influence interest rates, it simply changes the rate at which it will buy Treasury Bills seven or fourteen days from maturity – the very shortest time period – and the change cascades through the money markets.

This is the key to the motion of the system. Cash is permanently available at a price. If the Bank wishes to change the level of interest rates, it changes that price; and if it wants to keep the system short of cash then it charges a premium over its indicated interest rate to signal to all the actors that if they need liquid cash they must pay a penalty. Bank and markets are in a permanent cat and mouse game, second-guessing each other over hourly moves in interest rates.

What the Bank never does, under the current rules, is to confiscate cash or financial assets and put them into cold storage if it thinks liquidity is growing too rapidly, or vice versa if it feels it is growing too slowly. And while other central banks actively manage the entire structure of short-term interest rates across the maturity range of government debt by buying and selling and so shifting liquidity in and out of the system wherever it sees pressure points, the Bank of England operates solely at the very short end of the market – and lets market forces dictate interest rates.

Its attitude is exemplified by its approach to reserve requirements. Every other central bank in the industrialised world (except Luxembourg) requires its financial system to lodge a certain amount of cash with it as a kind of float – known in the jargon as minimum reserve requirements – and it adjusts this to modify liquidity as it sees fit. But not the Bank of England. It lobbied for the abolition of reserve requirements in 1980 (and so unleashed the 1980s credit boom) and runs the system wholly through shifts in interest rates.

In the rest of the world, central banks have direct leverage over the banks' balance sheets, and have the right to use changes in reserve requirements to supplement interest-rate movements in altering the banks' ability to lend. If reserve requirements are increased, the banks have *less* cash to lend; if they are decreased then they have *more* cash to lend. All banks experience equally any changes in reserve requirements. One system is a codified structure of disciplines; the British is a free for all in which the only constraint is the price of money.

This has far-reaching implications. The deep money markets that the Bank of England fosters not only enable the Bank to manage its financing needs with great skill and flexibility but also offer the banks the same facility. The banks follow the central Bank in playing the short-term money markets, keeping their liabilities short, always watchful for a trading opportunity and knowing that come what may there will always be cash to borrow, if at a price. But that need not worry any particular bank if it can pass the cost on to its customers. If the rate of interest on the loans it has made can be adjusted in line with the cost of the deposits, then the bank behaves like a classic intermediary, never itself at risk of losing money. It raises short-term deposits in London's money markets. It lends the money, trying to keep the loans as short-term as possible to match the short-term deposits. It tries to secure the loans it makes with property collateral which can be confiscated if the borrower defaults. And it makes sure that interest rates on the loan fluctuate in line with the cost of deposits – because banks even have to pay interest on the dwindling proportion of deposits raised through the branch network.

When banks themselves have to borrow large amounts of cash in the short-term money markets, it is not very attractive for them to lend longterm to industry at fixed rates of interest. Prudent banking practice demands that the kind of bank loan financed by short-term borrowing should in itself be short-term, self-liquidating and with a variable interest rate – with the bank guaranteed a profit by lending at a fixed mark-up over the rate at which it borrows. Thus is the character of British banking determined, with banks displacing the risk of interest rates changes on to their customers, who take on dangerously open-ended commitments.

The short-term structure of British bank lending does not come out of thin air. The way the Bank of England manipulates and guarantees the vast short-term money markets is the first of many incentives that forces the banks into keeping their lending as short-term as they can. The attitude is profoundly embedded and is part of the clearing banks' culture. It even figures in banking exams for recruits and rising executives. Banks must match their liabilities and assets; and so they must not lend longterm to support industrial investment if they only have short-term deposits. This cardinal principle of British banking was underlined in the 1830 edition of the *History and Principles of Banking*, was repeated in the 1970 edition of *The Lending Banker*[9] – and can still be seen today in the structure of bank balance sheets. In 1992 for example, more than 60 per cent of National Westminster's lending (excluding personal mortgages) was for less than a year; and under 20 per cent was for more than five years.[10]

Comparison between Britain and the rest of the world is difficult because unsurprisingly British banks do not like to disclose the degree of their short-term lending and the Bank of England makes no effort to insist that they do – a fact little commented upon by defenders of the system. However, there are clues. Deutsche Bank is Germany's largest bank, and its loan profile is the opposite of National Westminster's; half its lending is for more than four years.[11]

This loan profile matters, and is reflected in the level and sustainability of corporate debt. One of the few international comparisons available, from 1992, shows that 58 per cent of all lending to British small and medium-sized companies was in the form of overdrafts, compared with 14 per cent for Germany, 31 per cent for France and 35 per cent for Italy. Moreover virtually the entire stock of British company debt was at variable rates.[12]

The more short-term the lending, the higher the annual debt service requirement – just as the shorter the term of a house mortgage, the greater the annual repayment. When British companies are tempted to borrow heavily, as in the 1980s, their debt is less easy to service when cash flow gets squeezed – which is all the more painful because with variable interest rates their debt service requirements rise as interest rates rise. They are caught in a double bind and obliged to conserve cash by reducing investment, R & D and, of course, their workforces. British companies need to have the least demanding labour standards in the OECD, because without that flexibility they are much more likely to get into financial difficulty than their competitors whose debt structure is more longterm.

British companies, knowing this very well, are more reluctant to undertake borrowing than their competitors. In a league table assembled by the management consultants Coopers and Lybrand for the European Commission, British companies had the lowest proportion of debt in relation to equity of any industrialised country except Ireland.[13] Companies do not want to incur debt on such dangerous terms and instead rely on financing their operations through retained profits.

But debt is a much cheaper form of capital than issuing shares, and by borrowing so little the average cost of capital in Britain – including debt service, dividend payments, shareholders' profit requirements and tax payments – becomes, according to Coopers and Lybrand, among the highest in the world. While other countries' companies offset the high cost of equity by borrowing cheaper bank debt, which then lowers their cost of capital again because interest payments can be offset against tax, British companies do least to offset the high cost of equity capital with cheaper bank debt. Over the period 1983–91 the overall cost of capital in Japan was 14.7 per cent, in the US 15.1 per cent and Germany 15.7 per cent, but in Britain it stood at 19.9 per cent – and Coopers tested their result over time and found the same pecking order.[14] In manufacturing industries such as cars, steel, chemicals and paper where goods are traded internationally, differences in financial structure which lead to a varying cost of capital become pivotal determinants of the capacity to invest and innovate and to sustain longer production runs and lower unit costs.

British companies, compelled to set their prices to earn enough to pay back their expensive capital, have to surrender market share to competitors whose financial structure allows a lower cost of capital and who can set their prices accordingly. So while overseas competitors can climb on to a virtuous circle of expanding output and investment, British companies are forced into a vicious circle of static output and lagging investment. The apparently imprudent borrowing that foreign firms incur looks prudent enough when their output and revenue climbs. But even prudent levels of British debt begin to look imprudent as the companies' underlying competitive position weakens.

So it is that British companies have retreated in international manufacturing industries which have mass production and high fixed costs. In general they have instead adopted niche strategies where they have the chance to charge higher prices and earn higher profits. As John Muellbauer and Anthony Murphy[15] have shown, the more British industry was exposed to international competition in the 1980s, the lower its investment. Investment in the motor, mechanical engineering and mineral oil processing industries have all lagged; while domestic banking, communications and distribution sectors enjoyed an investment boom.

The analysis by Michael Porter in *The Competitive Advantage of Nations* underlines the point. Between 1978 and 1985 (the period for which the latest figures are available – tellingly, no British academic has followed up Porter's trail-blazing work) many more internationally competitive industries in Britain lost market share than gained it – but even more worryingly, the few gains were in petroleum products and low technology metal products, while the losses were experienced in most of the country's sophisticated industries. 'Large net losses in machinery', writes Porter, 'and in industries serving other industries (transport, office equipment, telecommunications, and power distribution) signal an inability to upgrade, a shrinkage of clusters and a narrowing of competitive industries in the economy.'

The British economy, as in the decades before the First World War, is again suffering from a financial structure that prevents it from exploiting a new generation of technologies. From bio-technology to semi-conductors there is a scant to non-existent British presence; the few exceptions have some unique technology or innovation which allows them to charge higher prices. Britain's share of patents lodged in the US is falling as the sinews of technological innovation weaken. Mobilisation of finance by the City or government to exploit the new opportunities is conspicuous by its absence.

Yet continental Europe and Japan have in general equipped themselves with longterm development banks whose mission is to mobilise precisely the longterm finance upon which any sustained investment effort depends. Japan has its Industrial Bank of Japan; Germany its Kreditanstalt für Wiederaufbau (KfW) or reconstruction bank; Korea a state development bank; France the Crédit National and various specialist *crédits mobiliers* and so on. All are organised to avoid the liquidity and commitment problem. They are given tax privileges which allow them to pay attractive interest rates on longterm deposits, equipping themselves to make longterm loans; but the crucial additional factor is the structure of their share capital. Normally their shareholders, which include the state in some form, either do not require dividends at all in the British sense or only at some distant time in the future.[16]

The reason why the German KfW can risk not being as liquid as a private British bank is that it does not have to pay dividends to its shareholders; all its profits are ploughed back into the bank to boost its capital base – which is then larger again for the next round of lending. The same is true of the German public

savings and development banks at regional state level. Nor does
the KfW, any more than the Industrial Bank of Japan, have to lend
every investment pound in Germany. Normally it provides only
a fraction of the total loan package for any investment, but that
encourages the German private banks into improving their own
lending terms. Even if the private banks only lengthen their loan
schedules marginally, the overall package is much more relaxed
and committed than those offered in Britain.

But British companies have no longterm development bank.
Nor is there a private industrial banking system, as in Europe
and Japan, ready to provide longer-term loans. Instead Britain's
companies confront banks who themselves have private institutional shareholders setting very demanding targets for the rates
of return.

This is the second and perhaps even more important bias
to disengagement and short-termism. The banks have to make
high returns to satisfy their own investors. As a result they have
to maintain a high margin between the funds they borrow and
lend, to charge high fees for loans, to take the maximum property
collateral, and to retain the capacity to switch the bank's lending
to more profitable operations. The demand for quick profits is
fundamental to their relationship with industry.

Stephen Zimmer and Robert McCauley, two economists at the
Federal Reserve Bank of New York, calculate that over the last
thirty years the British stock market has required British banks
to make returns of 9.8 per cent on average – compared with 3.1
per cent for Japanese banks, 5.3 per cent for Swiss banks and 6.9
per cent for German banks. The freer and more dominant the
stock market, the higher the returns required from the banks –
US banks have been asked to make 11.9 per cent. And like the
British banks, American private banks lend short term with an
accent on immediate profitability in their lending – but American
companies, unlike their British counterparts, have a wider range
of local financial options. Above all the US has, until recently,
forbidden state banks to lend outside state boundaries – and as a
result companies have a captive banking system, forced to offer
attractive terms even if its share capital is expensive. Britain does

not even have this let-out. It remains as centralised as any oligar-
chical eighteenth-century state.

One of the other important advantages of the American system, like the German, is that its federal government structure
has supported regional banks and regional financial markets. The
banks thus have local knowledge of their customers, their business strategies and the future viability of their businesses; they are
not reduced to a series of financial ratios held on the head-office
computer as they are in Britain. This allows US and German local
banks to tailor loan packages to individual company needs to a
much greater extent. It also gives these banks a sense of belonging to the cities and regions in which they operate. If economic
decline hits any particular locality, not only does it adversely affect
the business prospects of a particular bank, but the employment
prospects of the bankers' associates and relatives. No such emo-
tional pull touches the British system. South Wales or Durham
might as well be in Latin America for all the effect their decline
has on the directors of Barclays or Lloyds. The London financial
institutions make their cold-blooded judgement; and it cannot be
contested.

The stock market and the commitment problem

The London stock market is regarded by the Bank of England,
the City institutions and the financial pages of the broadsheet
newspapers as a source of great economic strength – and constant fascination. The value of the shares quoted exceeds £600
billion, ranking only after New York and Tokyo in size. Its
daily movements are charted by TV, radio and the press and
the weekly diet of bids, deals, takeovers and power plays provide
the staple content of most business news coverage. Its values are
pervasive; the *Financial Times* ranks companies not according to
their turnover or assets, but by the value of their shares on the
stock market. Thus 93 of the world's top 1,000 companies ranked
by stock market value are British: ranked by sales or assets this
number is halved.

The Stock Exchange's daily business is the buying and selling of shares, whose fluctuating prices flicker on the screens of
the market-makers in the London investment houses. Insurance
company A, deciding that it can make higher returns in another
financial asset, sells its shares in company XYZ to Pension Fund B
which, with fresh inflows of pension contributions to invest, needs
to top up its holding of XYZ. The intermediary, the stockbroker,
takes a tiny cut as a commission for executing the transaction –
but because each transaction involves tens of millions of pounds
even tiny commissions quickly mount up to substantial sums.

The daily juggling with pre-existing financial assets – shares, or
equity, entitling the holder to own a share in company assets and
the profits they produce as dividend – is presented to the nation as
a vital social function. The great institutions who receive some 6
per cent of GDP in the form of pension, life insurance or unit trust
investments need to be able to buy and sell shares rapidly as their
responsibilities demand, it is said. They need to raise the promised
cash for their customers as their policies mature; they need to be
able to invest the incoming payments freely; they need to adjust
the shape of their holdings to reflect profitable opportunities and
their changing assessment of economic conditions. Indeed, under
the nineteenth-century trust law under which they operate, they
are obliged to maximise the profits of their investments as a
fiduciary duty – and an effective stock market is an indispensable
tool for achieving this.

For stock market apologists this restless daily adjustment in
prices is a constant process in which the market is trying as
efficiently as it can to reflect the economic value of all the
information it has to hand. Share prices rising in one industrial
sector while they fall in another is a signal that investors favour
one branch of economic activity more than another. If the market values a pound of profit from a business importing electronic
gadgetry from Japan more highly, for example, than it does a
pound of profit from making leather goods in Halifax, then an
entrepreneur is better off trying to make profits from importing
Japanese gadgetry. When he brings his company to the Stock
Exchange for flotation, the market will value his profits more

highly and he will be richer; in economic terms the market will
have done its job by attracting talent and resources into an area
of economic vitality.

Moreover, argue the system's defenders, managers have to
assure their shareholders that nothing more can be done to boost
profits and dividends in the future given the circumstances in
which any particular company finds itself – that the stewardship
of the shareholders' assets is unimprovable. This acts as a continuing spur to efficiency because the directors are always at risk
of being expelled from their position by the shareholders at the
company's annual parliament – the annual general meeting. And
above all there is the threat that shareholders, disappointed with
the company's performance, will sell to a buyer who thinks that
more 'shareholder value' can be extracted from the assets than by
the incumbent management.

The stock market therefore encourages a market in corporate
control, just like a street market in vegetables; to the highest bidder
the management of a company falls. In Germany, according to
Professor Julian Franks and Colin Mayer, there have only been
four contested takeovers since 1945; in Britain there has been an
average of forty a year. It is the abiding feature of the London
stock market.

Defenders of the system insist that takeover is the ultimate
guarantor that shareholders' interests will be respected by company managements, and that in a market economy the only
arbiter of corporate strategy can be profitability, defined as
'maximising shareholder value'. Here, as elsewhere, the promotion of a market produces allegedly the best outcome for
society and individuals alike. At the height of the takeover boom
in 1986 and 1987 there was growing concern that takeovers, far
from being an economic boon, were frightening companies into
making absurdly high dividend payments and forcing them into
focusing only on immediate profit growth – but the view that
markets could only be efficient ran very deep.

The CBI, in response to these concerns, set up a City/Industry
Task Force of leading industrialists and bankers to investigate
but the report could only remark tamely that some takeovers

improved efficiency while others did not, that there was some evidence that the threat of takeover spurred efficiency and that in a survey conducted by the task force only 12 per cent of 109 top chief executives said that threat of takeover deterred them from longterm investment. The process might be expensive – costing on average 9 per cent of the value of the company – but it was effective.

But the same survey acknowledged that easily the most effective deterrent to longterm investment was the cost of capital and/or fears of an inadequate rate of return. The evidence about the true cost of the British financial system was staring the task force in the face if it had chosen to look; it examined particular aspects of the system and not the way it operated as a whole.

For if the stock market offers flexibility to shareholders in arranging their assets, it also brings costs that can offset those benefits – and are rooted in its very nature as a market. The more intensively shares are traded, the more widely dispersed ownership becomes; the greater the threat of contested takeover, then the higher the premium companies feel they must earn in order to keep their shareholders happy. This is the fundamental weakness of the British system. British companies not only suffer one of the highest costs of capital in the world, but the febrile stock market compels them to earn a very big mark-up over even that cost of capital to fend off the threat of takeover and keep their shareholder base stable. In a survey of 500 manufacturing companies by the CBI, it found that two-fifths of them aim for a nominal or real rate of return in excess of 20 per cent; more extraordinarily, two-thirds expect the project to finance itself within two to three years.[17] These are extremely demanding financial returns which need to be lowered if the level and type of investment undertaken by British firms is to be improved.

Yet as Colin Mayer has argued these demands also originate from the owners' lack of commitment to and responsibility for their assets.[18] It is because they are always ready to walk away from the companies they own by selling their shares, that the companies feel compelled to make high returns to lock them in. The more owners can forego the temptation of exit that the market provides, the better the relationships and strategies that ultimately produce better returns. The issue is 'the fundamental deficiency of the UK economy; a systemic failure to commit'.

Free-market theorists argue that this freedom to buy and sell should improve market efficiency; but that assumes both that the markets accurately value future returns, and that there are no efficiency losses from the continuing re-evaluation of a company's worth. But markets do not value companies' future prospects rationally, often placing a heavier emphasis than is justified on the short-term future, and ignoring the destructive effects of this endless change of valuation on the firm's longterm relations with workers, suppliers and customers. The mismatch of time scales makes it difficult to sustain the committed relationships which are at the core of productivity growth.

The lack of rationality about the future which is at the heart of the problem is a well-known psychological phenomenon. The 'matching law' shows how individuals are wholly inconsistent in the way they rank rewards over time. Robert Frank cites Richard Hernstein's work[19] which shows that individuals place a heavy emphasis on rewards in the present, while rewards in the future have to be very much higher than they should be rationally in order to persuade individuals to accept them. This irrational 'time-discounting' feature of the matching law is one of the most robust laws of experimental psychology – as true of rats and pigeons as it is of human beings.

This same irrationality is of fundamental importance in setting the costs of capital in stock markets. Suppose there is a company with 100,000 individual investors each owning one share in the firm. All agree that the current investment programme, dividend prospects and business strategy of the firm are unimprovable; and they have all given them their formal approval at the annual general meeting.

Now suppose that another investment prospect turns up, which offers returns that are actually worse than those of the first firm when measured over the life of the investment – but are higher in the immediate future. Influenced by the matching law, people will sell their shares to reinvest in the new prospect. As a result the share price in the first firm falls, even though all its shareholders were perfectly happy with its optimal business strategy. As the share price falls, the company has to issue more shares to new buyers in order to raise a given amount of money; its cost of capital has risen. And because the cost of its capital has risen, it must change its business strategy. Either it must compete with the alternative investment to which its old shareholders have moved by producing more returns in the present, even at the cost of sacrificing very much better returns in the future; or it must cut back its current investment plans.

But as Colin Mayer explains, this is not the end of the story.[20] All the company's stakeholders – sub-contractors, bank creditors and workers – will also need to adjust to the new situation. If investors feel unable to make the requisite commitment to the firm, then workers who were on the point of engaging in new training to work in new facilities will have to change their plans too. What commitment can they make to their own training – or the firm to spending money on their training – if owners are less committed to the enterprise than they were before?

So two destructive forces are at work here; the first is that immediate profits in an alternative investment are being rated more highly than bigger, but deferred profits (in the jargon the discount rate is lower); the second is that the change in shareholders' valuations has profoundly destabilising effects on the entire structure of what was and probably still is a good firm. It makes no difference if, as some argue,[21] pension funds and insurance companies keep a stake in the same company for years, providing a continuity of ownership in the British stock market comparable to that in Germany or Japan.

That is unfortunately not the point. British institutional shareholders are not bound into the company's strategy through a skein of social and legal commitments such as the German supervisory boards or Japanese *keiretsu*. Every day that dawns there is a market in individual company shares which allows shareholders an escape route if they choose to use it, and although the core holding may remain unchanged most institutional shareholders are willing to increase or decrease the size of that holding. These marginal changes in ownership often set in train destabilising and irrational changes in share valuations.

For in reality the stock market does not price future income rationally; the matching law proves to be a measurable fact. David Miles shows that for returns which stretch beyond a year, the stock market consistently values them less highly than it should, so that profits expected in five years' time are undervalued by 40 per cent.[22] Cash flows more than five years in the future are discounted at twice the rate of shorter term flows. 'Even on the loosest definition of what constitutes clear sight this counts as serious myopia,' he writes. Companies know that this mispricing takes place, and adjust their business strategies accordingly.

The issue is not, as some stock market apologists hysterically insist, that critics of the financial markets are trying like socialists to control dividend payments, which are shareholders' legitimate rewards for risk.[23] The issue is that payback periods are shorter, target rates of return are higher and dividend pay-outs bigger than in other industrial countries so that British shareholders are disproportionately highly rewarded for the 'risks' they run. For example, dividends in Japan as a proportion of industrial companies' profits are a quarter, and even in the US run at half of British levels.[24]

The aim of high pay-out ratios is clear – to retain the loyalty of otherwise fickle shareholders – which is why, when firms are quoted on the stock market, their dividend distributions more than double.[25] In the theory of corporate finance this should not matter at all, because the dividends will be reinvested in the stock market and thus the cash will find its way back to the companies which need it. Indeed, free market theory says that companies which cannot attract the paid-out cash now available for reinvestment are inefficient, so that reinvested dividends will flow to the 'good' companies – another spur to efficiency.

This is only another aspect of a much larger argument between two schools. Professor Paul Marsh of the London Business School, in a book paid for by institutional investors, argues that short-termism derives from management behaviour and remuneration structures rather than the attitudes of investors; and

high turnover in company shares is part of a continuing attempt
to price the underlying assets accurately – i.e. the market is simply
doing its job. It is not a sign of investors' lack of commitment.
He rejects out of hand industrialists' claims that the clamour of
their shifting band of shareholders for ever higher dividends leads
companies to look for short-term returns. That could not be
true, he says, because if any firms could produce high longterm
returns, then investors would be more than willing to back such
companies.

This is a classic circular argument. We know markets tend to
work perfectly; the stock market is an efficient market; ergo there
can be no problems associated with its operation. Professor Marsh
is saying that David Miles's proof that the market undervalues
future profits cannot be true, because the stock market could not
make a mistake of that type. Here, rather as in Soviet Russia, one
confronts not reasoned argument but pure ideology.

It is the same story with takeovers. There is plenty of proof
that shareholders in target companies do well from the process,
says Marsh and, that while the evidence about predator companies
is more mixed, there is not enough evidence to disprove the overall
judgement that takeovers work to the shareholders' advantage.

But his criterion is not market share, innovation or production;
it is shareholder value – a measure which is much more likely to
give him the answer he wants. As long as shareholder value has
at worst not been damaged and at best been improved, takeovers
cannot be a damaging process. And so the evidence as to whether
a market in which corporate control can be traded promotes efficiency is drawn entirely from share price movements: the only
permissible yardstick of performance. Marsh and his allies chose
precisely the measure which is least likely to express the damage
that a market in corporate control causes.

But if the optic is changed, the picture is very different.
The real case against the stock market is precisely that its sole
yardstick of measurement is shareholder value and short-term
corporate profitability – because it has no way of valuing all
the co-operative contracts between a firm's various stakeholders,
which also contribute to its efficiency; or the wider benefits that

the existence of clusters of independent, self-governing firms bring
to their workforces and communities. In the textile industry, for
example, the growth of Coats Viyella by takeover has forced all
its competitors to adopt business strategies that stress short-term
profitability to protect themselves from the predatory market
leader; but that has not protected them or helped the industry
raise its investment and productivity. The corporate strategy of
the textile company Tootal, finally swallowed up by Coats in the
late 1980s, was dominated for years by the unsuccessful attempt
to fend off the predator – cutting back R & D, innovation and
investment to support the share price. It is an experience repeated
many times every year, and it is unmeasurable by assessments of
stock market efficiency on the basis of share price performance.

Industries perform best as dense clusters of competing firms,
creating highly skilled labour forces and transmitting information
about new techniques between them. They collaborate as well as
compete. Investment in new techniques may mean deferred profits
and slow growing dividends; but serious industrialists know that
the end result will be upgraded production and a capacity to move
into higher-value-added markets. These are industrial rather than
financial values.

But if one company defects from this entrepreneurial, industri-
ally-based strategy and decides to grow by stock market acquisition, then all firms are trapped by the new rules of the game. The
trouble is that there will always be more immediate profit to be
made in an industry with a multiplicity of factories by taking over
a rival, closing down spare capacity and rationalising production.
This boosts profits, improves shareholder value and on Marsh's
definition, is a public good – and the nature of the UK stock
market means that there is a permanent temptation to go down
this avenue.

Takeover reduces the critical mass of the industry; reduces the
level of competition; and sends signals to the remaining companies that they must make do with less investment and training in
order to boost immediate dividends. But shareholders will defect
to the growing company, enhancing the value of its shares and so
making it easier still for it to grow by acquisition – exchanging

its highly valued shares for the cheaper shares of its competitors. This process works for a Coats Viyella or BTR growing in one industrial sector; and it also works for a Hanson that makes bids wherever there is perceived to be 'shareholder value' that can be unlocked.

Indeed Hanson plc, a company with £10 billion sales and 80,000 employees, is a classic creature of the British stock market – and perfectly exemplifies the biases in the system. It began as the Wiles Group in 1965 and it has grown by takeover, culminating in the purchase of Imperial, the tobacco giant; by 1990 Lord Hanson, founder and chairman, could boast of twenty-five years of uninterrupted profits and dividend growth. Yet this is an operation driven by financial manipulation. Lord White, Lord Hanson's partner, has boasted that he has never set foot on the shop floor of any of the companies that he has bought. As long as assets can be sold off for more than was paid for them, or made to yield returns higher than the cost of financing the takeover, then the exercise makes financial sense. Imperial's net cost, for example, after all the asset disposals had been made, was £200 million; it now produces £300 million in annual profits. Taxation is kept to a minimum via a complex structure of Panamanian companies.

Alex Brummer and Roger Cowe quote Lord White as saying that his interest in a company as a candidate for takeover is first aroused if its investment spending is greater than it would be if it were simply writing down or depreciating its assets; this instantly opens up room for 'savings'. After the company has been bought, then any investment has to pay back within four years, a period recently relaxed to five years. The target rate of return is 20 per cent. Hanson says that this makes the assets work hard; another view is that financial engineering exploits companies in the short term before they are discarded. The name of the game, as Hanson acknowledges, is to get hold of 'tomorrow's money today'; financial values predominate over those of industry.

The 1982 takeover of the battery maker Berec, manufacturer of Ever Ready batteries, is an instructive example. Instead of building up the company's international market share in order to sustain its production, investment and R & D, Hanson sold off the European division to its chief competitor, Duracell, financing most of the cost of the takeover. Then the prices of its products were boosted to get quick profits, but continually surrendering market share, while Hanson insisted that any investment had to meet the staggering targets for returns. By 1992 Ever Ready was no longer the market leader, even in Britain, and could not set high prices and margins, and Hanson sold the business to another competitor, Ralston Purina, who found the company 'a number of years behind the times . . . a business in decline . . . the whole infrastructure was pretty thin'.

Berec was not doing very well in 1982 when it fell prey to Hanson – it suffered from infighting and internal bureaucracy. But it was trying to build a global business and it did believe in R & D. Ten years of the Hanson treatment left it a mere shell; milked for profits and starved of investment. Britain's financial institutions got their required dividends from Hanson but the national economy is the poorer for it.

Hanson is only the most extreme example of a general trend. Financial considerations not only dominate industrial strategies, but financial preferences are expressed precisely as Hanson interprets them. Twenty per cent target rates of return, and an insistence that projects finance themselves within four to five years, are exactly what the stock market demands; indeed the recent evidence that the average payback period is two to three years means that many British companies are being even more demanding than Hanson. To argue that the market is efficient within these parameters, as defenders of the system insist, is not what the argument is about. It is rather that these boundaries are themselves destructive, and are created by forces that markets themselves generate.

The British authorities have at last begun to recognise the impact of these high returns; both the CBI and Bank of England were concerned by the results of the surveys cited earlier. But instead of looking to reform of the system to address the problem, they hope that lower and stable inflation will unravel the conundrum. Companies, they argue, set these target returns because historically inflation has been high and volatile. But even if inflation

fell, that would only marginally affect the processes described –
and to the extent that low inflation and interest rates are falling
everywhere, the cost of capital is lowered everywhere. Britain's
relative position, given its financial structure, will remain just as
bad – so that British companies will still invest less and have to
set higher prices than their competitors. This financial nexus is
at the heart of the British economic malaise.

Making it worse: the New Right revolution

The characteristics of the British financial system have developed over centuries. Centralisation of political power in London
aided and abetted the centralisation of finance; Britain's 'spontaneous' industrial revolution relieved the financial system of the
obligations of the supportive role it had to take on during
the development of industrialisation in other countries. This
historic disengagement from industry is reinforced by the market principles upon which every aspect of the financial system
is organised. While it may encourage the development of new
financial instruments, it also accentuates the lack of responsibility
to the wider economy.

The Conservative years have reinforced all these negative
trends. The financial system is even more market-based, in the
name of deregulation and liberalisation. In the capital markets, for
example, the preoccupation with liquidity has been worsened by
the slew of new financial instruments or 'derivatives'. The large
financial institutions can bet on the changing value of the stock
market, interest rates and foreign exchange rates; some of the
biggest betters against sterling, when it was forced out of the
European exchange rate mechanism, were British pension funds.

The London markets' ability to accommodate huge buying and
selling orders has developed with the vast increase in turnover;
ownership of 5 or 10 per cent of a major company can change in a
morning. The invitation to 'exit' has become even more tempting
and shareholders are more than ever uncommitted owners. Dividends as a share of national output doubled during the 1980s – and

carried on rising even during the recession of 1990–92. Over the five years between 1989 and 1993 dividends grew by a cumulative 7 per cent in real terms; capital investment fell in real terms by 14 per cent. And while profits in 1994 rose to a post-war peak of around 17 per cent of national output, output itself will barely have climbed back to pre-recession levels. The financial armlock on the economy grows ever tighter.

Nor is cheap debt likely to come to the rescue by lowering the overall cost of capital – the trends are in the other direction. The relationships between individual banks and companies have become more distant, narrowing the information flows upon which large build-ups of longterm debt are dependent. Banks have weakened their ties with companies and developed new markets in their loans so that they can be bought and sold just like shares. This turning of bank debt into securities is, of course, yet another manifestation of the London financial institutions' historical commitment to liquidity and disengagement. The inability of British banks, for example, to emulate Sumitomo's support for Mazda, is even more marked in the 1990s than it was in the 1970s.

The abolition of exchange controls allowed London to take the lead in developing a new global capital market. Sterling may rank after the dollar, yen, mark, French and Swiss francs as an international lending currency,[26] but London's status as the least regulated of world financial markets has allowed it to become the centre of global finance. It has the biggest number of international bond dealers; it tops the table of international bank lending (just ahead of Tokyo);[27] and it is comfortably the world leader as a market for foreign shares, well ahead of its nearest rivals in the US and Germany.

This international position means British companies have to compete (as they did before the First World War) with the highest returns in the world if they are to get financial support. British pension funds and insurance companies have the highest proportions of foreign equity in their portfolios of any industrialised country; and the returns they achieve become the benchmarks for British companies.

These returns are startlingly high. In the fifteen years up to 1994 pension funds enjoyed dividend growth of 10 per cent and a total rate of return of 22 per cent on their UK equity portfolios. Here is another paradox. The public that is facing insecure employment prospects created by the restless search for sky-high returns is the same public that benefits, through its ownership of the shares by the great pension funds and insurance companies. The flow of institutionalised savings has increased by half over the 1980s as people have been encouraged to provide for themselves, and as the institutions become more powerful so the blocks of shares they trade grow in size and the volatility of the markets increases.

The twin forces of this institutionalisation of investment and the internationalisation of investment flows prompted the so-called Big Bang of 1986, when the London stock market allowed international financial institutions to become members and to make markets in stocks and shares. Their increased capital allowed the stock market to underwrite the explosion of turnover that the new institutions were generating – and by underwriting it, to propel it further.

Britain's top 200 companies confront a highly marketised financial system. Their shares, bond and bank debt are traded furiously. The advantage is that they can raise equity and bond finance at keen prices; the disadvantage is that afterwards they have to deliver insane rates of return to their owners. Britain's company law, offering no formal status in the company's management to either bankers or shareholders – let alone any other stakeholder – reinforces the capital markets' disengagement. In this respect the entire system – from auditing through merchant banking to the new derivative markets – operates as a whole. The vested interest in the status quo is immense.

But medium-sized and small companies do not even have the advantage of getting their finance on keen terms. Reliant on a banking system that is averse to risk, any company whose shares are quoted has to meet the same dividend requirements as bigger companies, but with less capacity to deliver because it is smaller. Even unquoted companies find that they have to meet the same requirements, especially if they are preparing for flotation and the personal enrichment of their owners. For small companies, financial support consists typically of the owners' equity and overdraft finance – a very expensive combination which allows for little expansion.

Britain's industrial and commercial structure is the product of this financial environment, and from it radiate the effects on everything from employment to housing that bring so much economic inefficiency and social distress. The disintegration of family life and the decline in the public realm that disfigure contemporary Britain may seem far removed from London's financial markets, but they are as linked to them as remote shocks are to the epicentre of an earthquake.

7. Why Inequality Doesn't Work

Since 1979, a uniquely powerful combination of forces has worked to promote the market as the sole organising principle of economy and society. The financial and employment systems have been deregulated, while the government has attempted to design the welfare and tax system so as to maximise the rewards for 'enterprise' and the penalties for 'idleness'. Wherever possible – from the National Health Service to the provision of pensions – market forces have been promoted and state intervention rolled back.

The economy has been opened ever wider to international trade and financial flows, on the same principle of loyalty to the market. The authoritarian capabilities of the state have been ruthlessly enlisted to serve this end, which neatly chimes with longstanding British values and institutional structures. The stated objective has been to improve efficiency, raise economic growth and so advance the welfare of all. Those at the top of the pile may do especially well, but the argument is that their enhanced efforts will improve the lot even of those at the bottom of the income scale – who will do better under this system than any other.

Yet this neat theoretical equation has proved a great deal more complex in practice than the New Right would have us believe. The welfare of a significant part of the population has been actively damaged by the implementation of the new regime, and the results have fed back into higher government social security spending, more violent economic cycles, a slowing of the long-run growth rate, permanent unemployment, mounting social distress and the exclusion of growing numbers of people from proper citizenship. In short, while there may have been some efficiency gains in a few firms, and more income and wealth for a few individuals, they cannot justify the wider losses. These are intensified by the end of attempts to redistribute wealth and income; instead, the welfare and tax system is organised so that the gap between high and low income groups has become more and not less obvious.

The most striking effect of the process by which society has been 'marketised' is the growth of inequality. The distribution of incomes after tax has been made more unequal by cutting top marginal rates of income tax and switching from direct to indirect taxation, with those on lower incomes having to pay the same for any given purchase as those on higher incomes – so that in relative terms the unskilled shop assistant pays more indirect tax on a litre of petrol than a company lawyer. The Institute for Fiscal Studies estimates that in 1995 the poorest 10 per cent of the population will forfeit nearly 20 per cent of their gross income to indirect taxes while the top 10 per cent will pay 8 per cent.[1]

At the same time social security benefit increases have been linked to prices rather than wages (which grow more rapidly), severing the link between income support and the general rise in living standards. The value of supplementary benefit as a proportion of full-time male earnings fell from 26 per cent to 19 per cent for a married person between 1979 and 1993, and proportionally as far for a single person. Much the same is true for pensioners, so that those dependent upon the state for support have found their income worth less and less in relation to the average wage. And these reduced benefits are more likely to be means-tested ruthlessly, especially for the young.

Although changes in the tax and benefit system contributed to the growth of inequality, the most important motor of division was the evolution of people's earned and unearned income before taxes.[2] Even if the tax and welfare system and unemployment levels had remained as they were in 1979 there would still have been a substantial growth in inequality, between the skilled and unskilled, the 'permanent' and the 'casual'.

There have been four key influences. The first is the scaling back of employment regulation: the attack on the powers of trade unions, the abolition of wages councils and the raft of measures taken to make the labour market more 'flexible'. These have allowed employers to bid down wages and working conditions for the unskilled and poorly organised – with the impact particularly marked in the high-labour-content domestic service industries like hotels, catering and cleaning.[3]

Two other influences have reinforced this trend. The financial system's demand for high returns has put increasing pressure on company managements to maintain the growth of profits and dividends – and one obvious route for the desperate manager has been to reduce wage bills and make them more malleable by ensuring that employment levels can be quickly adjusted to changes in demand. Reflecting this trend, companies as disparate as the British Airports Authority and Burtons have reorganised their workforce so that a growing proportion works part-time. Two part-time workers can produce the same as one full-time equivalent, but for a fraction of the overheads and with much more 'flexibility', and casual workers can be hired or fired as demand rises and falls. Profitability is maximised while the risk of fluctuating demand has been displaced to the labour force.

But it does not end there. The build up of low-wage, high-labour-content exports from the underdeveloped world has forced producers of high-labour-content products in the developed world to react – especially in countries such as Britain which are very open to imports. In an important study Adrian Wood estimates that the proportion of European and US consumption represented by low-cost southern imports has doubled over the last fifteen years, implying that in Britain the proportion is now over 5 per cent.[4]

This has a huge impact on employment patterns. In industries such as textiles, shoes, toys, and consumer electronics, British companies have transformed their approach to production. Either they cease producing in the UK altogether and surrender the market to cheaper imports, or they relocate production. Shoe and toy production, for example, is barely represented in Britain now while consumer electronics companies increasingly assemble their products in low-cost manufacturing sites in Asia.[5]

Firms that survive do so by moving upmarket, increasing the capital intensity of their labour and raising productivity. Firms not facing direct competition from southern imports are aware that they could soon be under assault, and begin to upgrade their production as a defensive measure: investing in

labour-saving machines and shedding unskilled workers.[6] Adrian
Wood calculates that some 8 million jobs have been lost in the
North through this quiet trade war. On that basis at least 400,000
and probably as many as half a million of these job losses were in
Britain.

Nor has the state felt the need to resume its post-war role as an
'employer-of-last-resort' for unskilled male labour to counteract
these trends. The pressure to cut public spending and contract out
public services to 'low-cost' suppliers has made local and central
government increasingly part of the problem, driving down wages
and terms of employment for the unskilled.

Put these related processes together and the result is that the
demand for unskilled male work has fallen, while that for skilled
work is rising. Within UK manufacturing the share of non-manual
workers in total employment has grown on average by 0.2 per cent
a year since 1979, while the share of workers with no educational
qualifications has been falling by 2.8 per cent a year – a cumulative
fall of a third in the numbers of unskilled workers since 1979.[7]

Wages have reflected this widening breach. The wages of the top
10 per cent of male earners have risen from 1.67 times the median
wage in 1979 to twice the median in 1993, while over the same period the wages of the poorest paid 10 per cent have fallen from 68.5
per cent to 58.2 per cent of the median. The gap between low and
high wages is now the highest since records began.[8] According to
the Rowntree Trust, after adjusting for housing costs and inflation
the bottom sixth of the population actually saw their real income
fall between 1979 and 1991 while the income of the top 10 per cent
rose by more than half.[9] By any measure Britain is a substantially
less equal society than it was.

Inequality hurts us all

Inequality, it is said, is the price that has to be paid for economic
efficiency. The argument is that attempts to divide the pie more
equally simply shrink it – and conversely, the more unequally the
pie is divided the bigger it will grow. A capitalist society is by its

nature unequal and so faces a trade-off: the more unequal it is, the more economically efficient it becomes.

Without the incentives offered by inequality, either as a reward or punishment, a capitalist economy simply loses its dynamism. Unless there is a hierarchy of profit, capital cannot flow to the areas with highest returns; unless there is a penalty for being out of work, workers will not seek employment. There needs to be fear and greed in the system in order to make it tick.

Attempts to change this are self-defeating. Even if the tax system were so penal that millionaires were eliminated, the improvement in the circumstances of the rest would be minimal; a million pounds spread between 60 million people is worth only a couple of pence per person – but at the same time the system has lost the capacity to reward enterprising individuals by offering them the prospect of becoming millionaires. Everybody is poorer by their loss.

But worse, as neo-liberal social theorists in the US have argued, attempting to narrow inequality by redistributing income from the rich to the poor creates a dependency culture. The poor, instead of trying to improve their position by their own efforts, expect the state to underwrite them. This diminishes them as individuals, making them less responsible; with poor attitudes to parenting, work and wider social obligations. Beyond offering a minimum and targeted safety net, society should make no morally corroding commitment to transfer income from rich to poor.

And attempts to build systems of social solidarity between classes demand the intervention of the state. However effectively equality can be created it is always at the expense of individual liberty. The wealth and freedom of action of the better-off are qualified by state intervention, constraining their liberty in a vain attempt to promote equality. The distribution of income and living standards in society should be left to the market: here as elsewhere there is only trouble in store for those that meddle with market processes.

Although notions like the dependency culture and the need for incentives may seem modern, these are ancient concerns, which have dogged efforts to ameliorate inequality for centuries. It was only in 1948 that the Poor Law, with its distinction between the deserving and undeserving poor, and its system of relief doled out locally on the basis of means-tested household income was formally abolished, to be replaced by what was then called national assistance and is now known as income support. The boards of guardians throughout the nineteenth and early-twentieth centuries were haunted by the conviction that their attempts to provide minimum levels of subsistence would succour fraud and idleness, as the classical economists had predicted. The deserving poor should be helped; but wastrels and indigents should not be subsidised by the better-off.

'Modern' anxiety about the consequences of state action is thus at least a hundred years old. In 1988, Ralph Harris in *Beyond the Welfare State* wrote: 'In Britain, I have no doubt that improved social benefits have increased the incentive for the people to make some kind of a living out of being poor', unconsciously echoing *The Times* in 1902. Reacting to Seebohm Rowntree's revelation in his landmark study that 27.84 per cent of the people in York were living in poverty, the Thunderer insisted that a large proportion of the poor were 'miserable mainly from their own fault'.[10] Herbert Spencer's impassioned accusation in *Man Versus The State* (1884) that liberals were deserting their principles in favour of restrictive legislation would have found equal favour with Harris and other representatives of the New Right a century later. Spencer saw collectivism asserting itself and believed that the concessions already made to state intervention would destroy liberty and ruin the system of *laissez-faire*. Citing the Chimney-Sweepers Act, prescribing the size of chimneys up which sweeps could send young children in an attempt to prevent their maiming or death, and the Acts insisting on compulsory vaccination, Spencer fulminated against such limits on the liberty of contract.

At the end of the nineteenth century, across Europe and the United States, governments legislated to limit the workings of *laissez-faire* — first by inspecting factories and offering minimal standards of education and later by providing subsistence income for the old and out of work. From Bismarck in Germany to the British Liberal government of 1906–14, the state began to put limits on the degree of inequality that the unregulated market threw up, against a background of dire warnings from the economic liberals that the market system was being irretrievably endangered – even when it became transparently obvious that it suffered hardly at all and such intervention if anything raised the growth rate. In truth the danger lay in allowing the system to continue without such intervention; and this tension has remained to the present day. Today's New Right do no more than repeat the ancestral warnings of the *laissez-faire* economists over the last two centuries: interfere in the operation of the market at your peril; inequality is the price we pay for efficiency; liberty of contract is an indivisible principle; the poor will always be with us; help is self-defeating.

But fifteen years of redesigning the tax and benefit system so that it conforms to such principles has not borne very impressive fruit. Britain has certainly become a more unequal society than it was in 1979 but the pie, rather than expanding more quickly, is if anything expanding more slowly. The collapse of social cohesion that comes when the market is allowed to rip through society has produced a fall in the growth rate; marginalisation, deprivation and exclusion have proved economically irrational.

The social consequences are profound. The virtual stagnation of incomes for people in the bottom third of the population has infected the very marrow of society. Holding families together has become more difficult as the wages and conditions of unskilled adult males has deteriorated. And this has had major implications for public expenditure.

Market rule has recoiled on the state's finances; as the polarisation of society has worsened, public spending on crime, health and specialist education has increased – and social security spending itself, even though rates are meaner in relation to average earnings, has ballooned as poverty drives millions through the drab waiting-rooms of the rump welfare state.

Government efforts to extend the operation of the market in a plethora of areas ranging from housing and pensions to television and sport have not been a notable success, even in their own terms. Instead of extending choice, individual liberty and the general welfare there has been a secular increase in risk, insecurity and cultural impoverishment.

'Marketisation' has seen the growth of private forms of power and the entrenchment of the old class structure that Tory radicals affected to despise. Higher disposable incomes for the top 10 per cent have allowed them to afford ever more expensive private education for their children, with the numbers enrolled at private schools growing substantially over the decade. At the same time state schools have become more discriminating in their intake, in order to maximise exam results and therefore funding. To be born poor means to stay poor and ill-qualified; while to be born rich brings with it educational attainment and career achievement. Class hardens subtly into caste – and economies do not prosper in caste societies.

Inequality and economic performance

The case linking inequality and the economy is simply put. Inequality between classes and regions adversely affects both demand and supply. Demand becomes more volatile and unbalanced while supply is affected by underinvestment and neglect of human capital. Economic cycles are amplified; firms become more like opportunist traders than social organisations committed to production and innovation. As a result, the long-run growth rate tends to fall, unemployment rises and the government's underlying fiscal position deteriorates, and a vicious circle intensifies the volatility of demand and the weakness of supply.

Economic management should be designed to produce a predictable and stable growth in demand over time. This allows firms to budget for returns from new investment that promise to be stable, and encourages them to innovate, train and invest in order to capture these predictable returns. The anticipated rise in demand and the confidence that it will continue attracts the investment in capacity that will both meet the rising demand and is itself part of that demand.

Unfortunately there is a complicating factor – the economic cycle. There is a rhythm in economic life in which the promise of an improving economy leads to more investment, spending and optimism and so causes the economy to surge above its average growth rate. It approaches a peak in which there is so much pressure on capacity, which lags behind the rise in spending, that inflation or interest rates or the trade deficit rise either separately or in combination. This tends to slow down demand, which now starts to fall – the mirror image of the earlier improvement. Because expectations deteriorate, firms cancel or postpone their investments, consumers fearful of redundancy build up their savings and the whole economy slips below its average rate of growth – or even, in a recession, actually contracts.

All capitalist economies experience this rhythm but the less volatile the up and down movements, the more firms are able to sustain the capital accumulation and husband the skilled labour force that lifts the growth rate of a successful economy. The problem with the deliberate encouragement of inequality as a matter of government policy is that it exaggerates the economic cycle in important ways and seriously unbalances the pattern of demand. The events of the 1980s and early 1990s demonstrate the point perfectly.

In the long seven-year upswing from the trough of the 1981 recession to the peak of the Lawson boom in 1988, the distribution of income in Britain became progressively more unequal – a trend that continued into the subsequent downturn. Rising consumption was fuelled in part by the rise in real wages helped by cheap import prices from the increase in sterling; but an important factor was the tax reductions and expectations of more adding to the already rising pre-tax incomes of the top 40 per cent of the population. So if financial deregulation, and the avalanche of credit it unleashed, was one part of the equation, the other was the ability of the richer groups to borrow ever greater amounts. This triggered the housing boom, a key link in the self-reinforcing spiral of credit and spending.

If the inequality of income helped support the housing boom, it also skewed demand towards imports and luxuries. The higher earners paid up for private education, yachts, high-performance cars, race horses, fine arts, and designer clothes. Imports poured in. The boom moved to its climax in 1988, with the reduction in top tax rates to 40 per cent particularly overheating the south-east where most higher rate tax payers lived, emphasising a regional as well as social bias to inequality which had wider malevolent economic consequences.

The consumer boom had its genesis in the south-east because incomes were higher there, as were house prices. The inflation in house prices and property wealth was never matched in the north of England, Scotland and Northern Ireland – yet economic policy had to focus on cooling the south-eastern economic cauldron. It was the uneven geographical nature of the boom, as much as its overall ferocity, that made it so unstable.

The government could not respond with tax increases, still less with tax increases aimed at curbing the spending of the better off in particular regions which would have been in flat contradiction of its doctrine of promoting incentives for the rich. The only policy response that ideology could allow was to raise interest rates, which took a long time to work, and once in operation released powerful deflationary forces that again were intensified by the new inequalities.

With the fall in house prices, the 'feel good' effect that had been supporting consumption was depressed rather sharply. A great deal of evanescent economic activity had been supported by the bubble of housing wealth, and employment in these areas now fell dramatically. But while the south-east might have needed the medicine of 15 per cent interest rates to cool it down, the same rates were fantastically inappropriate to the relatively depressed British industrial regions – as was entry, at around the same time, into the ERM at a rate overvalued to curb inflation. The south-east powered the boom: it now propelled the recession.

The only offsetting measure open to the government as the recession deepened was to allow social security spending to rise automatically. It could not proactively spend its way out of the recession; the doctrine stated that the motor of recovery had to be the private sector and the market – a private sector which, aggressively laying off workers, cutting investment and preserving dividends, found it exceptionally difficult to rekindle economic growth.

Here again the dogmatic commitment to inequality had deleterious economic effects. Firms' employment of part-time and casual labour began to have destabilising effects on overall levels of demand. In the upturn the new 'flexible' labour market allowed employers to suck new workers into the workforce on terms they could quickly break if the economy turned down – and those higher participation rates, especially for women, had increased incomes and hence spending power. But in the downswing the same flexibility saw a sharp rise in unemployment – up 1.5 million over three years – and led to a particularly sharp fall in demand, which reinforced the downturn.

For not only were enormous numbers of people falling out of the labour market, but their loss of income was even more dramatic. With income support worth 7 per cent less in relation to average earnings than during the previous recession in 1979–81, demand fell by some £4 billion or 0.66 per cent of GDP more than it would have done had the old relationship between income support and average earnings held.[11] The government had made a rod for its own back.

The newly unemployed were not the only group to lose their purchasing power over the decade. The failure to index state pensions to wages meant that by 1994 pensioners' spending power was £6 billion a year lower than it would have been. At the same time the relative drop in incomes of the bottom 10 per cent of wage earners by some 7 per cent meant that their spending power had been cut by an additional £3 billion. Rising inequality had robbed the economy of at least £13 billion of spending from those sections of the community whose capacity to save is minimal. They must spend what they receive in income. On the ebbing tide of previous recessions the small boats had been able to float; now they were part of the wreckage.

Free-market theory claims that this should not happen, because in an economy with perfectly functioning markets, losers should be balanced by gainers; in other words, if pensioners and the unemployed receive less benefit, then taxation is lower and those in work should have higher incomes to spend to compensate for the reduced spending by social security recipients. Equally, the growth of low pay should be offset either by higher pay or greater profits, so the level of final demand should be the same.

But those at the bottom of the income scale save less and spend more for every pound of income. Thus redistributing income from the poor to the rich tends to lower effective demand and increase saving. The onus is upon the financial system to ensure that the higher saving from the higher income groups is recycled to maintain the level of final demand.

In reality, of course, markets are not perfect, the economy is not at equilibrium, nor is it closed, and the financial system does not work perfectly. The more unequal the income distribution, as Keynes, Galbraith, Myrdal, Kalecki and Malthus all recognised, the more likely it is that the economy will suffer from periodic crises of underconsumption.

In the 1990–92 recession, the economy had to rely on demand coming from those whose incomes had improved relative to the average; but these were precisely the people who had incurred high levels of debt in the boom. With most mortgages carrying variable interest rates, the same top half of the population that had propelled the boom now found themselves having to retrench severely to meet interest payments that had nearly doubled. Again the south-east was in the vanguard, its income falling back sharply against the national average.

Firms faced a fall in demand more severe than any they had experienced in post-war history. Whilst consumer spending had only stopped growing during the 1979–81 recession, stabilising at around £247 billion (in 1990 prices), in the recession years between 1990 and 1992 consumer spending actually fell by £7.6 billion – the sharpest drop since the war. Industries as disparate as television – dependent upon companies paying handsomely for advertising – and furniture – dependent upon rising consumer spending – found they had made investment decisions upon unrealistic assumptions; and launched into second and third rounds of retrenchment which in turn prolonged the recession. ERM membership prevented the fall in interest rates, which was the only acceptable policy tool available to the government.

But the new inequality, and the attitude towards the welfare state from which it had grown, had other subtle and damaging effects. For example, with the government signalling that public provision of pensions would become progressively meaner and telegraphing its belief in private provision by providing big tax incentives, pension funds mushroomed – but their new size and dividend demands rebounded on company strategies. Business investment fell to a thirty-year low as companies twisted and turned to find the cash to meet the pension funds' demands – and the weaker people in the labour market, the unskilled and non-unionised, were offered worse and worse pay and working conditions.

The dogma of inequality lay behind every gyration of the wild spiral of boom and bust, and the colossal misallocation of resources that it represented. There had been too much investment on the basis of rising consumption and too little on the basis of winning overseas markets. The economy entered the next upswing crippled by a legacy of excessive consumption and underinvestment. Saddled with growing institutional share ownership, firms' investment strategies would be driven by their owners' financial demands; the next boom would be no more sustainable than the previous one. Inequality had not delivered for the economy; and it had pretty disastrous consequences for the state too.

Inequality and the state

In the 1993–94 financial year Britain's public sector borrowing requirement reached £45.9 billion – the second highest figure as a proportion of national output since the war. Lowering marginal tax rates, while overseeing an explosion of public expenditure driven by the growth of poverty which the state had itself created, proved irrational for the state as well as the larger economy, burdening it with an inbuilt budgetary crisis.

Here, as elsewhere, indifference to the growth of inequality has proved counterproductive.

Although comparatively modest plans for public expenditure growth have been continually reined back since the mid-1970s, with some programmes like housing and trade and industry cut to the bone, overall public expenditure in Britain as it emerged from recession was only fractionally lower than in the comparable stage of the economic cycle a decade earlier. For cuts in domestic programmes are instantly cancelled out by the growth of inequality and the demands it makes on the public purse – from sickness benefit to troublesome schools.

At the same time the lower marginal tax rates have not delivered the supply-side goods. The belief was that lower tax rates would, by increasing risk-taking and entrepreneurship, so dynamise economic activity that overall tax revenues would not be impaired. Indeed the famous Laffer curve predicted that tax cuts would raise revenue, partly through the resulting increase in economic growth and partly because people would be less inclined to avoid or evade tax.

This theory always owed more to ideology – and the intrinsic appeal it had for the rich – than to responsible theory or observation. Economic theorists have conventionally claimed that the impact of reduced taxes had two effects. There is an income effect, so that an additional hour of work produces more take-home pay; but there is an offsetting substitution effect, because the same income can be achieved with less work, allowing more leisure. The New Right economists were assuming that there were only dynamising income effects, and no substitution effects. On their theory it could not be possible for a tax cut to persuade an executive to spend more time on the golf course than more time in the office – he or she would want to earn more. And this tallied neatly with the New Right's wider view that the only key to wealth generation is to encourage executives to manage and entrepreneurs to take risks – an idea of stunning banality and naivety. Wealth generation is as much a social as an individual act.

It is therefore no surprise that attempts to measure the impact of lowering marginal tax rates on improving the willingness to work should in general disprove the *laissez-faire* case. One study financed by the Treasury concluded in 1986 that the 'changes were small and it is likely that none differ significantly from zero':[12] this so offended the prevailing orthodoxy that the then Chancellor, Nigel Lawson, tried to prevent the report from being published. Atkinson and Mogensen, in a comparison of four countries – UK, Sweden, Germany and Denmark, could barely find discernible effects, with the exception of low-paid women for whom high marginal tax rates did seem to be a deterrent to work. Dilnot and Kell found a 1 per cent increase in the labour supply of the higher paid after the 1985–86 tax cuts – but were unable to work out whether this was because the demand for executives had increased in the run-up to the peak of the boom, or because of an increased willingness to work.

In 1994 the Policy Studies Institute (PSI) in a broad survey of more recently published literature came to the same conclusion, although for the very low paid there did seem to be an increased readiness to work as a result of low taxes, again especially among women. However, as the low paid tended to pay more tax during the 1980s through a combination of direct and indirect tax reforms this is hardly helpful to the New Right case, which is far more concerned with the need to lower marginal rates for the very well-off. Longer and more expensive lunches are not the precondition for entrepreneurship. In any case financial incentives, observed the PSI, were very much less important than social and psychological factors in determining people's working hours.

The claim that the Laffer effect has worked out in practice, with tax cuts paying for themselves because the revenue from higher rate tax payers has greatly increased, is also spurious.[13] What has happened is that the incomes of top earners have exploded, so that even lower tax rates produce a similar tax take. But that does not mean that their income has increased because they work harder with lower taxes; their income has gone up for the very different reasons outlined earlier. Skills are at a premium, and in a deregulated labour market insiders do well at the expense of outsiders. The tax regime has a secondary effect, but is not the motor of this process.

What the tax cuts *have* done is greatly to undermine the government's fiscal position, already under pressure from the big increase in social security spending. The interaction of rising current public spending and the drop in current receipts was to produce the largest current deficit since the war (excluding capital items) – around 6 per cent of GDP in the 1993–94 financial year. By contrast the current balance was in surplus in both the 1979–81 and 1973–75 recessions. As a result chancellors Lamont and Clarke had to raise taxes by the equivalent of some 2.7 per cent of GDP in their two budgets in 1993 to remedy the situation – the largest such rise of its type in modern times.

On the revenue side of the equation, the former adviser to ex-Chancellor Norman Lamont, Bill Robinson, reckons that the total loss to the Exchequer from income tax cuts (£9 billion) and the sale of public assets below their full market cost (£13 billion) is some £22 billion at 1994 prices, or 3.4 per cent of national output compared with the tax regime prevailing in 1986. The cost of switching from domestic rates to the poll tax and back to the council tax is put at 0.5 per cent of GDP or another £3 billion. All in all the government is at least £25 billion poorer from these three policies alone.[14]

In order to find some savings, the government has continually cut capital investment in the public sector. In relation to the total stock of public assets investment is barely sufficient to stop them wasting away. Investment in the railways per capita runs at a third of the European average; road investment per capita is 70 per cent of the European average.[15] By 1995 the public sector's net worth will be the lowest since the war.

The government has insisted that meeting its pre-announced public expenditure planning totals is a test of its credibility with the financial markets; but as a result it is trapped in a vicious circle. It is forced to cut other important programmes to accommodate the relentless rise in social security outlays. As Bill Robinson observes 'social security is at the heart of [Britain's] budget difficulties'. He tells us that in the autumn of 1992, for example, an unplanned increase of £3 billion in the social security budget demanded equivalent savings elsewhere. 'The inexorable growth of social security is a prime reason', he writes, 'why the government has continually to choose between making swingeing cuts in important programmes and failing to control spending.'

Social security spending, Maurice Mullard computes has increased from 9.5 per cent of GDP in 1979 to 12.2 per cent in 1992 and has been the principal reason why fifteen years of restraint have still not delivered decisively lower public spending as a proportion of national output.[16] Defence spending has shrunk from 4.6 per cent of GDP in 1979 to 4.0 per cent in 1992; housing from 2.3 per cent of GDP to 0.5 per cent; trade and industry from 1.3 per cent of GDP to 0.8 per cent; capital investment in all central government programmes from 2.2 per cent of GDP to 1.4 per cent. It is true that education spending has risen from 4.0 per cent of GDP to 4.7 per cent, and health from 4.5 per cent to 5.8 per cent – but in both cases most of the rise was in 1991 and 1992 in the run-up to the 1992 election and is projected to fall below the 1979 levels by the middle of the 1990s.

The phenomenal rise in social security spending has not come about because benefits have increased in real terms; it is because the economy has been run in such a way that the numbers living in poverty and eligible for benefit have increased dramatically. There used to be 7 million claimants of income support in 1979; in 1993 there were 11 million.

It is mainly men who are the cause of the problem. Not only are there 1.7 million officially unemployed and dependent upon income support – there are another 2 million who are no longer even seeking employment because they know there is none. Around a half are classified as 'longterm sick' and thus eligible for sickness and invalidity benefit. Since 1979 the number of supposed invalids has increased by nearly a million – and these people fall outside the government's net of make-work schemes and support systems for the unemployed – such as they are. Over 70 per cent of them are completely unskilled – exactly the category in which the demand for labour has fallen. Others have taken early retirement and qualify for other forms of income support. With each unemployed or non-employed man costing £9,000 a year in lost tax and income support, the transformation in the male labour market is costing the Exchequer over £36 billion a year.

The government sprang its own trap. It had a two-fold aim. It wanted to cut public spending in order to cut borrowing and lower marginal tax rates; and it wanted to encourage workers to become more mobile in order to improve the workings of the labour market. But the paradox is that the number of unskilled, jobless, male social security claimants has so increased under the impact of its policies, that the expenditure increases more than offset any of the savings. Nor, as the terminally demoralised stop looking for work, has there been any significant impact of the unemployed on wage-setting in the wider economy. The promotion of inequality has become self-defeating.

The approach pervades the public domain. The aim of housing policy, for example, was to raise public rents to market levels – but those who live in public housing are usually living on at most average incomes. As a result many of them are entitled to housing benefit to help pay their rents. Two-thirds of any increase in rents, estimates the Joseph Rowntree Foundation, are claimed back as housing benefit, and because rents inflate the retail price index they also inflate general social security spending which is linked to the RPI. Rent increases end up reducing GDP, and increasing unemployment and inflation.

For the way public money is spent has profound inter-relationships with the wider economy. In the US, for example, the failure to check rampant inequality has created a mutually reinforcing system of ghetto housing, racial discrimination and deep concentrations of poverty, with heavy implications for public spending. The growth of drug-taking and crime forces up prison populations while people in the deprived areas depend on state support – making social security spending structural rather than cyclical, a permanent overhead rather than a response to crisis.[17]

Any remedial programme becomes massively expensive, involving huge spending on education, housing and a corrective social infrastructure. Given that the economic gains from equality are so poor and the costs so heavy, the most prudent course is simply not to allow such no-go areas of self-sustaining and deepening squalor to develop. But the intoxication with *laissez-faire* economics in both the US and UK has permitted just that: laying up vast problems for the future in return for negligible advantages in the present.

Inequality and training

The British approach to training typifies the weaknesses of the neoliberal approach. The government has become aware that there are substantial returns from training, both to the individuals concerned and the wider economy, but has never felt that its own financial position could be so improved by raising skill levels that the investment could be self-financing. From the early abolition of the Industrial Training Boards through to the scrapping of the Manpower Services Commission its instinct has been to reduce state involvement. Nigel Lawson, for example, says in his memoirs that he always argued strongly in cabinet that training should be the responsibility of the private sector and that his contribution was to raise profits so that industry could afford it. Neither he nor any of his successors saw public money spent on training as a form of investment that might ultimately reduce the burden of social security – and indeed in his 1,086 page volume the subject of training merits no more than a few lines. A means of lowering the official unemployment claimant count, yes; an investment, no.

The aim, here as elsewhere, was to allow the market to do the job – even though decisions on training are more exposed to market failure than almost any other. British companies, David Finegold and David Soskice reported in a seminal article in 1988,[18] spent 0.15 per cent of their turnover on training compared with 1 to 2 per cent in Japan, France and West Germany – and the amount has not significantly changed since then.

Government efforts are equally lamentable. More British students finish their education at eighteen than in any other industrialised country;[19] fewer have formal educational qualifications;[20] and their mathematical ability is poor.[21] By international standards, there are fewer places for them on vocational training schemes and the levels of technical competence demanded to achieve any given qualification are at the lower end of the spectrum. Germany, for example, does not consider British NVQ Level 1 demanding enough to merit comparison with its own comparable qualification and insists on a better standard as the first building block in any common European norm.

Britain also ranks poorly in terms of institutional structures that support training. The failures in this area exemplify the malfunctions of the whole system described in this book. The political structures that might support properly independent public/private partnerships, so meeting local labour market requirements, simply don't exist; there are no incentives in the unchecked market-based system for individuals or firms to invest in the acquisition of skills; and the pressures from the financial system reinforce this trend by emphasising the gains from financial engineering, rather than investment in human capital. There is little political demand to invest in vocational training, because the middle class has its own inside track – public forms of education and training are seen as inferior and irrelevant compared to prestige private school and university education. Because there is no tradition of state initiative to develop the economy, there is consequently little willingness by employers to accept levies to pay for training. Permanently short of funds, training is the economic policy Cinderella to which ritual obeisance is paid but about which nothing effective is ever done.

The story of Training and Enterprise Councils – TECs – is a lamentable fable of the entire failure. Established in 1990, TECs were to be the means of establishing a market-led system of world-class training. They would be constituted as essentially private organisations with a majority of businessmen on their boards and were to take control of government spending on training and develop schemes for unemployment relief in their areas. With a businessman as chief executive, they would be closely in touch with local business needs. They would be free to establish local priorities, design programmes to meet them, place contracts with private training suppliers and cajole local firms into undertaking training they would not otherwise carry out.

At first there was considerable enthusiasm and businessmen rallied to the cause of what appeared to be a private-sector-led programme to develop UK plc. In keeping with the *laissez-faire* approach, there was no national plan or blueprint; TECs were simply established where local consortia wanted to establish them – some were too small and others too big – but no intervention to rationalise their scale was deemed ideologically justifiable.

Although some TECs have done a doughty job in improving levels of training, the experiment has failed to meet initial expectations. The British constitution does not admit the degree of local independence that the TECs were promised. Ministers were not prepared to insist that membership of TECs was compulsory, instead preserving the longstanding doctrine of voluntarism, relying on appeals to social responsibility and civic duty wrapped up with covert promises of honours for those who co-operated.

Without an element of compulsion, every TEC is exposed to the risk that firms who are not members and don't contribute at all poach trained workers from those who are more civically minded. Without constitutional independence from the state and no independent revenue-raising powers they cannot budget with their providers for any longer than the year ahead, which is the Treasury's only permitted time-horizon. Not only this, as Robert Bennett and his colleagues document in their extensive interviews,[22] the Treasury system of controlling spending by annual reviews means that budgets are allocated late and are frequently adjusted downwards after the financial year has already begun. Establishing the longterm relationships with suppliers that firms like Marks and Spencer have pioneered in the private sector is thus impossible for TECs and their training providers; they cannot expect more than non-renewable one-year contracts.

The government's avowed aim to privatise training spending as much as possible, with the Treasury taking the line that if firms want more trained workers they can pay for them is another systemic weakness. As a result, the lion's share of TEC budgets is eaten up by the programmes offered for the unemployed, which are generally poorly funded mechanisms for keeping them off the official register. There have been few additional resources for the much-heralded 'world-class' training programmes, with the Treasury instead constantly looking for efficiency gains from TEC spending on private trainers and always paring back spending levels. What little capacity there was to move money between programmes has been eliminated.

The entire structure of TECs is infected by the British disease. It is a short-term remedy. There is no independent power conferred on the local agents. There is no compulsion. There is no democratic legitimacy. The ideology says that public expenditure on it should be minimised. There is no national blueprint, so standards vary incredibly. TECs have no regulatory competence to ensure that qualifications are uniform throughout the country. They have no autonomy or revenue-raising power. The system is biased against those who are most in need. John Banham, then director-general of the CBI, warned in 1989 that there was a real risk that the TECs might wind up as reconstituted area manpower boards of the Manpower Services Commission simply administering centrally directed initiatives and, if so, the chance of keeping directors 'in the room committed for more than about 50 seconds are very slight'.[23] It was a prescient remark, for in the British context nothing else could happen. The constitutional structure allowed no other outcome and already businessmen are drifting away disillusioned by the whole exercise.

In short, training is in a mess, and highly inequitable in its distribution. Those without educational qualifications on low incomes and from unskilled families need training most. Yet it is precisely these workers who are least likely to receive training.[24]

The trouble is that for any teenager at sixteen who has no educational qualification, it is perfectly rational to get a job – if he (or she) can – rather than forego wages in order to train, because it is only by gaining NVQ at Level 3 that total lifetime earnings start to exceed those of the unskilled worker – and even then the break-even age is not until thirty-five.[25] But NVQ 3 demands intellectual skills equivalent to those needed to gain a GCSE and that is precisely the level of attainment at present beyond the unskilled. It is because they cannot obtain GCSEs that they are looking for unskilled work at sixteen.

Here the poor educational levels reached by most children in the state education sector intersects with the training system. If educational levels were higher, with better achievement in numeracy and literacy, then the system of vocational education would start from a higher base. But it does not, hence the hiatus in which the unskilled find themselves.

There is a mutual and self-destructive compact between the unskilled worker and the firm, in which it makes sense neither for the individual to invest time in training nor for the firm to offer it. As with so much else in the British system, the blind lead the blind. A teenager has to be very long-sighted indeed to want to undertake training that will raise his or her lifetime earnings only after the age of thirty-five and which, although it might help reduce the likelihood of unemployment, is for any individual an impossible risk to assess. At the same time firms are under pressure to maximise short-term profits, and incurring immediate costs for uncertain future benefits is equally irrational. In any case there is no certainty that the trained workers will stay with the firm that shoulders the costs. The rational approach, in terms of the system, is to minimise training and poach the skilled when market conditions demand it.

Yet there are strong positive returns from training and education if the *proper* levels of skill are attained. Vocational training provides a significant return for those who undertake it relative to those who have no qualifications at all. Men and women who succeed in getting at least one A level have higher lifetime earnings than if they had worked during that extra period of study and invested their surplus earnings in the stock market.[26] The pity is that the market-place does not and cannot signal clearly enough that this is the case.

If returns for individuals can be high, then the wider social returns on good education are high too, even if they are notoriously difficult to measure. If it has more skills available to it, the economy can grow more rapidly without reaching inflationary bottlenecks. With lower unemployment and a skilled labour force, social security spending is reduced, thus allowing a compensating increase in investment spending for any given level of public expenditure. Above all, productivity levels are raised as the human capital stock improves. The World Bank reports that the social returns from educational investment and training in underdeveloped countries are as high as 20 or 30 per cent; while some British estimates for post-school training have produced similar figures.[27]

The British government makes no serious attempt to compute what these social returns might be and therefore what the appropriate level of investment in human capital – people's knowledge and capacity – should be. As with so much public expenditure, the Treasury actively resists the very idea of such calculations, preferring instead to downgrade the existence of 'public goods' and 'social returns' and rely as far as possible on market judgements and individual incentives. In consequence the economy is dug further into the pit of a low skills, low wage equilibrium.

Economic efficiency is believed to arise only from individual responses to market signals; the relationship between social cohesion and wealth generation is consistently denied. But the urge to marketise every aspect of the way we live in the name of efficiency has eroded the fabric of our social life, which in its turn has weakened the economy.

8. Divide And Rule

The average salary in Britain in 1994 was around £19,000 a year – but the average disguises remarkable variation. Two-thirds of wage earners earn the average or below; only a third earn more than this. An imaginary parade of the entire working population dramatises the point. If the population of Britain were divided according to income, if income were made equivalent to height and if the population then marched past for an hour, it would take a full 37 minutes before the first adult of average height was seen. For the first 15 minutes there would be a parade of dwarves. Stature would increase gradually thereafter, but 57 minutes would have passed before we saw people of twice the average height. Giants of 90 feet or more would appear in the last few seconds, with the last one or two literally miles high.[1]

But earnings are not the sole yardstick of well-being and of the degree to which an individual is exposed to life's hazards; predictability and security of income are as important as its absolute level and along with growing inequality in the 1980s and 1990s has come growing insecurity, affecting all but the very richest groups. Insecurity touches the middle 30 per cent in the 30/30/40 picture of British society, so that while some of those in the last 23 minutes of the income parade may have larger than average incomes the unpredictability of that income leaves them at a disadvantage. The self-employed cameraman or the commission-earning pension saleswoman may enjoy above average income – but it is unpredictable and insecure.

On the other hand, some of those in the first 37 minutes of the parade may have safe and settled incomes, offsetting to a degree the fact that they are relatively poor. None the less a low paid job remains low paid even if it is secure, so that its holder still needs good state education, health care, and pensions.

Only the really well-off within the top 40 per cent can truly

declare independence from universal welfare provision and permanent full-time jobs. And even the well-off benefit from proper
health care and efficient, cheap public transport: for most of us
sudden illness and getting to work are challenges that only some
form of public welfare can overcome. Yet the direction of policy
over the last fifteen years has been to make work more insecure at
the same time as promoting more risk in welfare provision. To put
it crudely, the trains are less frequent and reliable and falling ill is
becoming more dangerous and potentially expensive.

For the vast majority of the population this is an irrational
state of affairs. They do not have the wherewithal to cover all the
eventualities that might hit them, from divorce to unemployment,
nor can they build up a cushion of savings against hard times.
To fund a modest pension, to insure adequately against sickness
and unemployment or to run the risk of a major investment like
house purchase going wrong demands affluence and predictability
of income. The extension of the market principle into wider and
wider areas, all in the name of individual choice and personal
responsibility, has begun to destabilise society.

Yet the existence of this risk creates a parallel opportunity for
the government – and it is this Janus-faced aspect of the market
revolution that has made the situation so difficult to reform. There
is little doubt that scepticism about politicians means that very few
people trust the government to spend their tax pounds wisely,
and at the same time the roll-back of the state makes individuals
properly more anxious to retain as much of their income as possible
in order to provide for themselves. If bus and train services become
unreliable, expensive and infrequent it is even more important to
have enough post-tax income to afford a car. If state provision is
being reduced year by year, everybody who has a job becomes an
ally in the crusade for tax cuts.

The model of the welfare state set up after the Second World
War assumed that there would be a relatively equitable distribution of income, full or near full employment and a decent average
standard of living. The need to guarantee the basics – food, cloth-
ing, light and heat – loomed large in the average family budget
and people were ready to accept standard welfare provision, from

council housing to a basic pension, offered by the state. After the miserly means-tested benefits of the 1930s, the new arrangements looked like affluence.

As average incomes have risen since the 1950s it has become easier to afford the basics, leaving more money free for individuals to spend on what used to be thought of as public goods like education and health, together with consumer goods that would have seemed like luxuries after the war. Technological innovation and productivity increases have brought what were once costly and prestige commodities within the range of those on average incomes. A car, for example, took eleven months of average earnings to buy in 1945; in 1995 a very much higher performance vehicle takes little more than eight months of average earnings to buy.

The state's conception of the average family plainly had to be remodelled to reflect these new realities and aspirations. An increased tax base could have been used to create better health services and education, and benefit rates could have been increased in line with the rise in living standards generally. The welfare state could have developed in complexity, offering a range of choices of provision in return for varying charges paid by people when they were in work, while honouring its promise to provide for everyone. This, after all, is roughly how the Scandinavian countries developed their welfare systems. There could have been a determined effort to make the system less bureaucratic and more consumer friendly. One of the more persistent complaints about the administration of social security is that it is authoritarian, rigid, centralised and hostile to claimants.

But reformism and modernisation on this scale did not appeal to the economic liberals running social policy in the 1980s. For the structure of the welfare system reflects fundamental choices about the relationship between the individual and society, and especially about the boundaries of public and private domains. Instead they used the buoyant personal incomes of those in work, and the sense of security built up during the previous thirty years of the welfare state to erode its boundaries and its vision – insisting that its inefficiency demanded change in one direction only. The state, Hayek claimed in *The Road to Serfdom*, could only enthral and entrap – and now the opportunity to roll it back must be seized.

The truth, as Mrs Thatcher's advisers grasped, was that sufficient numbers of the modestly tall and even the undersized in the British income parade were prepared to go along with this, even when it involved paying for their own personal pensions and conniving in the effective removal of free dental treatment and eye testing. Either they felt that they might benefit or, in baser terms, that any costs were so far in the future that they were not worth thinking about, or that the changes were inevitable so that there was no point in resistance. Certainly those who tried to resist the changes were portrayed as the conservative defenders of a status quo whose time was gone.

The political difficulty for the zealous neo-liberal crusaders against 'serfdom' is that the welfare state is deeply popular and entrenched. It satisfies a vague sense of justice, so that the free National Health Service and universal pension, for example, are regarded as inviolable. But this moral sense is not buttressed by any tradition of social citizenship. In Britain we are 'subjects' of the Crown-in–Parliament, and there is therefore no citizenship tradition to draw upon. The welfare state is no more a system of state social assistance, based on collective insurance and enacted by Labour when it had a parliamentary majority. There is no enduring value system, save Labour's collectivism, upon which its claims to universalism, social solidarity and inclusive values can draw; its legitimacy is simply that there had once been a parliamentary majority in favour of it. Although popular, it was uniquely exposed to the right's attack in the 1980s and the only coherent intellectual tradition available to defend it was the collectivist' one that was itself under furious assault around the world.

The right drew on another strong tradition in British life – the doctrine of self-help and the minimal state. The Treasury and the City were powerful voices of this orthodoxy, to which the articulate spokespersons of the Tory new deal were soon joined. Before the insistence that there should be no disincentives to work, no poverty traps, no excessive tax burdens and all the rest, the defenders of the status quo quailed – as Dennis Healey had in 1976–9.

Nor was there a convincingly principled response to the idea that state provision should be minimal and that people should make provision for themselves. The new notion of welfare combined more choice, more efficiency and more individual responsibility; apparently a winning trinity of ideas.

These ideas have been applied to a society in which there is a profound insecurity in the labour market. As we have seen, full-time jobs have shrunk so they are now occupied by fewer than 40 per cent of the adult population, with the balance in part-time or casualised work or no work at all. Full-time employment for men has plummeted by 20 per cent since 1977.[2] The trends are clear; full-time work is on the wane and people's lifetime earnings are punctuated by jagged spells of inactivity and hardship, and frequent moves from job to job.

At this time of tension and confusion the welfare structures and the institutions that radiate out from them have been weakened. Not merely the economy, but society has been 'marketised' – with an increase in anxiety, dread of the future and communal breakdown. The impact is nearly universal as the following survey shows.

Pensions

Providing for old age is one of life's elementary precautions. In a world without the state, each individual would have to build up a pool of savings over their lifetime and live off the interest of the accumulated capital in retirement. The level of the private pension would depend upon the level of saving, which in turn would depend upon both income and willingness to save, and on the interest rate on the savings.

In essence, this is how private pensions work. Regular premiums are paid to a company which invests them – typically in shares in the leading 200 companies at home and in other industrialised countries, as well as in a mixture of government securities and property assets. On retirement a fund has accumulated which is then used to buy an annuity, which gives a pension until death.

The size of the pension depends upon the level of payments, the size of the fund, the performance of the stock market and the competence with which the assets have been managed – and of course the prevailing annuity rate on retirement.

At the time of writing, annuity rates are some 9 per cent, so to produce a pension of £9,000 a year the accumulated funds would need to be £100,000. To be sure of a £100,000 fund in 2020 means having a remarkably prescient view of how the stock market will perform over the next twenty-five years and of how rapidly individual earnings (and thus potential contributions) will grow. The more your earnings and savings grow, and the better the stock market performs, then the easier it is to build up such a fund.

We should all be so lucky. In reality, the gift of prophecy is given to relatively few. For if we assume that earnings grow by 3 per cent in real terms and the stock market rises by 8.5 per cent per year, then calculations made by the *Guardian*[3] show that £2080 has to be set aside annually to produce a £100,000 fund by 2020 (the calculations assume nil inflation to simplify the underlying relationships). There will be almost 12 million pensioners in twenty-five years' time, all of whom will be aiming to have similar-sized funds, so cumulative funds would be £1,200 billion at today's prices.[4] Even allowing for a *doubling* of national output, this would imply that pensioners' assets would at least equal national output – three times more than they represent today.

This, of course, is impossible. It is impossible for everyone to save over £2,000 a year for twenty-five years continually because they simply do not have enough disposable income. After tax and national insurance, the average take-home pay is about £14,000; two-thirds of the population have this much income or less – income, moreover, that is increasingly unpredictable and insecure. To allocate more than an eighth of such income to accumulating a pension fund would lower the standard of day-to-day living. And it is not obvious that the economy could sustain the weight of such enormous funds or the demand for dividends they would store up. The British pension system has become a Jack-in-the-box that will not burst open cheerily when the time comes. Dividends have already doubled to some 5 per cent of GDP to meet the demands from existing pension funds. They would have to more than double again to meet the demands of the next century.

The reality is that unless there is some intervention by the state, average pensions will be very much lower than £9,000 a year, and that many people of pensionable age will have no pension at all and be forced to live on means-tested income support. The only way to avoid this miserable outcome is for the state to run a scheme which imposes a measure of redistribution from the better-off in work to the worse-off in retirement; in other words to maintain a reasonable state pension so as to avoid a huge population of mendicant poverty-stricken retirees. It is as well to be clear about this: to return to a state of nature and invite everybody to provide for themselves is to condemn the majority to penury.

Yet this has been precisely the direction of pension policy since 1979. The state pension has been progressively devalued in relation to average earnings and the right to top up the basic pension – the earnings supplement – has been made ever less generous. The argument has been that to maintain the level of real provision and improve it, would impose an intolerable burden of taxation, especially as the current four people of working age supporting each pensioner will fall to three by the year 2040.[5] The state is doing all it can to wash its hands of responsibility for future generations of old people.

People contracting out of the state earnings related pension scheme (SERPS) receive a rebate of 4.8 per cent (divided between employer and employee) on their national insurance contribution and they use the savings to contribute to a private persion. This will lower the future claim of pensioners upon the state, it is argued, even though people are thereby being encouraged to believe in economic impossibilities. The rhetoric speaks of fair pensions for all, but the game being played is a form of Russian roulette.

Pensions are not an isolated financial problem. The entire story reveals the *systemic* weaknesses of British institutions. SERPS had been painfully negotiated between the main parties in the 1970s to allow people to top-up their state pension with extra payments; yet the British constitutional doctrine is that no Parliament can bind its

successor. So in the mid-1980s the Conservatives could use their
majority in the House of Commons to knock out the keystone
of the arch leading, for most people, from a difficult present to
a relatively secure future, and greatly reduce the value of SERPS.
There was no redress, no discussion; it was taken as axiomatic that
taxes should fall as a proportion of national output and that SERPS
and the basic pension alike were too generous.

But, as John Hills of the London School of Economics has
explained, to maintain the level of the state pension in relation
to average earnings is not especially expensive. The ratio of
pensioners to the working population will rise in Britain over the
next thirty years, but by less than almost all other industrialised
countries. To maintain the current value of pensions in relation to
average earnings would imply taxation rising by some 2.3 per cent
of GDP at its peak in 2030 – less than the tax rises implemented by
Chancellors Lamont and Clarke in 1993. The tax level would then
fall as the rise in the population of elderly people declined. This is
not intolerable or unmanageable.

Instead, leading Conservative ministers openly acknowledge
that the state pension will become 'nugatory' through a continuation of current policies – as Michael Portillo put it when
Chief Secretary to the Treasury. Yet if the privatisation of
pensions for everyone is close to economic impossibilism in
terms of the macro-economy, at the micro level the individual
finds a barely regulated minefield. Because the value of the stock
market and its returns are unpredictable, as are future levels of
inflation, it is virtually impossible for the individual to make an
accurate judgement about his or her appropriate level of savings
towards a pension. At the same time the size of the ultimate fund
is dependent upon the investment performance of rival insurance
companies; the best company can produce funds 50 per cent higher than even average rivals – with one of the key determinants of
investment performance being the level of charges, over which the
individual investor has neither control nor information.

Then the investor has to run the gauntlet of estimating the value
of the stock market and annuity rates at the moment of retirement.
Some schemes give investors the value of their accumulated assets

on the day of retirement, so that the pension is dependent upon how high the stock market is on the 65th birthday; others gradually sell shares and acquire less volatile investments in the run-up to retirement so that the fund is less dependent upon the vagaries of the stock market. But as the state has not legislated to make sure this takes place, investors have to assure themselves that their investment is being appropriately managed. Pension funds are a complete mystery to most people and as this is the same public that redeems 80 per cent of endowment policies before their terminal date and thus loses enormously on them, it is improbable that such requests will be made. Not only that, annuity rates vary themselves by more than 40 per cent, and to get the best rate the new pensioner should shop around. Few do. The standard of living in retirement depends upon the spin of the stock market roulette wheel so that two individuals paying the same pension premiums could end up, if one chooses a commission-hungry insurance company and then makes the wrong purchase of annuity, with an income which is 50 per cent different.

The regulation of the entire business is spatchcock, based on nineteenth-century trust law and notions of self-regulation, despite the fact that the funds under management run into hundreds of billions, and that millions of people rely on them for their retirement income. Private pensions are sold largely by salesmen who themselves are tied into the same market-based system by being paid on commission, and who cannot make a living wage without sales. As a result it is scarcely surprising that their 'clients' end up holding schemes that are wholly unsuitable. As the highest commission paying companies tend to produce the poorest investment performance, the 'client' loses twice over.

For example, 2 million people have been persuaded to opt out of the state pension and into private pensions when their earnings were too low to allow them to achieve a comparable income in retirement for the kind of payments they had already been making to the state scheme. The Securities and Investment Board have estimated that as many as 450,000 people have left occupational pension schemes with guaranteed pensions related to final salary and with contributions from their employers, to buy private pensions dependent solely upon stock market gyrations and their own contributions. They have been sold a pup.

Customer and salesmen are bound together by the same market tyranny; one party is aware that public provision is increasingly inadequate and needs some form of private supplement – the other needs to close a deal. Improved disclosure requirements for commissions on pension and insurance products will begin in 1995, while the regulatory authorities have been imposing increasingly heavy fines on some of the best-known names in insurance: Legal & General, Norwich Union and Guardian Life have all suffered fines for malpractice, poor record keeping and bad advice – while other well-known names like Barclaylife, Nationwide and the Royal have all withdrawn their sales forces for retraining. The list grows inexorably. But even with tighter regulation the logic of the operation remains the same; an ignorant but worried buyer of insurance and pensions, and a seller who needs the business. The fact that some of the most famous names in British insurance have been shown to be shysters and tricksters casts a yet deeper pall of uncertainty and fear over the vast majority of people who are not rich enough to face the future without careful planning.

Occupational pensions are scarcely any better regulated. Robert Maxwell notoriously robbed the assets of Mirror Group Newspapers for collateral for his financial gambles. And companies regularly claim any so-called pension fund surpluses as their own. The surplus may have arisen from the rise in value of assets to which both employer and employee contributed – but the surplus is not passed on to the pension fund or pensioners. Instead the company makes it the excuse for cutting back on its own pension contributions, so that the purpose of many takeovers is to grab pension funds which have surpluses and so save on employers' contributions.

The Goode report into pensions was an attempt to stiffen up the regulation of occupational pension funds, but its conclusions were limited by working within the same basic framework that causes the problems. Under the 'reformed' regime, funds are not obliged to be placed in the custody of an independent trust to ensure their integrity; that would qualify the rights of sovereign company directors to maximise the interests of shareholders, and there is no larger public constitutional or legal model for such independence. Nor is there any tradition of corporate citizenship that encourages the establishment of occupational pension funds and the Goode Committee was rightly concerned that if it made its reforms too onerous, companies would scale back their provision of pension funds. Firms competed to offer them when labour market conditions were tight in the post-war period. With high and permanent unemployment there is increasingly less need to offer pension funds to attract staff and new companies tend to regard them as an unnecessary and expensive luxury.

More than ever people are on their own – left to the tender mercies of the scarcely regulated labour, capital, annuity and pensions markets. They don't know it yet – but the old age they face will be remarkably less affluent than that which their parents enjoyed. For that they can thank Britain's gentlemanly capitalists and their New Right accomplices in government.

Housing

Housing has been no less exposed to the blast of market forces. A majority of home owners are Conservative voters; a majority of those who rent public housing vote Labour. This makes for a neat conjunction of political and economic objectives. By reducing the public housing stock and increasing private ownership the Conservative government hoped both to reduce public expenditure on housing investment, encourage 'self-reliance' and enlarge its own political constituency. In the City of Westminster, home of Parliament and Sovereign, local partisans took the policy so literally that they spent public money to offer cut-price private housing.

Local authorities, as the custodians of the public housing stock, have been prime targets. They were seen as inefficient providers of housing and patrons of a Labour voting constituency, and thus doubly damned. By establishing housing trusts so that public sector tenants can manage their own housing, giving funds to housing

associations and limiting local authorities' capacity to use the proceeds of council house sales to build new homes, the government
has succeeded in greatly reducing their role.

There was enough truth in this New Right diagnosis of Labour
municipalities to warrant some reform. Local authorities have not
been impressive providers of housing. Many tenants feel powerless; standards of maintenance and renovation are often poor.
The housing association movement in the 1970s was expanding
partly because of these deficiencies, and strengthening it seemed
uncontroversial at first.

The attempt to staunch the decline in the private rented sector
and build up a third force in housing provision by deregulating
private rents was eminently justifiable. The control of private
rents, setting them at a fraction of their market value so that
they were affordable for the poor, displaced the cost of providing
social housing on to private landlords. Not surprisingly, the stock
of rentable accommodation has fallen throughout this century, and
many controlled tenancies are slums because private landlords cannot expect any reasonable return from their investment. Indeed, a
black market grew up between tenants in which the right to live
in a controlled tenancy was traded, with the capital value reflecting
the degree to which the controlled rent was below the open-market
value.

Yet paying rent, rather than servicing a mortgage ultimately to
own a house, does not make economic sense. The building society
movement grew up in the nineteenth century to help working men
and women to acquire their own homes, and in supporting this
strong tendency in British culture the Conservative Party was
going with the grain of popular opinion. Encouraging home
ownership established the party firmly on the side of upward social
and economic mobility, and attracted many working-class people
who wanted something better than their parents' way of life.

There are, of course, risks as well as rewards from ownership.
To buy a house is a longterm financial commitment, and housing
policy over the 1980s has fallen foul of the extraordinary volatility
of house prices and the new insecurity of employment. The interaction of these two phenomena has created vicious inequality of

gains and penalties as well as an unprecedented level of personal financial crisis as people with insecure jobs have found themselves unable to meet their commitments. One study in Luton showed that over 25 per cent of the town's owner-occupiers had lost their jobs between 1989 and 1993 – and unsurprisingly 23 per cent of those with mortgages had missed a mortgage repayment and a fifth were in arrears. Prices fell sharply, and one in three people in Luton knew somebody whose house had been repossessed.[7]

At the same time the obsession with private provision and the refusal to accept any role for planning has meant that the public housing stock – still a crucial provider of homes for low income groups – has become ever more second class and ghettoised. The celebration of the market and denial of a role for the state has here, again, been partially self-defeating.

The volatility of house prices has made *timing* the essence of successful home ownership. Those who timed their purchase correctly made fortunes while those who did not were left sitting on 'negative equity' – their house worth less than the cost of their mortgage. With most mortgages attached to interest rates that go up and down, home-owners are uniquely exposed to the vagaries of the economic and interest rate cycle – and those who bought at the top of the boom, and thus had larger mortgages, were more exposed than those with lower, older mortgages.

The sale of mortgages to the burgeoning new class of home owners has become one of the engines driving up the level of economic instability and personal insecurity. Over the 1980s, banks and building societies relaxed their terms of lending as the recovery from the recession of the 1970s seemed here to stay, offering loans at increased multiples of income and at ever higher proportions of already strongly rising house prices. This pushed up the price of houses in relation to average incomes but as long as there was a fresh wave of buyers and lending to buoy up current prices, the loan seemed safe enough to borrower and lender alike.

But the very particular structures of British housing finance and range of schemes created by the deregulated City of London accentuated the volatility. The rise in the stock market since the war had offered those investing in pension plans and endowment insurance policies annual real returns of 12 per cent or more, so that comparatively small monthly premiums produced substantial capital sums over the twenty-five-year-life of a mortgage. The stately endowment policy, in which the saver made regular payments over the life of the policy to receive a lump sum at the end, began to deliver returns well beyond the dreams of both the insurance companies and investors in the 1960s and 70s. Mortgage lenders began to sell mortgages that could be repaid – not gradually over their life but instead from the proceeds of endowment policies when they matured – and as stock market returns carried on growing, even from the lump sums that personal pensions offered their holders on retirement. This seemed a risk free and cheap means of paying back debt. Mortgage borrowers could play the same game as Lord Hanson and use these vehicles to get hold of tomorrow's money today and so reduce their debt service payments.

The lenders were not motivated by altruism. The attraction to the lender was that these policies offered substantial commissions whether or not they were appropriate to the borrower. Moreover, commission could be charged at the beginning of the life of the policy, so that anything up to the first two years' premiums of a twenty-five-year policy went in commission payments. Britain's system of self-regulation did not demand effective disclosure of the commissions; nor did it demand that insurance companies spread their commission over the life of the policy. Of the £17 billion premium income paid to life insurance companies in 1993, £2 billion was paid in commission.

Here again the ancient tendencies of British finance intersected neatly with the priorities of the Conservative government. It wanted to encourage private home ownership; and there were financial institutions and instruments in abundance that could serve that purpose. The building societies, mutual associations of small savers and borrowers whose ethic was to encourage self-help among ordinary people, were enlisted as allies in the New Right's political project. The banks, anxious to share in this highly profitable form of lending, insisted that they be allowed to compete with building societies on level terms in providing mortgages – and the anxiety to deregulate meant they were given what they wanted.

At the end of the 1970s around 90 per cent of new mortgages were repaid slowly by traditional means; by the early 1990s some 90 per cent of new mortgages were supposed to be repaid by stock-market related schemes with their astonishingly high commissions for the lender. It was the feeding frenzy induced by these juicy returns that contributed to the exponential growth of lending and the surge in house prices over the 1980s.

For if banks and building societies found the business highly profitable, so did the new lenders that could enter the mortgage market freely. They could borrow large sums in London's liquid money markets and then lend them as mortgages through a network of mortgage brokers and financial intermediaries to a public hungry to borrow. The key to their profits was to link each mortgage to a profitable sale of an endowment policy – and anxious to win market share rapidly, they lent even more aggressively than the traditional sources. They lowered their demands of creditworthiness, raised the multiples of income against which they lent and lent not only the full value of the house but additional sums to finance the legal and financial charges of assuming debt. In 1989 around a third of new mortgages were for 105 per cent of the valuation of the property concerned.[8] Millions of people, in other words, were staking their futures on speculative investment in the value of their homes. Banks and building societies were compelled to follow the new competitive rules or lose business.

As long as house prices and the stock market rose borrowers and lenders were happy. The commissions were good, the loans were secure against rising house prices and the premiums paid to the insurance company for stock market investments promised to secure the capital sum necessary to repay the final mortgage. But as soon as interest rates rose, house prices fell, new business evaporated and borrowers could not meet their now overvalued repayments, the lenders – especially the new arrivals – found themselves in serious trouble.

The same process now worked in reverse. The new lenders' cash flow position was insecure. Unlike building societies and banks they did not have a large number of small savers contributing deposits whose interest rates they could shave in relation to market rates as times got hard to sustain their cash flow. They had borrowed short term on the money markets at full market interest rates, and when they renewed their borrowing the large depositors, knowing that they were now at risk, demanded a premium over the regular market rates. The inflow of cash was more erratic because with unemployment or lower wages from casual work, the less cushioned borrowers to whom they had lent money in their chase for insurance business could not maintain the payments.

This would not have mattered if the volume of new business, with all those profitable commissions, was being maintained; but that too was falling away, locking the lenders themselves in a downward spiral. To cap it all the fall in house prices was gnawing away at their asset position and thus the sustainability of their balance sheet. With minimal reserves, they had to cease trading – and foreclose on distressed borrowers. The number of repossessions mushroomed from a mere 3,000 in 1980 to over 75,000 in 1991, most of them carried out by the new lenders. It was their additional lending that had helped fuel the boom; now it was intensifying the decline in prices, pulling down the more traditional lenders in their wake.

Even those in the top 40 per cent of the income scale barely understood the risks of the debts they had incurred and the real purpose of the financial instruments they woke up to find they owned; but earning relatively secure salaries they could survive the experience, with the longterm benefits of home ownership (ranging from the potential profits to personal autonomy) offsetting the risks.

For those in the bottom 60 per cent, the relationship between risk and reward is progressively more dangerous the more insecure and poorly paid they are. If they need to cash in their endowment policies before their full term, they will receive only a fraction of the potential full value. If they borrow too much or the value of their house falls, then they have no reserve. The alternatives are paying high rents to a private landlord with little attendant security, or to a public landlord in a ghetto of low incomes and social deprivation, so they are compelled to play the volatile housing market and negotiate unaided the hazards of how they finance and time their purchase.

Home ownership has, by closing down all other options, grown to nearly 70 per cent of the population. But according to the Joseph Rowntree Housing Review, around 30 per cent of those engaged in buying a house earn below average earnings; a quarter of unskilled manual workers are servicing mortgages. Close to 4 per cent of mortgage holders in 1989 simply could not sustain the cost of home ownership as the economy went into recession.[9] Many of the 1.6 million whose equity 'went negative' over the 1990–92 recession could not absorb the loss involved in moving house. For them housing has become an intolerable burden, a financial trap.

In the social, rented housing sector the cumulative sale of 1.45 million council houses at substantial discounts under the right to buy legislation – some 22 per cent of the stock of public sector housing in 1980 – has given the current incumbents a windfall gain, if their houses are sellable. But the absence of any significant construction programme has meant that many houses have dilapidated and not been replaced. The stock of social housing has fallen from 6.5 million units in 1981 to under 5 million and its character destroyed; the best houses have been sold whilst the least desirable remain in public hands, thus creating estates whose occupants tend to be the poorest. Three-quarters live on less than average earnings.

The housing associations, which began as non-profit-making voluntary organisations, have been forced to become the principal providers of social housing. Although they get public money, they have no formal constitutional structure that allows for accountability, either in the areas in which they operate or to their tenants. Public grants have been dramatically cut in the search for public expenditure savings so that while grants covered 90 per cent of new housing investment in 1988, they fell to 62 per cent in 1994 and are targeted to fall even further – to 55 per cent in 1995. As a result the associations have to charge progressively higher rents to cover the market interest rates at which they borrow. Rents, according to the National Federation of Housing Associations, are approaching 30 per cent of net income for their tenants; significantly higher than local authority rents and higher than housing costs for owner occupiers. But as housing association tenants typically earn a third of the average wage, government stinginess is almost completely self-defeating because it has to pay housing benefit; the Exchequer may gain in reduced grant but it loses through increased housing benefit payments.

Housing associations are obliged to let their houses to capacity so that homes designed for small affluent families become filled by large low-income families, and the houses themselves start to deteriorate very rapidly. These estates were never planned to deal with the social problems incurred by poor and poorly socialised people – so that crime and tension rise. Thin walls, close proximity, overcrowding, and lack of space disfigure many of the new housing association estates.

The decline in social housing together with the increase in the absolute numbers of poor people has inevitably led to a remorseless rise in homelessness. There has not been a single year since 1979 when the numbers of homeless people have not increased. In 1994 there were 200,000 of them, three times as many as in 1979. Two-thirds of the homeless have children, and they have jumped to the top of the queue of housing need. Around half of all current local authority new lets are to the homeless but this accentuates the extent to which local authorities have become home providers of last resort. Their financial constraints mean that they cannot discharge even this obligation properly, and so they are compelled to refer cases to housing associations who at least get some government grant – but as these cases tend to be very low income and particularly distressed the housing associations have become even greater sinks of the marginalised groups in society than council housing.

The privatisation of housing has intensified the breakdown of urban life and with it many of our most cherished notions of community and citizenship. 'Good' neighbourhoods become ever more expensive and exclusive, with their schools and doctors attracting more funding; 'bad' neighbourhoods are caught in a self-reinforcing loop of decline. The attempt to impose reliance on the market for housing has made cities more divided and dangerous, promoted inequality and directly contributed to the growth of crime.

Health

Pensions and housing were not the only areas exposed to market forces; formerly inviolable services have become subjects of the great experiment too.

The National Health Service was created as a monopoly provider of health. Its budget was centrally fixed and a network of general practitioners ensured that the patient would only get expensive hospital treatment if every other avenue had been explored – doctors thus standing as gatekeepers between the sick individual who would want to demand whatever care was available at whatever price, and the taxpayer who would otherwise be exposed to an open-ended financial commitment. Although Britain was near the bottom of the international league table of health spending, British life expectancy and the incidence of chronic disease were in the middle of the range. Treatment was free at the point of use, and everyone knew that medical care would be available to those who needed it.

Although there were variations between districts, and a few ignoble consultants had a vested interest in making sure that there were waiting lists as an incentive to private treatment, the system worked reasonably well. It was relatively cheap, efficient and helped to make the population healthy. But this was not enough for the idealists of the class of '79. The NHS did not conform to market principles; it was the seat of egalitarian collectivism and as a monopoly it necessarily had to be inefficient. The NHS did not have to compete to provide treatment, it was said; there was no overt pressure in the system to produce at lower cost nor any means by which efficient 'producers' could get more business or expand. So the NHS was reinvented as a market, with thinking influenced by failed US theorists who were confronting a genuine crisis of inflating health care costs, as the British were not. Not for the first time the US model was copied and misapplied by the New Right in Britain.

The awesome power of the British state is revealed at moments like this. The government insisted that the proposed changes were universal; there was no testing of the idea in particular regions. There was no argument that could make the state modify its position or institutions that could mediate the changes. They were introduced brutally and wholesale. Providers of health, such as hospitals, were classified as 'producers' who were to compete for health care business from those who hold 'budgets'. These are GPs and regional health authorities who contract with the 'producers'. GPs can opt to control 80 per cent of the per capita budget allocated to their practice and spend it on their patients' behalf to secure the most cost-efficient service. These are 'fund-holding' doctors.

The results, in improved efficiency, are difficult to assess, largely because the government refuses to release adequate statistics, but it is obvious that access to care has become markedly unequal. Hospitals agree contracts with fund-holding GPs, and then have to deliver on them – which means that fund-holding GPs have a prior claim on hospital resources for their patients over non-fundholders. There is growing evidence of this bias, with hospitals holding over routine referrals from non-fund-holding GPs to the subsequent financial year.[10] In this thicket of new jargon, the sick pay the price for redefining reality.

But even if all GPs became fund-holders there would be structural inequality, because the terms of individual contracts would differ. Patients from large practices with large budgets would benefit from their GPs' greater purchasing ability, especially if they lived in an area with high standards of health – such as a middle-class suburb where the GPs could afford to pay more for any given service; or where the hospital would be more willing to provide it, calculating that the demands would be less than from poorer, less healthy areas. At the same time patients' access to health care would depend on how profit-driven their GP was; for example, a GP anxious to boost his profits would want to offer the cheapest health care possible.

At the same time hospitals are forced by the logic of competition to specialise in 'profitable' lines of medicine in which they have a comparative commercial advantage. The general hospital attempting to provide a broad range of care for its locality will find itself under growing pressure from specialist competitors, often miles away, who offer heart surgery, for example, at a keen rate.[11] They will either be forced by fund-holders to bid down their own price, thus diminishing their capacity to provide other services, or discontinue the service because they lack the economies of scale as the most efficient provider. In all markets there is a tendency to concentration and specialisation; the same will be true in hospitals.

The prospect of being treated near home or even treated moderately quickly, will become much more remote. Access to doctors and hospitals will become increasingly dependent upon the general health of the catchment area in which one lives, the policy of one's GP and his or her skill in negotiating contracts with 'providers'. Inequality in health provision will become more marked, and the health of the poor will become worse. This will reflect itself in reduced capacity to work, increased isolation of the areas in which they live and greater public spending to try to relieve the deprivation. The search for efficiency through the market will once again have become self-defeating.

Education

British education has always been partially privatised, at least for the élite. In 1993 a *Financial Times* survey showed that 92 of the top 100 schools measured by A level results were private and 177 of the top 200 were private. Average fees at a private day school in the 1992–93 school year were £5,170; for a boarding school £9,400.

Fees of this size can only be paid by parents in the last few minutes of the income parade – and underline the degree to which private education has become a self-reinforcing virtuous circle for those who can afford it. Dominating the A level league table, the students from private schools occupy some half of the places at Oxford and Cambridge – and thus have an inside track to positions of power and influence, which then allow them to earn the salaries that can pay for their own children to repeat the performance. Private schools educate 1 child in 15 but account for more than 1 in 4 university students in Britain.

Anthony Sampson and Jeremy Paxman have amply documented the pervasive impact of private education on British society. It is the entry ticket into upper-middle-class life, and the lifelong appurtenances of class, and the personal networks it opens up – along with the benefits of high quality education – are essential foundations of Britain's caste-like élite.

The dominance of the public school system is a long-standing offence to any notion of democracy or meritocracy in our society; educational achievement is still more closely related to parental income than innate ability, and the country denies itself access to some of the best scientific and artistic talents by organising education in such an inequitable manner.

The defence, of course, is that private schools are the products of choice and the liberty of individuals to spend their money as they will. Even if only 7 per cent of pupils attend private schools, nearly 50 per cent of parents say they would send their children to private schools if they could afford to. They are not philosophically opposed; they just want what they perceive as the best education for their children.[12]

The wider processes of social exclusion and their dependence on privatisation are laid bare by these schools. It is not only that parental income becomes the crucial determinant of future status, but that the value system that justifies such inequality is compelled to reject ideas of citizenship, inclusion and universalism. To uphold these democratic values is to question directly the legitimacy of private education on the scale it is taken up in Britain. It is true that the freedom to educate one's child as one wants is a fundamental human right, as laid down in the European Convention of Human Rights; but the legislators of the Convention did not envisage the right being exercised by an entire class to establish a near monopoly of access to the higher rungs of society. A nation of fair citizens would demand equality of opportunity; a universal education system in which all were included, and could not justify an inside track for a few based on income.

The private school system becomes not only the hothouse of a privileged caste but also of an ideology that justifies its position. Its alumni necessarily believe in the primacy of voluntarism and choice. They do not think of themselves as stakeholders in a wider society, not only because they have set themselves apart from any commonly supported social structures in the quest for their own advancement, but because the justification for doing so is that stakeholding in the wider society is not important. This is why the voices reciting the incantation that the prime obligation of the firm is to its shareholders and that the state has no business to intervene tend to speak in the modulated tones of the privately educated.

The grip of the private schools on the education system is profound. To justify their fees they have to provide results; and these are measured by the highly focused and academic system of A levels. A level results are the route to social and economic advancement, and their principal steward and advocate is the private school system which now educates nearly a fifth of all sixteen-year-olds and over. This puts pressure upon state schools to compete, so that A levels become even more important. Academic examination results become identified with success; and vocational training, already the Cinderella of the system, becomes even more socially devalued as the preserve of the second best.

Our education system is becoming three-tiered. The top layer is the private schools. The state system is fractured into two further tiers by yet another wave of market-based reforms and attacks on the powers of local authorities. Schools which opt out of local government control receive favourable grants directly from central government, leaving behind more poorly financed schools under local authority control. Some opted-out schools select pupils by examination, like the old grammar schools. Yet even for local authority controlled schools funding is dependent upon the total number of pupils, so in order to receive the grant schools have to attract more students; and to attract more, they have to succeed in the examinations game and perform well in the published league tables of academic success.

Although these reforms have produced some increased efficiency by delegating the management of resources to the head teachers of individual schools, the larger issue is the inequality now built into the system. Like the Health Service this is generating virtuous and vicious circles – which increasingly correspond to the physical catchment area of the school. Opted-out schools in well-to-do areas perform well in the league tables, attract more pupils and thus more funding and expand further; comprehensives in more down-at-heel areas find themselves with less money and fewer facilities. With teachers' salaries falling from 137 per cent of the average of non-manual workers' salaries in 1974 to 99 per cent in 1992,[13] good teachers are harder to find. Inevitably they gravitate to the schools with fewer educational and social problems; and schools in poor areas with greater problems find it hard to afford the pay premiums required to compensate for the additional stress on their staff.

This same search for efficiency savings and measurement of performance has extended to higher education, where there has been a huge increase in numbers but little increase in funding. Not all students can afford to take up the offered places, reluctant to start their working lives (if they can find a job) on average £4,000 in debt to the government, since grant expenditure has been exchanged for loans, and prefer to take their chance straight away in the market-place. Universities and the old polytechnics, now all 'universities', have been turned into factories for the production of degree-holders, their teaching staff ranked by their publications in specialist journals in a competitive system of performance tests upon which funding and even job prospects depend. Spending on science has grown negligibly, and universities have been compelled to attract 'virtuous' private-sector funding in order to sustain their scientific establishments. Competition for funds is universal.

In the wider social domain housing, education and health policy reinforce one another. It pays to be born well and to live in the better part of town which market forces will make better still. Living on the wrong side of the high street means the risk of being caught in a market-driven cycle of deprivation.

The more these divisions grow, the more urgent is the necessity to join the privileged – and the more second-best and undesirable state provision seems. Too many vested interests are created by those who do well from the new system (and those who are disadvantaged are necessarily less vocal and powerful) – a process described elegantly by Galbraith as 'the creation of a constituency of contentment'. Marketisation may be economically inefficient; but the political consequence is a world in which the New Right can divide and rule.

The privatisation of the public domain

The extension of the market has gone well beyond the formal institutions of the welfare state. It now extends into the very quick of society. Bus services have been privatised and deregulated. Urban development has passed from the hands of public authorities to private companies. Television broadcasting licences have been auctioned and the old duopoly between the BBC and ITV broken by the arrival of satellite TV. The rail system has been partially privatised. Mutual building societies owned by their members have turned themselves into joint stock companies. Internal markets have been established in public corporations.

In all these areas the expressed motive is for increased economic efficiency, with the extension of private ownership – typically the establishment of a company with a stock market quotation – and market relations seen as the only means to achieve that end. Trade-offs and potential costs are ignored.

But efficiency is a slippery concept, particularly in areas where public goods are involved. A TV company may produce more programmes at lower cost, but the quality may be worse. A hospital with fewer nurses may have lower labour costs, but is the quality of health care better? The heart of a city can be redeveloped by a private developer more cheaply than by a public agency, but if there are more shops and less 'public' space is the result really more efficiency?

Markets can produce perverse results. There is an inbuilt tendency to cherry-pick. Social functions are executed poorly.

Short-termism becomes endemic. Markets are not value free. Passengers, viewers, and patients all become homogenised as 'customers' and 'clients' who consume 'products'. But the importance of customers is that they spend; the capacity to be a citizen depends upon spending power, without which citizenship disappears.

Deregulation of the buses has been in many ways a classic example of the process. The operation of local bus services by local authorities and county councils was deemed to inhibit entrepreneurship. Competition would be extended by allowing new companies to become bus operators, offering services between cities and within them.

The results are mixed. After the first round of deregulation comes an explosion of new entrants and competition; fares drop and a bewildering number of buses career around the city in question with no integration of timetables or other transport services. Then follows a period of consolidation until the service is run again by one or two companies in either a monopoly or duopoly. Fares rise, and the services concentrate in peak times; services catering for passengers at off-peak times or in rural areas are unprofitable and are discarded. Valuable sites in the city centre are sold to private developers, and bus services instead of radiating out from central depots operate increasingly from the margins of towns. Deregulation has led to the emergence of private bus monopolies, a patchier network, higher fares, older buses, lower wages, poorly trained workforces, and chaotic timetables.

Between cities the story is different. Intercity coach services, formerly neglected, have become very successful. Exploiting the motorway system and the relative expense of rail transport, coach services offer a cheap, flexible and efficient form of mass transport. Competition has improved standards and lowered prices. Yet there are signs that the same process of consolidation and monopoly is at work here – and in any case part of the reason for the long-distance buses' success is public transport policy. The motorway network is free; comparable rail investment gets little subsidy.

Markets can work well; or badly. There is no iron law – and behind success, like that of inter-city coaches, usually lurks an institutional advantage that has been shaped by public action. But public creativity in this instance as in all others is not acknowledged to have played any part; the injunction from the centre has been to privatise indiscriminately and roll back public authority, which is deemed to be inefficient and bureaucratic.

The results of this dogmatic refusal to accept the legitimacy of public action or the proper existence of the public realm are all around us. For example the privatisation of publicly-held property in city centres and the surrender of development to private companies has changed the character of British towns and cities. Local authorities, starved of cash, have been compelled to permit private developers to reshape city centres around shopping malls – but that has meant passing over public space to private ownership. The malls open and close during shopping hours, so that access to the heart of towns can be denied at night. The malls are privately-policed, with the owners anxious to avoid anything that might disturb shopping – for example, in a Basingstoke mall owned by the Prudential Insurance Company this led to the attempt to prohibit Salvation Army Bible reading and the banning of the sale of Women's Institute jam because it would prejudice sales by existing retailers. BBC's 'File on Four'[14] described how in Luton's shopping mall the security guards prevent old people from resting too often on the few benches because, the manager says: 'Market research had shown that the general public was particularly distressed by the sight of old people sitting down.'

What is once again at work is Britain's weak tradition of citizenship combining with the tradition's mirror image – the celebration of the private. It all adds subtly to the processes of social exclusion. Bus services to rural or remote areas are unprofitable; but so are shopping malls if shoppers are deterred by too many people who lack the wherewithal to buy, especially if they are the apparently yobbish young or homeless huddled in blankets. In rural areas the poor find themselves cut off from the town; the non-consuming classes find themselves excluded from the city centre. The already marginalised and disaffected become more marginalised still.

The process has extended to the mass media. Television has not stood aside from the wider trends. The auctioning of the

TV licences in 1992 for the regional independent franchises was driven by the same version of market ideology. The new licences were allocated to the highest bidder, although there was a quality threshold which was meant to act as a guarantor of minimal quality. The prices paid for the franchises varied, so that companies had conflicting commercial interests – some having the funds to make quality programmes with others chasing cost reduction and market share – making it impossible to harmonise their operations in the ITV network.

The arrival of satellite TV further destabilised the system, creating an additional competitor for advertising revenue and audience. The regulatory framework which had required the companies to broadcast some informed and informative programmes, including current affairs programmes and news bulletins at prime viewing time, together with quotas for homemade productions, began to come apart at the seams. Such 'public service' transmissions had higher costs and reduced audiences and the imperative was to maximise profits in an increasingly competitive market.

Here the new deregulated City and labour market had a huge impact on TV. The companies needed to make high short-term profits to satisfy their shareholders, this pressure coming at the same time as the industry itself was opened up to deregulation while the power of its unions was being weakened. The labour force is now substantially freelance and on short-term contracts; programme quality has suffered and the regional companies are consolidated into larger groups. Choice has been expanded; but the breadth and quality of programmes has been narrowed.

BSkyB, the satellite TV company owned by Rupert Murdoch, was freed from the regulatory standards applying to terrestrial broadcasters in part as a political favour to Murdoch, in part in recognition of the higher set-up costs and risks it was running. Its principal shareholders, notably News International, were able to sustain its losses through the profits from their other worldwide media interests.

BSkyB needed and needs to offer programmes that will justify consumers paying the higher subscription costs for its services together with the installation of a satellite dish. The new holders of the TV franchises need to increase market share to sustain the revenue that will meet their shareholders' demands for dividends and the prices they paid for their franchises. In this competitive maelstrom it is hardly surprising that the character of the programmes offered to the TV audience has changed so much.

In essence programmes have become commodities. They are calculated to attract mass audiences and are constructed with that in mind. Drama must have continual action. Comedy must have immediate laughs. News must be short and sensational. The complicated and demanding must be relegated to off-peak viewing times. When 'News at Ten' comes on the audience figures fall. The leading current affairs programme, 'World In Action', does not command a mass audience. Their survival in prime time is therefore under threat. Programme makers look for sponsors and co-producers to finance the making of TV 'products': inevitably the content is affected by the sponsors' commercial objectives.

In order to lower costs, build up their power to buy in programmes and sell advertising space, the regional companies are consolidating: Granada in the north-west has bought LWT with its franchise for weekend TV in London; Central and Carlton have merged; MAI, based in the south of England, has taken over Anglia. Notions of public service to a region and televison as a cultural asset are weakened; the idea of TV as a product strengthened. TV becomes less a means of creating events together with a flow of information, education and entertainment that is considered a public good; and more a vehicle for broadcasting commoditised segments whose content is exactly calibrated to attract audience and advertising. The public realm is weakened: the private realm strengthened.

The television rights for sporting events are sold to the highest bidder with only a handful of events protected by legislation, furthering the same mix of extending individual choice while deepening social exclusion. BSkyB owns the exclusive right to broadcast live Premier League Football, overseas cricket test matches and the Ryder Cup; and it would like to have Wimbledon, international rugby and whatever else is on offer to make its network more attractive. For individual sports the auction of their

TV rights offers resources for development. But for viewers the entry ticket to this world is the money to afford the subscriptions that are three times higher than the BBC's licence fee as well as the initial payment for the satellite dish. Great national sporting events – the Ryder Cup, a record test innings, the qualifying game for the World Cup – cease to be shared by us all; they become the property of those who can pay, typically in the top half of the income parade. Both the sport and national life are thereby diminished.

The BBC, the natural counterweight to these developments, has been kept starved of resources, its licence fee indexed only to the increase in retail prices, and its future as a public corporation made deliberately uncertain right up to the months before the review of its charter in 1994. Should it take advertising? Should it be privatised? Would its charter be renewed? Partly to generate finance and partly to convince successive Conservative ministers of its commitment to a market value system, it has reorganised itself completely to maximise economic efficiency and programme savings. But the means to this end has not been the thinning of the bureaucracy of control, co-operation with the workforce to promote productivity, or capital investment; it has been to create an internal *market* so that programme makers buy services from the BBC's infrastructure of production – negotiating payments for studios, make-up and use of the film library etc.

The results are ambiguous. Powerful forces bear down on costs, so the first effects are cash savings. At the same time the organisation has to set up a complicated and expensive bureaucracy devoted to auditing, controlling and evaluating what its costs are, and above all to monitor the myriad of internal transactions. The establishment and management of this audit trail is an expense in its own right, thus offsetting some of the savings.

The internal market brings an important cultural change in the organisation. Audit becomes the *raison d'être*, rather than programme making. The relations of trust and co-operation upon which any great corporation is built are broken down by the new reliance on formal monitoring mechanisms. The relentless downward pressure on costs forces managers to lower wages and worsen employment conditions. It becomes harder to build any culture of commitment to the organisation. The initial cost savings are offset by the collapse in the corporate ethic. The BBC has suffered strikes and a drop in morale, but the government approved of its approach; in July 1994 its charter to operate as a public broadcaster was renewed for ten years.

The forces observable in the BBC and British commercial television are at work everywhere. Across the Civil Service similar initiatives have been launched, with the culture of the audit becoming universal.[15] Public goods are privatised or submitted to market constraints, with all the attendant demoralising consequences. It might be the privatisation of the prison service, with the Home Office 'contracting-out' the management of prisons and prisoners to the private sector like Group Four; it could be the pressure on state-funded science laboratories to find private sector finance and commercial outlets for their research. In the government-sponsored arts the experimental gives way to the safe and bankable. Museums advertise their shops and cafés, while the old ethic of curating and scientific merit is down valued. A building society becomes a joint stock company; a government training company is floated on the stock market. As order breaks down in towns and cities, there is even a market in social control – private security guards are commonplace.[16] Values held in common but not viable in the market are in retreat; the inexorable march to a full-blown market society now appears unstoppable.

Living in a market society

Inequality and marketisation may be abstract concepts, but their impact on everyday life is real enough. Inequality is not only about income, where real poverty has grown, but about self-esteem. The more housing, pensions, education, health, transport and even television become market-based, the more points there are in the system where it is vital to be part of the virtuous upward spirals unleashed by market processes – and not the vicious downward ones.

It is hardly surprising that those at the short end of the

income parade suffer increasing despondency at their lot and
sense that their position is unchangeable. The dice are loaded
against them. With this realisation comes a collapse in one's sense
of worth. What matters is relative position; and as this gets worse,
the disadvantage is more keenly felt.

For some this manifests itself in an actual loss of the desire
to live. Research by the British Medical Association shows that
life expectancy for those at the bottom end of the income scale
has fallen, while Richard Wilkinson shows that life expectancy
in Europe, where the income distribution is fairer, is two years
longer than in Britain. The key to personal well-being, argues
Wilkinson, is not *absolute* but *relative* position. He shows that the
self-esteem of the poor falls the more that incomes are unequal,
and with the fall in self-esteem comes socio-psychological stress
which shows up as increased illness and can reduce life expectancy.[17] Over the 1980s, as inequality of income deepened, the rate of
life expectancy declined. He noted that suicide rates for young men
aged between fifteen and twenty-four rose sharply as their relative
earnings deteriorated, unemployment rose and benefit entitlement
was reduced.

But if conditions are intolerable for those at the bottom of
the pile, there are processes as destabilising impacting upon
those in work and whose incomes may be higher. Labour market
deregulation has made work insecure and the flow of income
unpredictable and financial deregulation has allowed households
to incur much more debt.

Burdened by debt and worried about the security of their
jobs, many parents with children feel that they both have to
go out to work while they can whether they like it or not.
They subcontract their parenting responsibilities to others; those
few who can afford it hire nannies, those on lower incomes
rely on baby-minders or their families. For some it is all too
much and children of school age have a latch-key and fend for
themselves while their parents work. Richard Wilkinson reports
a decline of children's reading standards between seven and eight
years old, which appears to be concentrated in the least parented
group.

As Amitai Etzioni, the leader of the American communi-
tarian movement argues, economic liberalism has not provided
any effective response to the parenting problem as both parents
are drawn into an ever more demanding work environment and
thus have less time and energy for their children. Having children
is a moral act, he says, demanding parental commitment – but
the labour market has been designed to make this very moral act
increasingly difficult. The commitment of being a good parent
in market societies is becoming more and more difficult. Etzioni
reports on studies in the US showing that parents spent 17 hours
a week with their children in 1985 compared with 30 in 1965. This
has seismic implications for the socialisation and upbringing of
children and their own future capacities to become good parents.

There are more and more poorly-socialised children, teenagers
and young adults. Their employment chances are almost nil.
Market processes are excluding them from good education and
the shopping malls alike. As Anthony Bottoms and Paul Wiles
argue, these processes are closely connected with the growth
of crime. The poorly-socialised resent their own relatively low
status, lifechances and income. With the collapse of local communities there is less stigma attached to criminality, the informal
sanctions and expressions of disapproval which offenders fear are
no longer there; and they have little reason to empathise with their
victims. There are fewer inbuilt deterrents and greater incentives
to criminal behaviour. The ugly growth of child prostitution[18]
is a testimony to the growing desperation as the marginalised
attempt to make ends meet.

A market society takes a terrible toll of the social groupings
that represent the building blocks of our humanity – from the
parenting of our children to the reliability of public transport. That
is what has been fashioned in the service of a pure market economy.
Irrationality, economic inefficiency and mounting unfairness result
– all forgiven by a value system based on exclusion and systematic
inequality. But why the obsession with promoting markets? For
some answers we must next visit the dreams of the economists.

9. Why Keynesian Economics Is Best

Men and women are social animals, but with conflicting demands and passions. They seek association with each other and value the esteem of others; they desire health and autonomy. They thrive on the stimulus of competition, they recognise the value of co-operation, the importance of security and the need for boundaries to individual action. They seek happiness and a good quality of life, but these are not absolutes – they are substantially influenced by culture and by social mores.

The elegance of market economics is that it cuts through such confusing ambiguities and offers a robust model of what governs human behaviour instead of slippery ideas about co-operation and the quest for happiness. The controlling idea is that the human being is a trader, constantly weighing up the advantages and dis-advantages of various courses of action. And because the essence of a market is that courses of action have a price tag, every act can be reduced to an economic calculus weighing up the costs and benefits of each action.

Happiness may mean eating an apple rather than a pear, but if a pear is half the price of an apple, then the happiness to be gained from eating a pear and using the spare money to buy something else may equal the pleasure from eating an apple. Marriage should not be seen as a celebration of love and mutual commitment, it is a contract between two parties to maximise their returns through rational specialisation of roles; if the returns prove disappointing then there is divorce and remarriage which is an attempt to make a new contract – only executed if the benefits outweigh the costs.[1]

The market economist does not have to make a value judge-ment about, say, divorce, but he or she can predict that if the costs are raised then divorce will fall. Indeed, economists need not make value judgements about anything. All that is required is that confronted with relative market valuations economic men and women make rational choices. It is up to them what their choices and preferences are. As economists ranging from Alfred Marshall through Lionel Robbins to the authors of contemporary textbooks argue, economists simply study what is revealed by actions in markets – not why those actions take place.

Market economics is an intellectual edifice built upon this belief – and requires four key assumptions. The first is that all human conduct can be reduced to a ranking of economic choices in which costs and benefits are accurately and consistently weighed up one against another. The second is that men and women are in a state of nature. There are finite limits to their options, and as they approach them the costs rise and the pleasures of unmined alternatives seem increasingly attractive. The third is that the results of such trade-offs – as long as they are freely arrived at – are optimal for everybody and cannot be improved upon. And the fourth is that the existence of money does not change the fundamental processes at work. If all this holds then the market economy can be viewed not only as conforming to our deepest instincts as human beings, but as producing an unimprovable way of producing outcomes that reflect our rational choices. The economic world is an extension of the natural world, governed by the same natural laws, and if left alone will achieve the same harmony as nature.

This is an attractive philosophy. It is simple; it describes an important aspect of human behaviour; it corresponds to some deeply held intuitive feelings about human conduct; it yields some robust principles for organising both economy and society. The doctrine seems rooted in the actual behaviour of markets. And it is an important justification for minimal government and maximum personal freedom. It has been the animating intellectual force behind the rise of the New Right and the policy prescriptions of the last fifteen years.

But it is also wrong, or, more precisely, it fails as a formal theory to describe the actual behaviour of actual people in a modern money-based exchange economy that produces goods over time. Try as they may, free-market economists (or neo-classical economists, as they are known professionally, because their views descend from classical free-market theory) have been unable to box human and economic activity into the same constructs that make the ideas work in theory. The complexity and variety of rationalities of human response do not fit the narrow requirements of economic rationality.

In the real world in which goods are produced, rather than the state of nature in which they are hunted and gathered, it turns out – contrary to the theory – that production can be increased without returns falling. It can be difficult to soak up demand. And it proves impossible to provide a watertight account of how the simple exercise of choice and its impact on market prices can bring the market economy to an unimprovable outcome. Markets turn out to be unstable, irrational and quite capable of producing perverse results – exactly what happens in real life. Yet they are also capable of producing great wealth, productivity and of sponsoring innovation. The problem is to tease out why they go wrong and how they can be corrected. The answer is not to let them do what they like.

First mistake: defining economic rationality

The economic man of free-market theory is an amoral fellow. He is the descendant of the natural savage. This Robinson Crusoe is the antecedent of modern economic man, who at root is the same being. His God has skimmed Darwin, or at best Tennyson's famous gloss on *The Origin of Species* . . . 'Nature, red in tooth and claw'.

The rational economic man exists to consume and indulge his pleasures. To satiate his wants he must forage, hunt and gather. He barters with other natural savages who bring the results of their hunter-gatherer expeditions to the local market. The relative prices of all the produce reflect their varying quantities and the varying demand for them; and the savages will trade with each other until each has the range of goods that exactly corresponds to his capacity to meet his wants with the goods at his disposal to trade. Nor do these savages entertain any doubts about what they want, or make mistakes, or want any less than the maximum available. The whole exercise is a diversion from the real purpose of life, which is pleasure and leisure (this is where economic woman enters the scene). The less time spent in hunting and gathering the better. Work is burdensome, and economic man shares the view of the Greeks that it is a curse placed upon him by the deities for his hubris. It is in our leisure time that we civilise ourselves and practise our art.

It is this creature that has to lurk inside every one of us if we are to behave as we must to allow the market economy to work as the market theorists say it does. We must regard work as a disutility and leisure as a utility. Wages are what we are paid to make us forego leisure – because if there were rewards other than pay from working, the contract would cease to be reducible to an economic calculus. The job of wages is to reflect an exact trade-off between workers' desire for leisure and the value of their production to an employer; only thus can the optimal use of resources be guaranteed. But if we work for other motives the perfection of market trading is not guaranteed, for some workers may have succeeded in meeting those other objectives better than others – and who is to know?

We must also be trading creatures, with just as perfectly formed a view of our wants as the natural savage, despite the sophistication of our world. For example, if we do something that appears uneconomic – like giving money to charity – it must be assumed that we are gaining some market value from such activity, otherwise the amount we give is unpredictable. And above all we must want something because we want it – and not because we have learned that it is cheap. We bring our desires and our goods to the marketplace to trade so that after we have traded we are left with the best possible result. The theory has to pretend that our desires are formulated completely independently of the marketplace and what is available in it. What the theorists cannot accept is that deciding our preferences is bound up with the act of trading, because then the argument in favour of markets would become circular. If preference were part of the market process there could be unused resources, unbought goods and wild swings of enthusiasm that made the market unstable and perhaps undesirable.

Unhappily for the neo-classical economist we do allow market prices to affect our judgement of worth because in a market economy there is no means of discovering what is available on the market without at the same time knowing its price. Even worse, we cannot be relied upon to make judgements that are rational. Daniel Kahnemann has shown that human recollections of pain and pleasure do not correspond to the actual pain and pleasure experienced. In the 'peak and end rule' he demonstrates that our memory of an event is conditioned by the peak of emotion we experienced during its course and how we felt when it ended; how long it lasted and thus what the true full experience was has little impact on our recollection.

A long operation which was cumulatively painful may be remembered favourably if there was a nice moment during its course and it ended pleasurably, with the relief of pain; while a short operation that had a peak of pain and ended painfully, but was cumulatively less painful will be remembered unfavourably. 'There is compelling evidence', he writes, 'that the maintenance of coherent beliefs and preferences is too demanding a task for limited minds. Maximising the experienced utility of a stream of future outcomes can only be harder.' Rationality, in short, is too difficult for human beings to cope with; and he advocates that the assumption that it is always possible should be dropped.

A host of psychological tests support Kahnemann's view. If we prefer Coca-Cola to lemonade and lemonade to fizzy water, it might be supposed that we prefer Coca-Cola to fizzy water – in other words that the choice is transitive. But when consumers are confronted by such choices they end up making wholly inconsistent rankings. They may choose rationally between a pair of choices, but the addition of a third choice transforms the perceived value of the alternatives. They may choose Coca-Cola when lemonade is around, but as soon as fizzy water is offered the consumer will compromise between the three drinks and opt for lemonade. There simply is not sufficient predictability to assume that choices will be transitive.

Above all in a modern economy it cannot be assumed that modern man has the same approach to work as the ancient Greeks (whose urban leisure class had slaves to endure the curse of labour). For work is not a disutility. It is a means of acting and interacting with the world that fulfils an individual's humanity. Work is a supremely social act. As Robert Lane has argued in an important book, *The Market Experience*, to engage in work is to employ hand and brain in the exercise of production in association with others. It brings self-esteem. It demands the acquisition of skills. It sharpens the capacity to be and to do. A thousand surveys show this, not least those which reveal the anxiety of people who are unemployed to work again.[2]

This does not mean that men and women are indifferent to what they earn – but the supposed free market calculus that they work up to the exact moment when the disutility of working offsets the loss of utility from leisure fails to capture the nature of the bargain over work. Employers value a tried and tested team, so they will disregard the attractions of paying outsiders less to replace known insiders. Equally some may continue to work for less than is available elsewhere because they value the status they have achieved in their current job.

What all this does is to impart uncertainty to our actions. We cannot be rational about whether we have executed the right market bargain because we do not always know enough about ourselves to know whether the choice will prove durable. Are we happy to work for this wage? Does this choice of good truly reflect our priorities? To what extent is any choice attractive because it appears cheap or because it reflects our intrinsic sense of value? And above all how certain can we be that today's price gives an accurate picture of what prices will be tomorrow? Unlike savages who have to trade every acquisition before it perishes, modern economic man has money and can decide not to purchase today – or, by borrowing, bring forward tomorrow's planned purchase.

The best free market economics can do before this onslaught is to concede the impossibility of assuming *individual* rationality but to assert that there is a *collective* rationality. While individuals may be fallible or respond incorrectly to market signals, there is none the less a rolling process of actual market outcomes through which individuals can test what they have done and change their behaviour if it is mistaken. The doctrine of rational expectations claims that, on average, outcomes prove to be rational because we are in a continual process of adaptation.

But this is a major modification of the notion of rationality. It disproves the thesis that market outcomes are unimprovable because it concedes the possibility of mistakes and that individuals cannot be reliably expected to make a priori rational judgements. It is an intellectual retreat. Instead the theory asserts that markets have an inherent capacity to correct themselves once they have produced an outcome that was not desired by the participants. But this requires assumptions about the capacity of market prices to send signals that modify behaviour – and that in turn requires assumptions that prove impossible to sustain.

Second mistake: the laws of diminishing returns

If markets are to correct themselves and achieve a point of balance, they have to send signals that market participants can act upon – and which then provide the basis for convergence around a new balance. In the great Victorian economist Alfred Marshall's formulation, the market is the forum where the forces of demand interact with the forces of supply; these are the two great blades of the market scissors that produce a price at which the quantity demanded equals the quantity supplied. At this point the market has 'cleared'.

Again the basic image is of a market place peopled by Robinson Crusoes. There is a supply of produce; there is a demand for it; and at the close of trading the forces of supply and demand have interacted to produce a price at which the market clears. Such a market is like any market for agricultural produce in any of the world's market towns. There is a multitude of buyers and sellers and prices rise and fall to reflect the availability of supply and the intensity of demand.

The key is the movement of prices and the way in which demand and supply can be assumed to respond to them. Put simply, the more the price falls the more will be demanded and the less will be supplied; conversely, the higher the price the more will be supplied. Thus the upward and downward movement of price will make supply and demand converge to the point at which the market clears. Prices will have produced self-correcting behaviour.

This image of smoothly-closing scissors is predicated upon the pattern of supply and demand mirroring each other, so that their responses to price are opposite. To get this result economists have to assume that supplying more goods becomes at some point progressively more expensive and that demanding ever more goods becomes at some point less attractive. In other words that there are real scarcities and real possibilities of satiation, and that the world is characterised by falling or diminishing returns – and this applies to industrial production as much as it does to the world of hunter-gatherers. It takes progressively more time to forage to collect some fruit, for example, so that costs rise; the manufacture of the extra widget is marginally more expensive than its predecessor. On the other blade of the scissors there comes a point where consumption starts to have diminishing returns – and even falling prices cannot coax the consumer to buy more because his or her wants are satiated. The market clears.

But do we live in a world of diminishing returns? Can we suppose that in a production-oriented economy firms' incremental costs must necessarily rise? And are there really limits to consumers' desires? Paul Ormerod, in *The Death of Economics*, sets out the detailed research that contests these assertions. Modern capitalism is characterised not by falling but by *increasing* returns. He cites Alfred Chandler's massive work, *The Scale and Scope of Industrial Capitalism*, which traces the histories of the top 200 manufacturing companies in the US, Britain and Germany for the century after 1870. In industry after industry what happened was not that costs rose as production increased but that they continually fell. Ford, General Motors, Siemens, Procter and Gamble, and AEG were giant combines which used their early start to entrench a position that proved unassailable for decades. They invested in long production runs; they invested in marketing, distribution and purchasing networks; and they recruited managers who could operate the firm efficiently. They had lower costs than their competitors; and kept them that way.

The same phenomenon has been noted by a new generation of American economists. W. Brian Arthur, Professor of Economics at Stanford University, writes that 'to produce a new pharmaceutical drug, computer spreadsheet programme or passenger jet, many hundred millions of dollars must be spent on research and development. Once in production, however, incremental copies are comparatively cheap. The average cost of producing high technology items falls off as more of them are produced . . . high technology is subject to increasing returns.'[3]

The key is an early start that 'locks-in' advantage, argues Arthur. New firms and industries grow on what is already there, building on the cost advantage of the initial firm and then creating further advantages for themselves. In his latest book, *Peddling Prosperity*, Paul Krugman cites the QWERTY format of modern typewriter keyboards; such a format is irrational but it would take too much investment in human capital everywhere to change it – so it sticks. A contemporary industry now revolves around the historic accident of the format – an exact parallel with what happens generally. Industries are locked into a virtuous circle based upon some initial advantage so that increasing production lowers costs, builds markets and spins-off new allied firms and a fresh round of innovation. There is no moment when an upward move in prices automatically obstructs the working of this virtuous circle.

Nor, as Ormerod claims, need there be diminishing returns from consumption. The possession of one car does not mean there are diminishing returns from owning a second, so that 'for some people at least consumption is often subject not to diminishing but to increasing returns to scale. The more one has, the more one wants and the greater the satisfaction obtained from having it'.

Such a structure of costs and potential benefits is lethal to the free market theoretical structure. It suggests that in some industries production can carry on rising without any necessary upward movement in costs; and that demand for any given product can rise for years before there are diminishing returns. There may be extensive periods in which the market's self-correcting capacities do not exist.

Third mistake: the system regulates itself

The great ideological attraction of market theory is its demonstration that any form of state intervention is unnecessary and counter-productive. The market will, if left to itself, find the optimal solution. Armed with price signals from the marketplace, buyers and sellers will carry on experimenting with production and purchasing until there is a point of unimprovable balance – a general competitive equilibrium.

But the devil is in the detail. How in practice can this experimentation take place? Paul Ormerod makes a useful analogy, comparing the task of an economic actor seeking equilibrium using only price data to a blindfolded man trying to find the deepest hole in a huge field by trial and error – having to clamber in and out of all the various holes that represent all the possible market bargains, one of which represents the equilibrium outcome. If the assumptions of rationality and the law of diminishing returns as described above do hold, then the task is simple. There will only be one hole and the blindfolded Crusoe can walk effortlessly to the bottom of it.

The trouble is that those assumptions do not hold and as a result the field will have as many craters as a First World War battlefield – representing all the many possibilities for market bargains. The blindfolded economic actor has to clamber in and out of most of them – even those so deep that no exit is possible – before finding the deepest, which represents equilibrium.

If the craters were static then the task might be feasible, but if there are increasing returns to higher production then they are constantly mutating, expanding and contracting. Moreover, as the future unfolds, the craters on the field will change their configuration, while there is still supposedly one particular hole that represents the optimal result.

Thus, finding a competitive equilibrium by reliance on prices alone, is a fiendishly difficult job; indeed it is exactly akin to solving simultaneous equations for changing variables in an infinite plane – which is impossible. The only way that general competitive equilibrium models can be made to work is in one of three ways: suspending time; assuming that there is an invisible auctioneer who can instantaneously find the prices that will match all buying and selling plans optimally; or by inventing markets in future plans and intentions so that economic actors can trade in the future as if it was the present – which is a way of stopping the craters from mutating and the variables constantly changing.

Some readers may find this account of free-market theory implausible. It surely cannot be true that the ideas around which the British (and much of the world's) economy and society have been organised over the last fifteen years are as flaky as this. The answer is that they are. Leon Walras, who first invented the notion of an 'auctioneer' to solve the problem of equilibrium determination in his *Element of Pure Economics* written in the early 1900s, openly recognised that the passage of time wrecked the whole free-market model. Goods were being produced all the time the auctioneer was trying to clear the market, so forcing constant changes in price. Walras's answer was clear. 'We shall resolve this difficulty,' he wrote, 'purely and simply by ignoring the time element at this point.'[4]

Roy Radner set out in 1968 in a paper in *Econometrica* to prove that a general competitive equilibrium could exist, and explored the assumptions it required. Radner found the job impossible. Only if everybody could work out what they wanted beforehand – our Robinson Crusoe bringing his clear, well-worked-out, desires and preferences to market – and then negotiated bargains for each market at each point of time in every possible state of the world could a competitive equilibrium exist as the result of free exchange. Yet even to get this far all economic actors must have an infinite amount of computational capacity to explore all the consequences of the options open to them. As he concluded, the model of competitive general equilibrium 'is strained to the limit by the problem of choice of information. It breaks down completely in the face of limits on the ability of agents to compute optimal strategies'.

Indeed the famous Arrow and Debreu General Equilibrium Model depends upon the same construct: markets in future contingencies and plans. But beyond the future markets developed by the financial markets (and even those do not extend much beyond two years) such markets do not exist. And, as Kenneth Arrow conceded in a seminal article in the *Guardian*, the existence of increasing returns and new evidence about human capacities for economic rationality mean that the other restrictive assumptions upon which equilibrium theory depends break down. The Nobel Prize-winning father of the general equilibrium theory admitted defeat.

In other words, the major tenet of free market economics – that unregulated markets will of their own accord find unimprovable results for all participants – is now proved to be nonsense. It does not hold in theory. It is not true. Yet on this altar British industry and social cohesion have been turned into sacrificial offerings. It may take generations to expiate the effects of the mistake.

Towards a new theory of capitalism

Throughout the twentieth century a different account of the behaviour of markets and of wealth creation has been struggling to establish itself. There is a long line of democratic non-free market economists who have insisted that unmanaged capitalism is inherently unstable as a system and that successful enterprise is a social rather than an individualist act. To visualise the firm as an organisational natural savage combining capital and labour in a pitiless competitive struggle, which requires no state intervention, management or regulation to produce the best result, is the legacy of an historic world view justified neither in theory or practice. We have looked at the shortcomings of the theory; but also in practice the twentieth century is littered with great inflations and violent oscillations of economic activity which reinforce the criticisms of free-market economies.

The flaws in free-market theory are not more widely recognised because the twentieth century, at least until the collapse of the

Soviet Union, has been riven by great ideological competition. Part of market theory's job was to offer a view of capitalism at least as rosy as that offered of a planned economy by Marxism. If socialism claimed to know a route to wealth, freedom and human happiness, then free-market capitalism – as long as it conformed to the dictates of free-market theory – could do better.

Yet, paradoxically, the capitalist economy prospered most in the three decades after the war when it was managed and regulated according to the theories of Keynes, even though what was practised fell a long way short of what he preached. His ideas had grown in stature in the 1930s and 40s, in part because capitalism was working spectacularly badly and something had to be saved from the wreckage. He was able to argue that unless capitalism was managed as he proposed, it would lose the ideological and political competition with communism – and then all private property could disappear.

Since at least 1979, but especially since the advent of Reagan and Thatcher, there was growing confidence that the shaky Soviet system could not last. This sense of imminent victory increased after Gorbachev's appointment as Soviet leader, and reached a climax in 1989. But there was also a growing conviction, on the part of economists and policy-makers, that the Western corporatist consensus, which bastardised Keynesianism had helped produce, was the chief begetter of inflation. Social democracy was seen as the soft version of communism. There was a desire to return to capitalism red in tooth and claw, and a hardening of the view that the real world can be made to correspond to the nostrums of free-market theory – complete with flexible prices, an atomised labour market purged of trade unions, and firms as little regulated as possible in their quest to maximise profits.

Yet again there is a paradox. With the collapse of communism it is possible to argue that capitalism does indeed need to be managed and that wealth creation *is* a social act – without being labelled a communist subversive. At the very moment of capitalism's triumph there is a crisis in its dominant theory and a renewed willingness to examine alternatives. And where better to begin than with a reassessment of Keynes.

The properties of capitalism – as a system

John Maynard Keynes offered the outstanding alternative theory of capitalism. In a series of tracts and books in the 1920s and 30s he pulled down the free-market edifice and erected something more powerfully explanatory in its place. Recognising that a competitive equilibrium was a logical impossibility, he invented new concepts to describe economic activity and thus a means governments could use to achieve better outcomes than the market alone could. In particular, he identified investment as the volatile motor of the economy, which (to develop the earlier metaphor for equilibrium determination) was the crater whose depth and shape most readily mutated – and the one that did most to change the motion of the economic 'field'. It was an intellectual *tour de force*, and although Keynes' policy conclusions were only partially implemented by his interpreters they none the less offered the world an unparalleled period of prosperity.

Keynesian theory is rooted in the real world. It incorporates time as a key element in its account of market behaviour, rather than trying to conjure it away, or invent wild fantasies like 'auctioneers' or 'markets in future contigencies'. It acknowledges that money and production give an economy a wholly different motion from the barter economy of hunter-gatherers. It accepts the limitations of human rationality, and recognises the mood changes, errors and myriad agendas of producers and consumers alike. It regards the possibility of the market economy reaching an optimal outcome of its own accord as remote, and worries more about how the economy can get trapped into self-sustaining booms and busts, explaining why and offering a means of moving to better out-comes. Quite simply it attempts to account for the actual realities of capitalism.

The first building block of the theory is uncertainty. As Keynes himself explained: 'We have only the vaguest idea of any but the most direct consequences of our acts . . . our knowledge of the future is fluctuating, vague and uncertain.'[5] The notion that we can reduce the future to a calculus of advantages and disadvantages, each multiplied by its appropriate probability, is absurd. 'Human

decisions affecting the future, whether personal or political or economic, cannot depend upon on strict mathematical expectation,
since the bases for making such calculations do not exist.' We live
in a condition of uncertainty, 'calculating where we can, but often
falling back for our motive on whim or sentiment or chance.'[6] Not
for him the contortions involved in trying to impose an artificial
economic rationality upon human beings – rather a straightforward
recognition of what we are and how we behave.

But production in a modern economy generates uncertainty
through time. Time elapses between production and the sale of
products. Thus 'the entrepreneur has to form the best expectations
he can as to what the consumers will be prepared to pay when he
is ready to supply them after the elapse of what may be a lengthy
period; and he has no choice but to be guided by these expectations
if he is to produce at all by processes which occupy time.'[7] Expectations of price changes drive decisions as much as today's prices,
for Keynes knew what Radner was later to prove more rigorously
– namely that the system cannot find its own way to equilibrium.

A crucial reason for this is the existence of money. In the
realm inhabited by neo-classical economists there are real values
thrown up by what amounts to the bartering of goods, reflecting
real wants and scarcities; and there are a set of money values set
by the supply and demand for money. Money does not disturb
the basic motion of the economy, although it determines the price
level, with too large an increase in money supply causing inflation.
But for Keynes, money transformed the dynamics of the economy
because it allowed the expectations generated by uncertainty to
manifest themselves in a way that was impossible if goods and
services were bartered. Money and the real economy were not
somehow independent of each other; they were interdependent,
and that interdependence, when linked to uncertainty and changing
expectations, changed everything.

For it means that consumers and producers have the means of
acting upon their expectations of the future. If they are optimistic
they can borrow and bring forward their purchases, investment
and production; if they are pessimistic they can defer purchases and
investment until tomorrow. In bullish times there is a build up of

credit; in bearish times a build up of unused cash balances. The free-market idea is that the rate of interest acts as a price with cash being traded like any other commodity. By lowering the price idle savings are drawn back into circulation by consumers borrowing more. By increasing interest rates money is used to save and not to spend. It does not matter whether an individual consumes now or saves in order to spend later; his or her savings will be borrowed by somebody else so the overall level of demand in the economy will be unchanged. Keynes argued that this orthodox account missed the point about the role of expectations in an uncertain world.

An act of saving, he wrote, is not as good for effective demand as an act of individual consumption. Saving does not imply 'placing a specific order for future consumption'; nobody knows when the future spending might take place. So if the savings are not going to create a hole in current demand, they have to be borrowed. And here is the rub. Those who add to the economy's productive capital stock by investment will be the borrowers of those savings, but the rules governing their decision to invest are wholly separate from those governing the decision to save – and the rate of interest is helpless to match the two. Rather, savings and investment are influenced by 'two sets of judgement about the future, neither of which rests on an adequate or secure foundation – on the propensity to hoard and on the opinion of the future yield of capital assets. Nor is there any reason to suppose that the fluctuation in one of these factors will tend to offset the fluctuations in the other.'[8] In other words the entrepreneurs who invest are primarily concerned with their profits in the future, which is determined by their expectations, while savers are putting aside cash for entirely different reasons. The price of money – the rate of interest – is unable reliably and continually to make sure the two balance in such a way that demand is the same as if there had been no saving.

Time, money and uncertainty pervade Keynesian theory – and they are what sets him apart from the free-market or classical tradition. The focus of his attention in explaining how the economy moves as a system is where time, money and uncertainty intersect and have the greatest impact – the point at which the financial system, which marshals savings, translates them into investment. It is in the financial system that savings accumulate and from where credit is advanced. It is here that the instabilities of the market economy show up in excessive hoarding of cash or excessive granting of loans. It is the act of investment that is most dominated by time, because the interval between investment and profit is the greatest – and where expectations have a pivotal role in confirming or cancelling investment decisions.

Investment is not only volatile, it is the key motor of the economy's prosperity because it has a snowball effect, what Keynes called the multiplier. Investment is the part of national output which raises future productive capacity; and the process of raising it so boosts employment and demand in the present that the process becomes self-justifying. Investment, for example, creates jobs in the construction or machine-tool industries; that in turn creates demand for domestic goods, clothes and food; and that creates more investment.

Investment is financed by saving, so in any system of national accounts the two magnitudes must match; they are an accounting identity. But for Keynes that is a useless piece of information, for what matters at any moment in time is the traffic between them. A low level of investment and saving will balance; so will a high level of investment and saving but the latter will produce higher income and employment. If investment rises it can produce income growth that leads to higher savings – a chain of causation which turns the static free-market view on its head. It is not high savings that produce high investment – but high investment that produces high savings.

What happens in the labour market is thus dependent upon factors outside workers' control. The notion that workers can 'price themselves' into work in a low-investment, low-activity economy is for Keynes inherently absurd. An individual employer cannot know if he hires a lower priced worker that other employers will or will not do the same: if they did the wages paid would help generate demand for the extra production; if they did not the extra worker's production could not be sold – however low the wage. The price mechanism unaided cannot resolve this dilemma.

Nor is there any way that workers in aggregate can lower their wages sufficiently to price themselves into work, because the only uniform way is to raise the general price level thereby lowering their wages in real terms – but the factors determining this price level, such as monetary policy, are outside their control. They are *involuntarily* unemployed, and the origins of their problems lie in what has happened in the financial system, to investment and to the character and level of economic activity it has generated. In short, most of the economic cannonades of the past decade and a half have been firing at the wrong target.

Axel Leijonhufvud, perhaps the greatest interpreter of Keynes' theories, sees the clash Keynes describes between savers' and investors' interests within the financial system in terms of their willingness to commit to the future. Savers want to be able to get at their savings instantaneously in order to spend the money on unforeseen eventualities. Investors in real capital assets are in a trickier situation. They know that they have to commit to real machinery, bricks and mortar from which it is difficult to unwind their involvement. Savers want 'liquidity' and investors the stability that 'illiquidity' brings – and the rate of interest cannot readily broker the best outcome between these irreconcilably different desires.

'In Keynes' grand conception the basic function of Finance in modern systems', writes Leijonhufvud, 'is to reconcile the desire of households to be liquid with the technological necessity for the system as a whole to carry vast stocks of physically illiquid capital goods.' The more illiquidity that the financial system can sustain, the greater the level of investment. But a market-based financial system like the British, as Keynes knew well, obsessed with the desire for liquidity, had an essentially low-investment, low-growth bias.

Thus Keynes was the father of the argument that the financial markets are inveterately short-term; that their preference for liquidity oppresses the real economy. His famous dictum that 'when the capital development of a country becomes a by-product of the activities of a casino, the job is likely to be ill-done' captures the essence of his position (and those with any doubts should read Chapter 12 of *The General Theory*). It is one of the most devastating critiques of the stock market as a means of channelling resources into investment ever written – and leads him to conclude that he expects the state, 'which is in a position to calculate the value of investment on long views [what he called the marginal efficiency of capital] taking an ever greater responsibility for directly organising investment.'[9]

The pivotal role of the financial system in destabilising the market economy is the unifying theme in all Keynes' work. In *The Treatise of Money* which he completed in 1925, he is preoccupied by how the Central Bank can manipulate financial flows by altering bond sales and interest rates to change the overall price level; in *The General Theory of Employment, Interest and Money*, his greatest book, the target is the larger one of mobilising idle funds for investment by manipulating business expectations about future returns. If the government can assure private businessmen that demand will be rising in the future, they can be more confident about borrowing for investment – idle finance can be utilised after all. Low interest rates cannot do this by themselves; there needs to be the promise of demand in the future.

The aim of policy is to find ways of acting upon the financial system – the true commanding heights of a market economy – so that the real economy functions efficiently. Monetary and fiscal policy, and active direction and control of the financial markets are a continuum; the Keynes who designed an international financial system in 1944 is the same Keynes who ten years earlier wanted Roosevelt to borrow to pay for public works, and the Keynes who inveighed against Britain's return to the Gold Standard in 1926. The target changes, but the search is always the same: to get some purchase on financial flows – from varying the price level to boosting effective demand. The means might be interest-rate manipulation, changing taxes or even directing private lending – but the end game is influencing financial flows and acting upon expectations.

For the free-market school, Keynes' ideas were and are anathema. The presumption that markets were inefficient was plainly wrong – and it led to Big Government. In the late 1960s the New

Right counter-revolution began, insisting that classical theory stood the test of time. Keynes' majestic insights about money, time and uncertainty amounted to no more than the mildly interesting point that wages were slower to adjust than other prices in some circumstances like the 1930s. This might cause temporary problems of unemployment, but it was in no way a general theory. In any case ever increasing government spending and borrowing, the result of Keynesian economic policies, were causing inflation and weakening long-run economic performance. Obviously the capitalist world had to return to its free market roots.

Keynes' ideas had been traduced (as this author has argued in an earlier book). A proper Keynesian programme would entail a transformation of the way the financial system operated – not running a permanent and rising budget deficit while leaving the financial system market-based and unreformed, which was what happened in Britain. The Labour Party, and a Conservative Party chastened by its inter-war reputation, found themselves with the means to generate full employment and to finance the welfare state without realising that the associated build-up of national debt imposed an economic constraint. Together with the short-comings of the British state in organising any effective economic co-ordination, this led to serious economic underperformance.

The Keynesian counter-attack

Over the last decade a new generation of Keynesians, American almost to a man and woman, have been mounting a vigorous fight-back resurrecting and updating Keynes' ideas – and devastating the free-market position as effectively as Keynes ever did. They show how the neo-classical idea that the world of money somehow stands apart from the real world of production and exchange is unsustainable; they demonstrate that markets necessarily have profoundly disruptive imperfections.[10] And their policy proposals, as we shall see, are more subtle than the diet of never-ending pump-priming through public spending increases and tax cuts, which governments in the UK followed after 1945.

There are three strands to their thinking. The first is to contest the notion that the timing of market adjustments makes no fundamental change to the motion of a market economy. On the contrary, if the speed of response to changed market conditions varies between economic actors with, say, the financial markets being fast and labour markets slow, then the whole economy can be thrown out of kilter because small changes can quickly be magnified.[11] It may be perfectly rational for firms and workers to be slow to respond to market changes; there are costs in constantly changing prices and if a firm has a measure of control over its market – which most firms do – there may be advantages in not immediately incurring these costs. Just as a restaurant wouldn't want to keep changing the prices of its menu from day to day, so firms do not want to keep amending their prices. The existence of these 'menu costs' forces a market economy to behave less than perfectly.[12]

Then there is the role of the financial system. Joseph Stiglitz, for example, develops Keynes' conception that a market-based financial system is itself a source of economic instability by focusing, like Keynes, on the role of uncertainty in unsettling the relationship between savers and investors. Banks ration their credit, making it harder to get when economic activity slows down and interest rates rise; and more available as activity picks up – so that bank lending rises rapidly as the economy improves and falls sharply as it deteriorates.[13] Other New Keynesians go further, with Alan Meltzer following Keynes in showing that the rate of return on private investment is necessarily lower than the wider economic and social benefits which it brings, and which the price mechanism above cannot capture; as a result there needs to be some form of government intervention to lift investment to its socially optimal level.

And lastly the New Keynesians explain how even if wages are completely flexible and workers completely unprotected there may still be involuntary unemployment – and that it makes rational economic sense for firms to pay their own workers above the market-clearing wage.

All in all this is a remarkable resurgence of Keynesian ideas; so much so that Treasury economists concede in an unpublished memorandum, that the free-market explanations of real business cycles are highly stylised and 'have a hollow ring'. Keynesian accounts, while still having to go further, attempt to mimic reality and 'contribute to our understanding'. Quite an admission from the fountainhead of neo-liberal orthodoxy.[14]

Keynes did more than open up a more persuasive account of the dynamics of the capitalist economy than that offered by classical economists – he turned economics on its head. For his focus of attention was on how the economic system worked as a system. Rather than accept that the economic whole was the sum of its component markets, he insisted that the whole had properties and dynamics of its own – what biologists call 'emergent' properties.

The conclusions for Britain and its institutions is very uncomfortable. Here is an economy and society predicated upon the perfectibility of the market mechanism and whose élite consider any restraint on their freedom by the state as an intrusion on liberty. The class system is founded upon the merits of individual choice which permit the scions of the upper class to send their children to privileged schools and to network amongst themselves in the pursuit of power and privilege. Free market economics is a powerful comfort, for it appears to legitimise such arrangements as natural and unimprovable. Keynes proves that they are not – and invites the state to make good the shortcomings. Small wonder he is held in such disdain.

The properties of capitalism – the merits of co-operation

Central to the new Keynesian revolution is a challenge to the Darwinian conceptions of competition and market clearing that imbue the whole of neo-classical theory. Readers will recall the first building block of free-market economics – that rational man is a trader weighing up all his options. The race to satiate those desires first is what gives economic life its vigour. Competition is the public-school ethic transposed to the national economy; only through being compelled to *compete* will firms be lean and efficient just as the first team will only hone itself to complete fitness if it wants to win the game. Businessmen call for 'level playing fields' so they can compete fairly. The first team cannot win if it is always kicking uphill; and neither can British industry. The sentiment has graced a thousand after-dinner speeches at employers' organisations over the decades.

But this simple-minded approach to economic life does not correspond to any conceivable reality. It is true that free-market economics demands as a prerequisite a level field in which all the players have an equal capacity to play the game and none of them can determine the rules – in the jargon, that they have 'perfect information' and that they are 'price-takers'. If they were 'price-makers' that would imply they had more market power than their rivals. The whistle then blows, and they start dealing with each other until they have arrived at the best outcome.

The trouble is that in reality no such level playing field could ever exist. Information is distributed unfairly between the players. Some are condemned to kick uphill, so economic efficiency may not result from competition, and the players are perfectly within their rights to attempt to play the game by different rules. Above all it may make sense to co-operate rather than compete – and the new Keynesians are spawning a whole new theory of the circumstances in which this is likely to be the case.

The starting point is that market participants have to spend time and effort acquiring information about the nature of the transaction into which they are entering before they can judge whether it is worthwhile. Before a bank makes a loan to a client it has to assess whether the client can repay it. A firm has to monitor its workforce to see whether it is worth the wages that are being paid. If it subcontracts business to a supplier it has to be sure that its orders will be met on time and to the appropriate standard.

This information is not available in the stated price; it has to be sought out and represents a cost – it is an investment in ensuring that the transaction will work out as intended. But this knowledge is necessarily distributed unevenly between the parties to any transaction. The borrower will always know more than the bank about his true creditworthiness; the worker will always know more than her employer about her commitment and energy; the subcontractor will know his own track record of delivery times and the difficulty of meeting them better than the contractor. In other words one party to the bargain is better equipped than the other to judge whether it is a good deal.

The point is that all market agents know this. The reason why firms exist at all rather than subcontract all their work to others is that there are costs attached to subcontracting that offset the advantage. Firms know that it is expensive to monitor work which they contract out, and even then that the results of their screening may be unreliable. After all, the very fact that a subcontractor or worker is available for work may imply that others in the marketplace do not want to use his or her services; availability may be signalling that the subcontractor or worker is not very good – rather as in the second-hand car market the fact that a car is on the market is frequently a signal that it is faulty.[15]

The free-market version of company strategy is that the firm in such circumstances should simply open up any contract for competition and accept the lowest price. But the firm knows that there is an asymmetry in the information that could determine whether the contract will go wrong; and it knows that it will bear heavy costs if it does so. Even if we accept it has the optimising calculus assumed by free-market economics, the best strategy is not to beat its subcontractor down to the lowest price, especially if it expects to repeat the business. Rather it is to co-operate in the search for a relationship that reduces such risks.

This is where game theory enters the lists. This is an intellectual framework for examining what various parties to a decision should do given their possession of inadequate information and different objectives. It attempts to describe the consequences of doing business with only partial information, when the parties to a deal have to guess what the other side's true motives and position actually are – in other words game theory gives insights into the dynamics of doing business in an actual market economy. For example there is always some profit in entering into a contract knowing that you cannot deliver – deceiving your interlocuter who cannot know this. So is this the best strategy?

The key is the value that is placed on the future. The more weight that is placed on future returns, the costlier the penalty attached to cheating or misleading your trading partner about your true intentions – because you will lose the value of all possible future business. As Robert Axelrod shows in *The Evolution of Co-operation*, the strategy that works best in hundreds of different simulated games is to be straightforward rather than dishonest, always to reciprocate what is done to you and above all to co-operate. Keeping your own integrity and imposing heavy costs on someone who has been dishonest, produces the best results.

The classic game is the Prisoner's Dilemma. Two prisoners have to decide without communicating how they should respond to their jailer's proposal. Confession to the crime will be rewarded by your going free and the incarceration of the other prisoner; if you both confess then the sentence for both of you will be reduced; while if you both decide not to confess the evidence will only be sufficient to put you in prison for a short period. The optimal strategy is for both prisoners *not* to confess, in other words to co-operate with each other, but that runs the risk of the other prisoner confessing, in which case you will end up being incarcerated. If you both confess, on the other hand, at least the sentence is reduced. You both confess.

The best way out of this dilemma is to pre-agree not to confess, with both sides understanding that if they betray the deal then the incarcerated prisoner will respond by asking his friends outside prison to make the freed prisoner's life hell. In other words the best strategy, as Axelrod demonstrates, is to co-operate but to impose immediate and heavy penalties on any defection from the agreed strategy. In commercial life, as in game theory and crime, there are always gains in behaving super-competitively – but there are risks from retaliation. The correct strategy depends on the respective value of the gains and losses, and as losses happen tomorrow the decision will be governed by the estimation of tomorrow's losses. Or, in the economists' jargon, the present-day value of those losses which in turn depends upon the discount rate that is applied to tomorrow's losses.

The point is that if information is held asymmetrically and your welfare depends in part on other people's strategies, the prosecution of undiluted competitive self-interest is often self-defeating. The twin keys as to whether co-operation is worthwhile are the market structure in which a transaction is taking place and the value placed on the future. If the market structure is one where market agents need to know lots about each other and expect the relationship to continue – like that between a bank and its clients or any firm and its workers – then there are big rewards for behaving co-operatively. And if the present-day value of future costs is high because the discount rate is low, then there is an additional reason to co-operate. A worker who expects a longterm career in a company with a low turnover of staff will not want to be found shirking, for example, while the opposite will be the case for a short-term worker who expects to be fired quickly.

Human beings tend not to value future rewards and penalties rationally. In *Passion within Reason*, Robert Frank cites the psychological evidence that we do not equate future rewards with present rewards. The 'matching law' states that the attraction of a reward is inversely proportional to the delay in receiving it, so that most people will opt to be paid a lower amount today than a greater amount in the future – even though by waiting they can enrich themselves. This happens even when the future payments come with a cast-iron guarantee. In other words, psychological tests confirm what we have already observed about the stock market's short-term approach to the valuation of future profits. Without strong countervailing pressures, there is a constant tendency to undervalue future rewards and penalties.

The perennial dilemma facing the participants in a market economy is that while there are genuine gains from co-operation, they can only be captured by commitment over time and the constant temptation in a truly free market is not to make such commitment. Any market-based contract – between worker and employer, firm and subcontractor – can be unravelled by the simple act of selling, which ends the commitment. The problem for the capitalist economy is that the competitive principle upon which it is founded makes it hard to achieve and to sustain the gains from commitment.

As a result, there is a permanent tension in a capitalist economy between the desirability of forming committed relationships where both parties co-operate and don't cheat on each other – and the temptation to cut and run, attempting to find a better deal elsewhere. But because the richer rewards tend to come from long run commitment and co-operation, successful capitalisms find a way to solve what is really a moral problem. In essence, parties to market bargains have to be able to trust each other. If there is trust, the transaction costs of doing business can be lowered because trust reduces the need to invest in costly information gathering. A basis for co-operation is more quickly established with trust so there is less danger of a party to any contract acting opportunistically. Ensuring that both parties are committed to a co-operative strategy is easier. Trust is the cement of non-competitive market bargains. It is the means of solving the commitment problem – of making people behave apparently against their immediate self-interest but in their true longterm interest.

But trust is dependent upon parties to a deal caring about their reputation as moral beings and monitoring their own conduct with integrity. Robert Frank argues that the range of apparently irrational emotions that we have developed – anger, love and jealousy, together with the bodily signals by which they are recognised – are in effect thoroughly rational tools by which human beings size up each other's trustworthiness and capacity to behave morally. Some are sanctions; others are rewards; others, notably love, are means of entrenching committed behaviour. They are tools with which we hope to create and police the morality without which it is impossible to interact with other human beings. So it is that firms cluster together geographically; it is important to meet, to know and to see how those you do business with react to evolving deals and contracts. Competition is not blind; it is thoroughly human.

This rich mixture of psychology, sociology and economics offers a complete reinterpretation of how firms behave in markets – and in particular, in the financial and labour markets. As we have seen, one of the puzzles for free-market economists is why firms persistently pay their workers more than the market-clearing rate so that insiders earn more than outsiders; and in particular why the trends in real wages have been so little affected by the massive deregulation of the labour market, the collapse in trade union power and high levels of unemployment. For the New Keynesians the answer is simple; employees whose performance is known to employers are worth more than those whose performance is uncertain. It is expensive to monitor workers' performance and build the relations of trust upon which co-operative relationships depend; it is this expense that makes it worthwhile paying more than the going rate to lock in the existing workforce: which is known as the 'efficiency wage'.[16]

Free market economists find it puzzling that performance-related pay frequently backfires as a means of improving labour productivity. The explanation is easily to hand once you understand the importance of trust in economic relationships. Workers have to trust that their performance is being fairly measured. Yet if that trust exists it will be easy to win co-operative gains in productivity without performance-related pay; if it does not exist then workers will not trust the basis on which they are being measured and the system will weaken morale and lower effort. The key to productivity is not the wage system, but the system of human relations within an organisation.

This, of course, is the central insight of much contemporary management theory – especially that which builds on the work of W. Edwards Deming, whose ideas on quality improvement are seen in Japan as a contribution to Japanese post-war success. Deming was a statistician who observed in the 1920s and 30s that statistical techniques for ensuring quality control did not succeed

in improving it. The issue was not assessing the statistical probability of faults within any given batch of products and trying
to root them out, but how the quality of production could be
improved over time. And for this Deming urged that workers
had to be incorporated into the improvement of the production
process.

He wanted to 'drive fear out of the workplace' and insisted that
management had to find mechanisms for enlisting worker commitment to improvement. Performance-related pay, productivity
bonuses, production quotas and the rest of the paraphernalia of
trying to improve performance within the tradition of mainstream
economic theory were inherently unfair and led to reductions in
quality – anticipating the efficient wage hypothesis by fifty years.
Workers' brains had to be enlisted in the achievement of quality
as well as their hands; and they had to be incorporated into teams
sharing a vision of continuous improvement. Executive dining-
rooms and carparks were invidious, driving a wedge between
managers and workers and preventing them from making common cause.

At the heart of Deming's position was the understanding
that the nature of work is fundamentally different from the
way it is conceived in the free market tradition and embodied in
the techniques of Fordist production. You have to win worker
commitment – and that requires communications, remuneration
packages and organisational structures radically different from
those of the top-down management represented by much US
business after the war. In Japan these ideas were taken up enthusiastically – but one of the reasons for their success was that Japan
has buttressing institutions that allowed firms time and deferment
of immediate profits to develop their human capital as Deming
advocated.

For if a firm is to establish co-operative and committed relations internally, it must have external supports – particularly
with providers of finance. Yet information is held asymmetrically
in this relationship as in all the others and the only way to get
around this is to establish relationships of trust and commitment
– just what are lacking in an increasingly market-based financial

system. The more distant the relationship between bank and firm, the more the bank resorts to using the firm's willingness to pay a higher rate of interest as the screening mechanism for deciding on whether the borrower is creditworthy. But as Joseph Stiglitz and Andrew Weiss have shown, the higher the interest rate that the bank demands, the less creditworthy and more opportunistic borrowers will become, the greater the risk of losses and the less useful the interest rate as a signalling mechanism. In other words using the price mechanism to solve the problem of imperfect knowledge proves self-defeating for banks. The more market-based and arms-length the relationship, the uneasier banks have to be about advancing large longterm loans. They know the inadequacy of their information and the difficulty of correctly charging the right price to their customers.

But financial pressures of this type will make sustaining efficiency wages harder as firms find their credit rationed and are obliged to lower their wage costs, to conserve internally generated cash flow as compensation for the shortfalls from the banking system. Market economies work as systems, and the biases of the institutional structure need to support co-operative behaviour if it is to be sustained. And reasonable wages for good workers are harder to pay if the financial system places a premium on rapid, high dividend distributions.

Successful capitalism demands a fusion of co-operation and competition and a means of grafting such a hybrid into the soil of the economic, political and social system. Where relationships are sustained over time there needs to be a means of capturing the gains from co-operation – but such co-operative structures must, of course, co-exist with the stimulus of competition, which gives an indication of what market-clearing prices and profits actually might be. Yet the entire British economic system – and increasingly the social system – is founded upon the idea that such co-operative gains do not exist and do not need to be nurtured.

Successful British firms usually have some shelters from excessive market pressure to abandon co-operative relationships and instead enjoy the benefits of worker and financial commitment – just as New Keynesians would predict. Their shares may be held

by a family or trust so they are not exposed to a constantly changing shareholder base – for example the Wellcome Foundation,
Pilkington, or Sainsburys; they may have a government buyer
or agency which allows them some continuity and security of
profit – GEC (the Ministry of Defence), Glaxo (the National
Health Service), British Airways (Heathrow Airport); or they may
have an active policy of promoting such co-operative structures
internally and externally because they have discovered that they
work – Marks and Spencer, Rover, the John Lewis Partnership.
All these firms are privately owned and operate in competitive
markets; yet all of them are successful.

The British problem is that our system makes such firms
the exception rather than the rule. In other successful capitalist
economies the institutional biases encourage the fostering of
co-operative and committed relations rather than their abolition
– and whole industries can reproduce what only a few firms
can achieve in Britain. Nor can such relations be expected to
appear from a Darwinian competitive struggle; they need to
be sustained by institutions ranging from the financial system
to the welfare structure. A prosperous market economy is not
simply the product of atomistic individuals and firms competing
fiercely in competitive markets with no state intervention. This
is an intellectual and practical chimera.

The urgent necessity is to construct an interdependent institutional structure in Britain that will permit commitment and
co-operation in the context of a competitive market. And that,
as we shall see, implies nothing less than a British revolution.

10. The Political Economy Of The World's Capitalisms

After 1945 American capitalism was the envy of the world. In five years the US had transformed itself into a war economy and had outproduced the Soviet Union, Germany, Japan and Britain combined – and not just in planes and tanks, for it increased production across a range of civilian industries too. Its productivity was legendary, its industrial riches apparently beyond peer; its technological lead seemed unassailable.

Yet since the 1950s the US's position has been challenged in two successive waves of industrialisation. First there was the rise of European capitalism; and then Japan, steadily growing throughout this period, became the forerunner of the remarkable rise of East Asian capitalism. The US, which accounted for some half of world manufacturing output in 1945, now accounts for only a fifth. But despite the doom-laden predictions of its decline theorists, the US is not regressing absolutely – its average productivity across the whole of its economy still remains higher than Japan's. In a range of high technology industries it retains and is even increasing its world market share; by any standards it remains a formidable capitalist power.

European, American and Japanese capitalism each have distinctive characteristics. They are all, of course, based on private property and the legal right to make private profits by production and exchange in markets; and they all possess stock markets, income tax and social security systems that make them seem part of the same generic type of society. These features have persuaded some to argue that Western capitalism is converging towards an Anglo-American norm – but that is gravely to misread the depth of the institutional and cultural differences between capitalisms.

For the similarities disguise vast differences between the social and economic purpose of apparently similar institutions, so that each capitalist structure ends up with very different specific capacities and cultures which are very hard to change. But what all do have – even, paradoxically, the US – are strong institutions that allow their firms to enjoy some of the gains from co-operation as well as from competition, and these institutions are created and legitimised by some broad notion of public or national purpose.

The industrial strength of the world's great powers originated not because they followed the injunctions of purist free market economists, but because they succeeded in combining vigorous rivalry between entrepreneurs with a measure of co-operation. When their systems are seen as a whole it is the interlocking of the political, economic and social that is striking, and the varying ways in which they intersect is the key to the puzzle of their societies. The British tragedy is that its system locks together to form the least fecund of all capitalist models – as the following survey of capitalisms will show.

The US Model

American capitalism is commonly regarded as the most individualistic and libertarian of all. Its financial system is highly market based; the returns it requires are very high; and it is therefore important that US corporations can hire and fire their workforces freely to produce the profits their shareholders demand. Unions are weak, employment regulation is minimal and the turnover of workers is high as companies trim their staff to market demands. One worker in five expects to lose his or her job within the next year, according to a 1993 survey, and another 20 per cent expected a spell of temporary unemployment.[1]

There is little spending on social welfare and levels of corporate and personal taxation are low. Welfare entitlements are tightly monitored and means-tested; social security contributions are at the lower end of the international scale. However the US has proved an effective generator of jobs – although by European standards they are astonishingly poorly-paid, with the bottom tenth of the workforce earning 38 per cent of median earnings (compared with the European average of 67 per cent of median earnings).[2] Workers are assumed to be willing to move home in order to work, and to accept low wages with social security acting only as a safety-net of last resort. Unemployment insurance lasts for a mere six months and replaces only 36 per cent of average earnings.

There are few co-operative industrial combines along Japanese and East Asian lines. There is tough anti-monopoly legislation, and the typical firm is owned by stock-holders, a majority of them financial institutions like pension funds, who trade their shares on the stock market while the company operates in a highly competitive arena for its sales. All companies can expect to be taken over or merged when predatory companies buy their shares on the stock market, and this puts a high premium on maintaining the growth of short-term profits and dividend pay-outs to sustain the share price at all costs. Firms' relations with their suppliers are strictly market-driven, with contracts put out to tender and allocated to the lowest bidder. There is little or no public ownership; whatever social objectives are deemed essential are prosecuted through federal and state regulatory authorities. The system is outwardly almost purely capitalist, its apologists celebrating its job-creating and innovative qualities and critics inveighing against its promotion of consumption over longterm investment, its systemic inequality and lack of social provision.

The US has, in fact, retained important institutional shelters against the full blast of competition and these have become ways of expressing co-operative common purpose. At the federal level many of these institutions were inaugurated during President Roosevelt's New Deal which, along with a security safety net and creative make-work programmes, put in place a system of financial regulation, innovative government financial institutions and a system of deposit insurance that has helped mitigate the worst proclivities of the US financial system to this day. The Reconstruction Finance Corporation, the long term investment credit bank whose role was revolutionised by Roosevelt, played an important role in financing the US war effort before being abolished in the 1950s. The range of state-run bodies created to manage the system of housing finance managed to survive into the 1990s, and these have consistently supported housing construction and home ownership. The separation of banking and the securities business by the Glass-Steagall Act forced banks, especially at state level, to become less market-based and so develop longterm relationships with their customers.

Indeed the existence of powerful state banks, entrenched under the New Deal legislation, has been one of the most important buffers between medium-sized companies and the full blast of the US financial system. Texas, California, Pennsylvania, Connecticut, Chicago, Detroit, Minneapolis and Seattle are all important centres of finance and industrial headquarters around which clusters of small and medium-sized firms have formed.[3] Individual states have been able, if they choose, to use procurement policy and subsidies to develop local industries, together with supportive local banks interested in longterm investment. North Carolina, for example, was one of the US pioneers in linking university research, soft loans and new technology in its famous high-tech 'triangle'.

At Federal level a variety of initiatives gives another layer of support to these efforts. Federal spending on research and development, especially on defence, is an important source of funding for high technology industry. Spin-offs from the space programme were crucial in encouraging the US electronics industry's capacity to make miniaturised components. The military-industrial complex built during the Cold War and sustained by the Pentagon was a kind of national industrial policy, using its enormous purchasing power in the late 1980s, for example, to support the US semiconductor industry.[4] The Buy America Act ensures that public procurement is focused on US suppliers, while the US has not been afraid to use trade measures openly to support its own industrial interests. The 'Super 301' trade legislation empowers the US government to take unilateral retaliatory action against countries it considers to be either unfairly blocking imports from the US or subsidising exports.

The best US universities remain world-beating centres of excellence, and skill levels for middle management and craft workers are supplied by a dense network of higher educational establishments. However, public education for the masses remains weak, made even worse because many poor US families are desperately deprived, in a market society that has gone even further than the British. Many children are reared badly and are incapable of learning without considerably more resources than the public authorities are prepared to offer. While skill levels in the middle and upper parts of the labour force are high, US society is crippled by growing numbers of barely literate and numerate workers.

In partial compensation there is a strong culture of participation and engagement and a willingness to use the full array of public institutions to provoke common responses – and this spills over into the private domain. Pension funds, for example, have been obliged to intervene constructively in company affairs, under the pressure of members insisting that their ownership be exercised positively. Individual states have used the provisions of the 1977 Community Reinvestment Act to insist that banks support community developments and minimum wage legislation is a feature of many states.[5]

The democracy of the public realm becomes in this way the yardstick for private action as well. A network of intermediate public institutions at state level intercedes between the individual, the firm and the market. The dominant factor of production in the US remains private capital in a highly market-oriented financial system, and there is little doubt that its search for ever higher financial returns and its short-termism has been an important reason for the hollowing-out of US industry. But with a strong tradition of public citizenship and system of decentralised government there are ways of constraining and regulating the market, and even on occasion turning it to economic and social advantage. Stock market imperatives may loom too large in the strategies of US companies, but by the same token there are demanding standards for transparency and provision of information to shareholders and the wider public – demands that are modelled on the injunctions of the US constitution. Although the value system formally celebrates individual rights, competition and the primacy of markets, there is also a powerful impulse towards charity and solidarity in US culture, signalling the co-existence of a more altruistic co-operative tradition. As De Tocqueville put it, 'The Anglo-Americans acknowledge the moral authority of the reason of the community as they acknowledge the political authority of the mass of citizens.'6

The US may be the home of pristine capitalism but it is qualified by a vigorous public and private morality. This is the home of the most aggressive venture capital industry on earth; but also of the largest private charitable foundations. Bill Gates, chairman of computer giant, Microsoft, followed Ford, Rockefeller and others in giving up almost all of his fortune to a private foundation. The Protestant ethic, although weakening, remains an important underpinning of the US value system and a source of co-operative economic strength.

Social market Europe

The second distinctive species of capitalism is that of Germany, its neighbours in the European Union and of Scandinavia. This is broadly the world of the social market, and once again the political, economic and social institutions hang together to form an interdependent web. Capital and labour operate in partnership; the financial system is less market-based than in the US and thus more committed to the enterprises it finances; the welfare structure is more all-encompassing and inclusive and the political system has a high degree of formal power sharing. Yet this social web still vibrates to the signals sent by the price mechanism; it may be regulated, but it conforms to market imperatives. It is a social *market*.

The great benefit of the system is that its institutional structures favour co-operation, high productivity and investment. The disadvantage is that when the external environment becomes more uncertain, the system finds restructuring more difficult because the centres of power are more diffuse and the bureaucratic regulatory network can slow down firms' responses. None the less restructuring is achievable eventually. In the recent German recession Volkswagen was able to negotiate wage cuts and reduce working hours in agreement with its unions, and Daimler Benz slashed its labour costs by over DMI.5 billion within a year.[7]

At the heart of the European model is the notion of a rule-governed, competitive market whose power to generate wealth is intimately linked with social cohesion. The partnership between capital and labour embodied in *mitbestimmung* (or co-decision making) at both board and works council level in Germany represents a bargain between manager and unions. Unions forego the right to strike and to pursue their self-interest regardless of the firm's plight; but management eschews the right to run the business autocratically in favour of the shareholders' narrow interests. Instead there is a compromise in favour of concerted and co-operative behaviour aimed at boosting production and investment.

Labour has to recognise the legitimacy of capital; and capital the rights of labour. Seventy-five per cent of German workers are covered by union-negotiated industry-wide wage agreements – which is a major concession by management; on the other hand the agreements are legally binding and a strike can only be called once the contract has expired – a major concession by labour. If the big unions represent a majority of workers, so the employers' organisations represent most of German industry. Both capital and labour are represented by all-encompassing self-governing organisations which are allowed to manage wages and industrial relations. As a result labour turnover rates are lower than in the US and wages considerably higher.

This collaboration is interdependent with the rest of the economic, social and political system. In order for managers and workers to run enterprises collaboratively, financial stakeholders have to concede that they cannot maximise their returns in the short run. Thus the pivot on which the German system turns, as Michel Albert argues, is the patience of the banks – 'the principal guardians of Rhine-Alpine capitalism'. The Frankfurt, Zurich, Stockholm, Vienna and Amsterdam stock exchanges are modest in size compared with those in London and New York; it is not in the stock market that companies are valued and raise money but through their respective banking systems. Contested takeovers organised through the Stock Exchange, so common in the US and Britain, are almost unknown in Germany, Switzerland and Holland.

The German banks are uniquely powerful, holding shares themselves and on behalf of others in the major German companies, making longterm loans, acting as information clearing houses and assessing industrial and commercial prospects in partnership with their borrowers. They are the stable backers of German industry and loyal longterm shareholders. They know the companies they finance, sit on their boards and can more accurately assess their risks. The system is orderly because its financial components give it the time and space it needs – and the situation is very similar in Austria, Switzerland and Holland.

This stability of ownership and financial support is matched by a welfare system – the *sozialstaat* – which offers a high degree of social protection, the visible expression of social solidarity. Pensions and unemployment benefit are high in relation to average earnings, and the universal health and education systems underwrite Germany's famous sense of social well-being. Education and training are enmeshed, and the 'dual vocational system' combines academic education with workplace experience, providing Germany with among the highest numbers of trained apprentices per head of population in the world. School leavers are educated to a high standard. Over 70 per cent of German employees are technically qualified compared with 30 per cent in the UK[8] and the status of the *handwerke* (craftsman) and *meister* (craftmaster) is deeply etched into German culture.

One of the inevitable consequences of the system is high social overheads for both employers and employees. Health, pension, and unemployment insurance together with taxation make up one of the highest tax burdens in the industrialised world; but, as Wolfgang Streeck argues, the 'social production' of skilled workers, powerful unions and the strong welfare system help to raise the general strength of the economy. The welfare structure, for example, is designed so that firms can hang on to workers during a recession with part of their wages paid by social insurance, keeping their workforces intact, while the constant supply of skilled workers has made German productivity levels the highest in Europe. Powerful unions have been important agents in restructuring German industry, using their dominant position in works councils and their role on supervisory boards to legitimise often painful programmes of job cuts and wage reductions.[9]

The partnership and solidarity of Rhine-Alpine social market institutions has not been built in a political vacuum. It is supported by a particular kind of state. Regional government is strong and culturally entrenched, with a strong tradition of autonomy and a vigorous regional media. Voting is by proportional representation, and the state is seen as part of civil society, rather than ruling from above it. Unlike the British system, where the state is coterminous with whichever party controls the government, the social market state represents a common or public interest in which parties are expected to share power; and this fosters the network of independent government agencies of which the most famous is the German central bank, the Bundesbank.

Many public agencies, even the state television networks, incorporate a similar conception of their responsibility. They are social partners as much as organs of the state; their constitutions allow them to govern themselves but within a mandate set by the state, which by obliging each institution to consider wider interests allows it to become a forum for building consensus within its own particular area of competence. The governing council of the Bundesbank, for example, consists of the presidents of the regional state banks, who are in turn appointed by regional governments. They reflect the broad range of political opinion within the country, allowing a consensus to develop over the direction and execution of German monetary policy.

As the great social market theorist Alfred Muller-Armack argued, a free market order is not a state of nature; it must be produced and regulated. Governance works best when it is as close to its area of competence as possible; hence the case for decentralisation and for independent public agencies like a central bank, or a regulator of competition. It is not only that price stability, a market that respects local custom and practice and real competition are central to an effective market-place; the markets' institutions earn legitimacy by being 'owned' by the wider citizenry, who trust that the fruits of prosperity will be shared fairly.

Wider economic policy is the outcome of negotiation between the various social partners – what is known as concerted action. The government proposes, unions and employers' organisations negotiate, while the Bundesbank acts as a guarantor of price stability – but it is also mindful, as a social partner in its own right, of larger economic and social objectives. The regional governments or opposition parties are not excluded; their participation is assured by their formal membership of the upper house of the parliament (*Bundesrat*) which they may succeed in controlling even if they do not hold a majority in the *Bundestag*. The German Chancellor is thus the conductor of a political concert, relying on power, persuasion and the force of argument to move policy in the direction he wants. To critics used to states where political authority is more clearly delineated, as in Britain, the system seems a glutinous corporatist mess; to its devotees it is a highly effective means of achieving consensus and cohesion.

The usefulness of Germany's system of decentralised power is revealed in the strength of the famous *Mittelstand* – the medium-sized business sector that is proportionally nearly twice the size of its counterpart in Britain. These family-owned companies are the backbone of German industry, but they owe their strength as much to the institutional support around them as to the dynamism of their flexible and innovative owners. At one level they are the quintessential independent capitalist owner-managers – relying on their wit, ingenuity and entrepreneurial light-footedness to win the Darwinian struggle in markets; at another they are the beneficiaries of Germany's unique institutional structure.

They enjoy longterm, committed finance from the regional state banks. They can fish from a stream of skilled workers. As smaller sub-contractors they can build their business around reliable contracts from larger firms who understand the gains from co-operative, longterm relationships – and are themselves financially secure enough to offer such relationships. They can group together in cities and towns in clusters and so reinforce their position, allowing them to share information, because German cities and regions have the autonomy to tailor an industrial policy to suit their companies' particular needs. The independent scientific research and technology institutions, like the Steinbeis Foundation or Fraunhofer Institutes for example, have a strong regional bias and regional governments have the financial power to support them by channelling technology and ideas to the *Mittelstand*. In short, the social and political system is itself a major source of competitive advantage, allowing Germany to develop comparative economic strength. The tariff walls of Friedrich List, father of German protectionism, may no longer exist but Germany's network of institutions offers a modernised form of shelter from unfettered market forces.

Under the pressure of globalisation and intense cost competition the *Mittelstand* has begun to lose ground, and there are fears that large German firms are being compelled to get their supplies in low-cost countries while overseas producers – notably the Japanese – are winning business in the *Mittelstand*'s heartland. German banks, under the same pressures, are allegedly becoming more short-term in their time horizons. Even more threatening is the rise of so-called lean production in which large firms, determined to emulate the Japanese and contain costs by sub-contracting out work and insisting on 'just-in-time' delivery to cut inventories, are asking suppliers to be ever more flexible. This requires heavy new investment even as prices are being pared to the bone, and many companies lack the financial muscle to adopt a more hard-nosed relationship with major buyers. Yet in front of these challenges the German instinct is not to abandon but to update and renew its institutional network – intensifying its training effort, improving systems of technology transfer and developing new networks to share market information. Above all the banks intend to stand by their industrial companies.

Underpinning the notion of the social market is a complex value system that emphasises both the values of order and solidarity. From the Prussian tradition comes a sense of the need for discipline and for a regulated order in human affairs; from Catholicism the tradition of social solidarity and 'subsidiarity' – the location of decision making as close as possible to those who are affected by it. These twin streams in German thinking unite with a third: an accent on the real values of production over those of finance. The rentier tradition is extremely weak in Germany – this is a country which industrialised late and had to marshal its financial resources consciously to achieve it. The country could not afford a large class of rentiers living off unearned income, and company law has never given priority to shareholders' financial interests over those of other stakeholders.

There are inflexibilities in the social market, and the relationship between finance and industry can become incestuous and open to corruption – while strong trade unions don't always behave rationally. In the move to 'lean production' many unions are resolutely opposed to contracting work outside the large firms. The *sozialstaat* is also expensive. Yet in the main the social market's success is testimony to its virtues, and the *schadenfreude* expressed in the Anglo-Saxon world over its difficulties during German reunification is undoubtedly premature.

The social market is a self-conscious way for a capitalist economy to blend the gains from competition with those from co-operation – and the new world of 'lean production', where so much depends on the collaboration between firms and their sub-contractors, will emphasise its strengths. Far from capitulating to the British and American style of capitalism, the social market economy is in the throes of adapting to changed conditions in a unique way. France has set out to copy its main strengths, and Eastern Europe and even the former Soviet Union are looking to this model as their disillusion with the Anglo-Saxon variant grows. It has not failed; the question is how far it can succeed in the new environment.

East Asian capitalism – 'Peoplism'

The third distinctive form of world capitalism, and currently the most dynamic, is that of Japan, the East Asian tigers and the emergent Chinese genre. Although again there are variants within this wider culture, there is enough common ground to attempt a descriptive synthesis under a common label. Here the attempt to capture the gains from co-operation in a competitive environment has been taken to its most extreme. East Asian and particularly Japanese capitalist structures emphasise trust, continuity, reputation and co-operation in economic relationships. Competition is ferocious, but co-operation is extensive; the juxtaposition of apparently inconsistent forms of behaviour may strike those schooled in Anglo-American capitalism as irrational, but for the Japanese the tension actually enhances the strength of each. There is even a widely quoted phrase for it – *kyoryoku shi nagara kyosa* – literally 'co-operating while competing', so that out of the subsequent chaos comes harmony.[10]

As a result human relations and the necessity of nurturing them are centre stage; the dominant factor of production is labour, so that one Japanese analyst has been moved to call the system 'peoplism'.[11] This is probably overstating the humanity of an economy which demands long hours and often demeaning working conditions,[12] but it none the less captures the important stress on personal networks and human relationships. Contracts are even less price mediated than in the European social market economy; wealth creation and productivity are seen to come from co-operative longterm relationships for which the Japanese are justly famous, and which Alan Blinder calls a 'relational market'. With Japan and East Asia growing explosively, its institutional structure and value system commands increasing respect and even fear; for example, if Japan maintains its current rates of investment as a proportion of national output, nearly a third as high again as the US, then it will be the largest economy in the world by 2005 while East Asia as a whole will become the dominant force in world output and trade by the first decade of the next century.

Given Japan's track record it is unsurprising that the Japanese model has been extensively copied. Its regulated financial system is the least market-based, most traditional, above all most committed to its customers, of all the three principal capitalist variants. Firms' shares are held tightly in a system of cross-holdings with sister firms in other industry groups, the *kigyo shudan* and *keiretsu*, and the required returns are low. Secure financial backing has allowed

Japanese firms to cultivate an extraordinary series of innovations in working practices with both shop floor workers and suppliers – and these efficiencies have placed the economy firmly in a virtuous circle in which growth, investment, financial commitment, worker/supplier productivity and continual quality upgrading become mutually reinforcing.

The firm is the core social unit of which individuals are *members* rather than simply workers. Unions are organised around the firm, which promises life-time employment, social protection and a pension, and the firm expects commitment in return. Taxation is at the lower end of the international scale, but so is income inequality; senior managers earn a mere two or three times the average wage. The culture is firmly production-oriented, rooted in Japan's anxiety to catch up with the West which was intensified by the trauma of losing the Second World War.

The state is the architect of these institutional relationships; it seeks to build consensus and then guides firms and the financial system in the direction established by the consensus. In this respect it is nearer to the German social market state, and British notions of parliamentary sovereignty and top-down governance are strikingly at odds with the Japanese conception of government by consent. The boundaries between government, society and economy are remarkably porous, and there is great emphasis on inclusiveness, on respect for various points of view and on the achievement of harmony, while at the same time ensuring that business objectives are at the heart of Japan plc's concerns. On the other hand it means that the country has no hard centre, and fraud and corruption are widespread. Responsibility is diffuse and accountability low.

None the less the leadership – or, as the Japanese would put it, the consensus building – provided after the war by MITI, the Ministry of International Trade and Industry, is justly famous. Even though it now plays a less overtly interventionist role than it did in the 1950s and 1960s it remains a formidable source of 'guidance', leading industrial restructuring and co-ordinating private firms' strategies. The build up of the Japanese ship-building and steel industry, the managed decline of the coal industry and the rise of cars, consumer electronics and information technology are all tributes to MITI's key role. It may no longer be so overtly *dirigiste*, but it remains the ultimate custodian of Japanese industrial and commercial interests.

The system, as with the US and German social market models, locks together as a whole. Without committed finance there can be no parallel commitment to suppliers and workers; but the productivity gains from such commitment justify the financial commitment and vice versa. So while the institutional structure respects the priority of human relations, it incorporates, as Masahiko Aoki has brilliantly argued, incentives for economically rational behaviour even though they are not mediated by price signals. Competition, in a sense, is confined to the market where goods and services are offered to the final consumer but in all the intervening stages of production there is an accent on nurturing longterm relationships and capturing the gains from co-operation that game theory and New Keynesian economics promise.

There are four overlapping series of relationships – with finance, employees and subcontractors and, of course, with government. The role of Sumitomo Bank in rescuing Toyo Kogyo has been described already, and this exemplifies the relationship between finance and business. Shares, which in the Anglo-Saxon tradition are titles to a claim on the company's profits in the form of dividends and which are expected to be bought and sold on the stock market, are in Japan tokens of a longterm commitment. The *kigyo shudan* are industrial groups that use shares to cement these relationships. Mitsubishi, Mitsui, Sumitomo, Fuyo, Sanwa, and Daiichi Kanyo Bank are each City banks which, along with a trust bank, life insurance company and trading company, sit at the centre of a constellation of cross-shareholdings. Forty per cent of the equity on the Tokyo stock exchange is held by *kigyo shudan* members. The banks act as presidents of each group, channelling longterm loans, chairing negotiations over joint ventures and generally sharing information and business advice. In cases of financial distress, as with Sumitomo and Toyo Kogyo, they organise the restructuring. Their role is similar to the German banks, but more formally embedded in their clients' business.

The group companies, because of the dense network of cross-shareholdings, in effect own each other and are impregnable to takeover – but the task of monitoring and improving company performance, which takeovers purport to play in the US and British system, is in Japan performed by internal and group pressures. Other features of the Anglo-Saxon system like executive share options are banned while in the event of bankruptcy the banks rank after the employees and subcontractors in having a claim on the company's assets.

Yet, as Aoki shows, the incentives built in to the system lead to rational outcomes. If banks have no prior claim on company assets in the event of bankruptcy then they have a double incentive to ensure that bankruptcy does not happen, which encourages them to establish institutional networks that permit effective monitoring of loans. More to the point, the system allows them to finesse the Keynesian conundrum that the interest rate cannot co-ordinate the demand for financial capital with the supply, so that the higher the interest rate the riskier the project. Intimate access to information means that there is less credit rationing and as Takeo Hoshi[13] shows, the supply of external credit to Japanese companies is made on more favourable terms than to firms outside the industrial groups. Indeed, Japanese banks will lend up to four times more in relation to a firm's assets than British banks. The respective fortunes of the two country's car and consumer electronics industries are a stark illustration of the competitive advantage that such abundant working capital and stability of ownership give to the Japanese.

The role of shares as tokens of relationship also extends into production and to the tiers of sub-contractors who, by allowing great flexibility of production, have allowed the Japanese economy to pioneer the new techniques of lean production. While US manufacturers effectively auction their sub-contract work, Japanese industrialists enmesh themselves in a network of cross-shareholdings with their sub-contractors. These non-financial *kieretsu* cross-shareholdings make up another 30 per cent of the Tokyo stock exchange, complementing the 40 per cent held by the *kigyo shudan*, indicating just how large the 'relational market' in Japan has become.

The cost gains from flexibility and minimal inventory are huge, but so are the co-ordination and design problems. Parts have to be made to pin-point accuracy and production modified with every change in demand, and once a manufacturer has taken a sub-contractor into his confidence over specifications the sub-contractor has every incentive to exploit the privilege by maximising profits because he has his buyer over a barrel. The advantage of the cross-shareholding is that it signifies that the relationship will continue over time and so gives the main contractor a way of responding to any blackmail. He can sell his shares and so tell the wider marketplace that the relationship is not working well – a damning indictment in an economy where such store is set by longterm relationships. But the shareholding commitment also gives the sub-contractor confidence in the continuity of business, and allows him to tie up large amounts of capital in meeting just one customer's requirements – which would otherwise be highly risky.

The other apparent irrationalities in the Japanese-based system turn out to have equal economic value. Lifetime employment and job security means there is little of the labour mobility valued by free market economists, while the compression of pay differentials would seem to offer little in the way of 'incentives' to Japanese workers. Nor are trade unions in thrall to company managements likely to be very effective fighters for individual workers' interests. Yet job security forces employers to develop different kinds of incentive which ultimately prove to be highly economically rational. The counterpart of lifetime employment and low pay differentials is a complex managerial hierarchy that rewards people instead with complex gradations of status, while security of tenure makes middle and lower management less threatened about delegating decision-making downwards. To solve the problem that lifetime workers may be shirkers or prove otherwise inadequate, Japanese firms take great care over recruitment, often talking to schools about the personality, intelligence and general demeanour of specific recruits long before they need to hire. As a result, parents and schools form an alliance to raise educational standards to the highest level to meet the companies' exacting requirements – and high levels of intellectual skills, even on the shop-floor, are the basis of the problem-solving teams that are the key to Japan's famously high levels of productivity.

Lifetime employment also carries a message about those who are unemployed; to lose your job implies that the original firm was in some way unhappy with you as a worker, that you are a 'lemon': an undesirable worker. Workers are under pressure not to lose their jobs, which means that their income in the long run will depend on the welfare of the firm which they will not want to leave. Hence the willingness to co-operate in teams to improve productivity, rather than piggy-backing on others' efforts. The same applies at the top end of the scale: chief executives will have peers who have been in the firm as long as they have so, as Ronald Dore argues, they will be aware of the general opinion that two or three of their contemporaries 'could have done the job just or almost just as well. This knowledge, on the part of CEOs, acts as a useful curb on both greed and megalomania.'

The firm has become the core social unit in Japanese society. It trains and retrains its workers. It offers them a measure of social security. It is the adaptive and creative organisation which constructs networks of finance, teams of workers, and relationships with subcontracting firms that are at the heart of the Japanese system. Paramount above all else is the desire continually to upgrade; Japanese firms could incorporate W. Edward Deming's ideas more easily than their American counterparts because they were in an institutional framework and a cultural value system that allowed them to.

This private institutional network is backed by a public infrastructure that supports economic growth and domestic industry. As in Germany, there is a system of devolved regional government with enough autonomy to draw up industrial policies to meet local needs. Technology transfer happens through the *kohsetsushi*, local centres for the testing of new innovations, similar to the technology transfer network in Germany. And at the level of central government there is the complex system of planning, state funded R & D and investment guidance led by

MITI. Telecommunications, transport and construction are all sectors where innovation has been aided and abetted by government action.

Yet this highly innovative, competitive, production machine is an extremely difficult trading partner. With so much internal trade taking place between the *kigyo shudan* and *keiretsu* members as the consequence of protecting rational longterm relationships, it is difficult for foreigners to penetrate Japanese markets even when they have saleable products. They are not part of the relationship network. Japanese companies, pricing their products incrementally off an already low cost base (given the low cost of Japanese capital) are formidable exporters. Consequently there is an inbuilt asymmetry in Japanese trade relations with the entire industrialised West.

The same is true of the emerging East Asian capitalist states, who have all constructed their styles of capitalism around what Ronald Dore calls 'community' firms on the Japanese model. Chinese companies are family-run networks based on ownership by kinsmen as much as on shareholdings across companies, while the South Korean *chaebol* incorporates within one organisation a vast cluster of related enterprises that are given overt state support by the South Korean government and state banks. Similar variants can be seen in Thailand, Taiwan, Indonesia, Singapore, and Malaysia and although Hong Kong is often regarded by neoclassical economists as the paradigm of free market, price-mediated, unallayed capitalism, its successful Chinese companies are based on the same relationship nexus as those in Japan. As James Abbeglen argues, these corporate structures interact with high savings rates and huge state investment in education, and have produced the most dynamic period of capitalist growth in history. There is a real sea change occurring in the world economic system.

In some respects the Asians have been lucky. Confucian conceptions of social harmony have allowed them to build up co-operative firms and networks that are congruent with these deeply held values, while in Japan veneration for age and the wisdom of the elderly can give the young a core of discipline and respect for others around which longterm relationships are easily constructed. Japan is also a profoundly ordered society in which it is understood as a legacy of its feudal past that reputation and the saving of face are important for everybody – another important element in sustaining trust over time.

The astonishing paradox is that Japan did not always have this kind of economic and social structure which we think of as quintessentially Japanese. Between the wars the financial system was more like the Anglo-Saxon model. Companies had large numbers of shareholders, and boards of directors were obsequious to their needs, distributing dividends with an eagerness that would satisfy any British unit trust. As Tetsuji Okazaki[14] demonstrates, the *zaibutsu* combines (parents of today's *kigyo shudan* and *keiretsu*) were comparatively unimportant, representing only ten of the top sixty manufacturing and mining companies. In the non-*zaibutsu* firms quoted on the stock market, R & D and investment took second place to immediate profits, while a multiplicity of banks offered commercial credits and short-term loans, refusing to offer more longterm loans to their borrowers. Senior management insisted on bonus and share option schemes as incentives to further effort, and a 'flexible' labour market was operated in which firms hired and fired workers as demand conditions fluctuated – the lifetime employment system was then very much less important. It all sounds very familiar to anyone who knows Britain and the US today.

But this style of economy failed the Japanese completely. There was widespread despair at the 'degeneration of firm management' and the 'high-handedness and short-sighted selfishness of large stockholders'.[15] In the run-up to the Second World War the government moved to a 'New Economic System' which recast the financial and labour system along broadly contemporary lines. Stockholders' rights were limited, dividends curtailed and firms were to become 'an organic organisation whereby employers and employees are bound together in their respective functions.' Workers' committees were charged with boosting production and the banking system was required to make investment loans, 'not on the certainty of repayment, but on the contribution the project could make to the national purpose'. Responsibility for allocating government and private funds to particular industries was given to specified financial institutions – foreshadowing the role played today by the *kigyo shudan*.

The changes were controversial and widely resisted. There were loud complaints from employers that the initiatives were quasi-socialist. One group opposing the changes cited the British Whiteley Committee as an authority, which rigorously distinguished between the rights of capital and obligations of labour to the firm.[16] There could be no watering down of capital's demands for returns, or advancing of workers' claims to share in management and the design of production processes. This was a corruption of capitalist economic law and would lead to perdition.

Yet the urgency of war and the desperate desire to catch up on the West allowed such complaints to be brushed aside. What mattered was effectiveness, and the contribution that the business sector could make to the war of conquest. After Japan's defeat the US was too distracted by opposing communist trade unions and Japanese socialism to follow through in its attempts to change the system, and the underlying institutional structure survived.

In other words, the constitution of the Japanese firm and its relationship with government, finance and workforce is not a 'natural' evolution. It has developed from a series of experiments about what works best, fired by an overwhelming sense that the country had to catch up – a determination only strengthened by losing the war. Britain, by contrast, was the first country to industrialise. It has never lost a war. The British élite has no sense it needs to catch up, that its system doesn't work and cannot recognise that what passes for timeless economic truth is no more than a particular economic ideology. Britain's chances of reproducing what is happening in East Asia seem negligible.

Can rival capitalisms co-operate?

European and Japanese capitalism did not develop in a political and financial vacuum. They benefited from a benign world trade order in which there was open access to the world's largest market – the US – and where until the early 1970s, the US itself was economically powerful enough to anchor a world monetary order which was in essence an extension of its domestic financial system. The first two decades after the war launched the western industrialised countries on the biggest economic boom for a century. And while that growth subsided in Europe after 1973, Japan and East Asia exploited their unique internal advantages, the relative openness of the US market and the increasing volume of credit available on the global capital markets to continue their own industrial boom.

The US did not, of course, establish and manage this system out of altruism. Frightened by the international economic and financial chaos that led to the war, it did not want a repeat performance after the Second World War – and the beneficiary of the political and economic tensions that would arise from any post-war recession was all too obvious. The communist bloc, led by the Soviet Union, was in ideological and economic competition with the US. If liberal capitalism could not flourish in Europe and non-communist Asia, there was a danger that communism could spread from Eastern into Western Europe and from China, Vietnam and North Korea into the whole of Asia. North America might confront a Euro-Asian landmass dominated by communism; a formidable foe in any conflict, operating from a strong enough strategic base to bid for global domination. To prevent this nightmare it was worth making considerable financial and trading sacrifices.

The US was thus prepared to make the dollar the centre of the world's monetary system, and run a defence effort along the whole of the Euro-Asian littoral, and to accept that its market should be open to countries that were developing their economies. There needed to be a successful western and Japanese capitalist community strong enough to act as a bulwark against Stalin and Mao and prosperous enough to beat off the ideological attractions of communism.

So it was that the US played a crucial role in both European and East Asian economic growth. From the Marshall Plan, through to underwriting the Bretton Woods agreement, the US put in place the institutional architecture that allowed Europe to organise its reconstruction. The significance of the collapse of the Bretton Woods system of managed exchange rates in 1972 was that the dollar ceased being overvalued in relation to the German mark, and the imbalance in the strength of the European and US economies was suddenly exposed. Europe had come of age, and the US was no longer willing to accept the same unequal trade and financial relationship, regarding its defence commitment in Europe as enough of an economic burden.

The US and Europe still continued to stand by the rules of international trade as set out in the Gatt, cutting tariffs on manufactured goods and insisting that trade preferences to any one country should be extended to all. At the same time European states, under US pressure, began to liberalise their rules on exports and imports of capital. The foundations of a global capital market were being laid together with the rules that would permit companies to extend their production and distribution internationally, confident that they would be allowed to move goods freely between nation states.

While Europe and the US had come to an accommodation, with Europe accepting a depreciating and volatile dollar as the price for US defence, and which led to a boost in US export volumes and decline in European exports.[16] Japan and Asia were able to use the new open trading rules to their own advantage. Japanese exports grew by 16 per cent per year during the 1960s before settling back to more moderate but still high growth rates in the 1970s, but in the 1980s the East Asian tigers began to follow in Japan's footsteps. Between 1981–86, argues Lester Thurow,[17] 42 per cent of Korea's growth and 74 per cent of Taiwan's growth could be traced to exports to the US market – and in the 1990s China is reproducing the same pattern. While Japan's export growth between 1985–90 had settled down to some 2.7 per cent, China's exports grew at 18.3 per cent – with exports from Indonesia, the Philippines, Thailand, Malaysia, Taiwan, Hong Kong and Singapore all in double figures. South Korea's exports growth had slowed to a mere 8.9 per cent!

The trick has been to use the ultra-competitiveness of Asian capital in the North American and to a lesser extent the European market, which allows Asian firms to build up investment and production runs and launch their economies in to a virtuous circle of growth, balance of payments surpluses, hard currency earnings and low inflation. While the US was able to respond to this threat in the 1970s by allowing the dollar to depreciate against the European currencies and counteract the trends, the same downward movement of the dollar has much less impact in the 1990s. Asian capitalist structures are much more competitive than European ones, and can accommodate their costs more flexibly to changes in exchange rates.

As a result the US is once again running a trade deficit in excess of $100 billion after moving towards balance in the recession years of the early 1990s. Over the 1980s the US ran a cumulative current account deficit of $893 billion financed largely by Japanese and German inward investment in both factories and stocks and shares;[18] but in the 1990s Japan and Germany are proving more unwilling to provide such finance. Germany has to pay for reunification of its state, and is directing funds to Eastern Europe and the former Soviet Union, while Japanese financial institutions, which had to accept substantial losses on their dollar holdings, are less willing to invest in dollar assets. The international financial system is finding it difficult to accommodate the instabilities caused by the relative strength and weakness of the rival capitalisms.

The end of the Cold War frees the US from any obligation to anchor the world trading system by keeping its own markets open, while the flood of cheap imports from East Asia is bidding down the wages of its blue-collar workers. The US has already responded to Japanese exports by imposing quotas and restraints which now extend to 30 per cent of all Japanese exports, and it is plain that other East Asian exports will suffer the same restraints. The political pressure to arrest the decline in living standards of US blue-collar workers is extremely intense.

If the US could increase its exports to Japan and East Asia

then there would be an improved chance of keeping both markets open, but as we have seen there is a fundamental asymmetry between them. East Asian 'community firms', embedded in their relationship networks, have an inbuilt protectionist bias and an aggressive attitude to overseas markets – and it is an uphill battle for American and European firms to gain reciprocal access on the same terms. There is no level playing field, and as a result trade tensions are likely to increase. The US is increasingly unable to finance its deficits; open up the vast Asian market; or control its capital outflows. Further US decline, and an ever weaker dollar, now seem unavoidable.

The optimistic view is that East Asia and Japan are maturing as industrial regions and will increasingly trade with each other and with Europe, taking the pressure off the US market. The pessimistic view is that their growth is unstoppable, and that their unbalanced trade relationship with the rest of the world cannot be changed. Regional blocks will form, with the US and Europe protecting themselves from the vigour of Asian capitalism. It is against this uncertain background that British options must be viewed – its structures must be radically overhauled in a world where the power balances are changing fundamentally.

Britain

The contrast between British capitalism and its rivals is marked. The financial system demands the same high returns from companies, with the same lack of commitment, as in the US; but there is not even the saving grace of statutory regulation and strong regional or state banks to moderate the consequences of such pressure: centralisation in London means that the entire economy suffers.

The labour market has many of the worst features of the US – ranging from high turnover to inequality of income – but without the compensating virtues of mobility and managerial dynamism. Nor is there an institutional structure which would allow firms to develop the co-operative, community-based

A comparison of four systems

CHARACTERISTIC	AMERICAN CAPITALISM	JAPANESE CAPITALISM	EUROPEAN SOCIAL MARKET	BRITISH CAPITALISM
Basic principle				
Dominant factor of production	capital	labour	partnership	capital
'Public' tradition	medium	high	high	low
Centralisation	low	medium	medium	high
Reliance on price-mediated markets	high	low	medium	high
Supply relations	arms-length price-driven	close enduring	bureaucracy planned	arms-length price-driven
Industrial groups	partial, defence, etc.	very high	high	low
Extent privatised	high	high	medium	high
Financial system				
Market structure	anonymous securitised	personal committed	bureaucracy committed	uncommitted marketised
Banking system	advanced marketised regional	traditional regulated concentrated	traditional regulated regional	advanced marketised centralised
Stock market	v. important	unimportant	unimportant	v. important
Required returns	high	low	medium	high
Labour market				
Job security	low	high	high	low
Labour mobility	high	low	medium	medium
Labour/management	adversarial	cooperative	cooperative	adversarial
Pay differential	large	small	medium	large
Turnover	high	low	medium	medium
Skills	medium	high	high	poor
Union structure	sector-based	firm-based	industry-wide	craft
Strength	low	low	high	low
The firm				
Main goal	profits	market share stable jobs	market share fulfilment	profits
Role top manager	boss-king autocratic	consensus	consensus	boss-king hierarchy
Social overheads	low	low	high	medium, down
Welfare system				
Basic principle	liberal	corporatist	corporatist social democracy	mixed
Universal transfers	low	medium	high	medium, down
Means-testing	high	medium	low	medium, up
Degree education tiered by class	high	medium	medium	high
Private welfare	high	medium	low	medium, up
Government policies				
Role of government	limited adversarial	extensive cooperative	encompassing	strong adversarial
Openness to trade	quite open	least open	quite open	open
Industrial policy	little	high	high	non-existent
Top income tax	low	low	high	medium

(adapted and extended from Alan Blinder)

capitalism of Japan and East Asia; examples of such networks are rare and are the exceptions that prove the rule. Arms-length, price-mediated relationships extend all the way from the shop floor to the Stock Exchange. The British medium-sized business sector – the equivalent of the *Mittelstand* – is fragile and small in size.

The accompanying table sets out the principal features of the four capitalist systems. It is not exhaustive and merely attempts to isolate the key features of each variant. Each is an interdependent whole, in which the character of one set of institutions interacts with the others; each shapes and is in turn shaped by the whole system. In Britain, profit-maximising firms that give the building of market share a low priority have to be run autocratically in order to produce the kind of shareholder returns that the financial system demands – and that in turn has consequences for the way the labour market is run: the less committed the financial system, the less firms are able to offer lifetime employment and the less willing they are to undertake training.

Firms whose relations with their workers and suppliers are mediated solely by price have to have low social overheads in order to maintain their competitive position; as a result the welfare system in Britain and America is necessarily less ambitious than it is in social market Europe. The same unwillingness to see the firm as an organic enterprise involving all its stakeholders extends to their attributes to the wider society: British firms resent levies to pay for training, for example, both because they seem to make their operations less competitive and because they are an attempt to impose obligations they do not feel they have. In this kind of market economy everybody looks after themselves.

None the less Britain does have the legacy of the social settlement of 1945. While welfare falls below mainland European levels it is still significantly more universal in scope and generous than in the US. The result is that the country once again gets the worst of both worlds; it has neither low enough taxes nor strong enough institutions of social solidarity and so falls between the American and European stools. The introduction of market principles into education, health, criminal justice, housing, television, pensions and social provision is actively eroding social cohesion, and undermining society.

The tradition of public spirit, common interest and national purpose which variously imbues social market Europe, the US and East Asian capitalism is absent in Britain. The private realm and the market are celebrated as the only efficient and responsive forms of organisation, while notions of public and common interest are dismissed as 'bureaucratic', 'interventionist' or 'socialist'. Nor is it easy to mobilise the country in the name of national purpose when it is not clear what purpose an increasingly divided and atomised society might have. The financial markets have no common cause with the medium-sized business sector, and neither have any sense of solidarity with the growing numbers of the excluded and marginalised. Nor is the parliamentary system a potential source of integration and national leadership.

The failure of this institutional matrix and value system to fit into the rest of Western Europe is clear, but in a world where the risk of trade tensions, financial instability and regional trade controls is growing it is apparent that Britain has no option but to stay a member of the European bloc. If that membership is not going to continue to be a source of tension, the structures of British capitalism will have to change. The élite do not want this to happen, yet change they must. How is change to be brought about? And what are the chances of success?

11. The Republican Opportunity

We have seen that in the world's generic forms of capitalism each institutional component is shaped by and helps to form the whole – and that economic performance, social well-being and political governance are interdependent, and dynamised by some notion of common interest or national purpose. If British capitalism is not delivering reasonable living standards and employment opportunities for the country's citizens, that is because the entire institutional structure is failing and there is a weak public tradition – not because 'markets' have been obstructed in their felicitous work by 'bureaucracy'.

For the market economy is not an act of nature. It is socially produced and politically governed. Free markets do not of themselves produce the 'best' institutions and outcomes; they must be carefully sustained by social and public action. If Britain wants better, then it has to rethink its institutional structure and how it can be re-oriented to longtermism, commitment and co-operation without losing the stimulus of competition. Co-operative capitalism does not spontaneously emerge from free markets – it needs to be designed, and to do that a properly democratic system of governance must be devised.

It has been obvious most of this century that such a project is necessary. In his 1951 Reith Lectures Lord Radcliffe launched a coruscating critique of the British unwritten constitution and the doctrine of parliamentary sovereignty. 'The old glories of the liberal tradition,' he said, 'the passionate belief that political liberties are the essential condition of the great liberties of thought, speech and action, have shrunk to a meaningless constitutionalism which asserts that anything is all right if it is permitted, nothing is all right if it is forbidden, by an Act of Parliament.' He went on to remark that the British had a 'habit of praising their institutions which were inept and of ignoring the character of their race, which is often superb. In the end they will be in danger of losing their character and being left with their institutions: a result disastrous indeed'.[1]

Forty years later Lord Radcliffe's warnings are still timely. The public spirit, tradition of fair play and respect for opponents that leavened Britain's medieval political system have been trampled underfoot leaving us only the institutions, in all their resplendent awfulness. Britain needs to redesign its state, overhaul its financial system, vitalise its companies and reinvent institutions of social solidarity. Its producers need to commit themselves to innovation and the development of human capital. And the UK needs to play its part in the construction of an international financial and trading system in which renewal is not undermined by rentiers moving offshore – a system required across the industrialised West. But the very first precondition for any of this is the democratisation and republicanisation of the state. Britain must start by writing a constitution.

The public sphere

The state remains the fountainhead of political authority and democratic power. It is the standard-bearer of nationwide collective action and the embodiment of the community's values. It constructs and polices the law. It represents the nation's concerns, legislating for change and administering what the community holds in common. How it is structured is a matter of huge importance.

British institutional problems start here. The British state conforms to no agreed rules nor clearly articulated principles; in other words, there is no written constitution, carefully setting out the functions of government and the rights and obligations of citizens. If the state is careless about its constitution and thus its relationship with those in whose name it purports to rule, it can hardly be a surprise that such carelessness imbues the whole of civil society. Notions of community, of membership, of belonging and of participation are established here or not at all.

This carelessness is not accidental. Our official culture regards existing public institutions as perfectly adequate. It has no complaint about the centralisation that is the hallmark of the British state. It endorses the doctrine of parliamentary sovereignty and executive discretion. It sees no need to ensure that the executive, legislative and judicial branches of government are kept formally separate. It is satisfied that the Treasury and its book-keeping values are at the heart of the British system. It is quite prepared to countenance the mushrooming of unaccountable quangos. It turns a blind eye to abuses ranging from party funding to the conferring of honours. It colludes in the notion that the majority party in the House of Commons, in effect, is the state.

This approach to public affairs reveals itself in a hundred different shortcomings. Successful capitalism and socially cohesive societies at bottom incorporate the idea of membership; that workers are members of firms and that individuals are citizens of the state. The two conceptions go hand in hand – but not in Britain. Here Parliament and the firm are sovereign; individuals are subjects and workers. They have no formal stake in the society and economy of which they are alleged to be part.

Britain needs what might be called a *republican* attitude to its culture and institutions. To argue for a republican approach is not the same as calling for the abolition of the monarchy, although implanting a republican tradition and institutional structure will mean stripping away prerogative powers and the hereditary principle, which are both aspects of the continuing royal influence on the constitution. But the first republican step is to recognise that constitutions are guarantors of the continuing contract that must exist between governors and governed. Critics say that constitutions change, but this is simply evidence that the rules of governance need to be negotiated constantly. And it is likely, although with the current crisis in the monarchy no longer certain, that in any such negotiation the British would want to retain the monarch as titular head of state. Too many generations of Britains have fought and died for King and Country for this unifying symbol to be thrown aside lightly. But the placing of the monarchy in a constitutional role within a wider settlement, in which the

principles of governance were articulated and agreed, would do
more to legitimise the institution than a thousand speeches, well-
intentioned princely gestures or sermons from the self-appointed
guardians of the House of Windsor.

Reform will have to respect the situation from which Britain
starts, but there is little doubt about where it needs to end up.
Political power and authority needs to be firmly rooted in the
people; the secrecy and executive discretion that pervade the
British system, from the calculation of the annual budget to
the regulation of privatised utilities, must be overcome. The
business of government needs to be more transparent and more
accountable. The executive branch of government needs to be
embedded in a formal system of checks and balances. This will
involve denying the system as much as possible of its capacity for
patronage.

Apart from making the actual day-to-day business of governance more democratic, this will have three fundamental effects.
The rentier culture of the state will be weakened, while the
state itself will be rejuvenated; it will become possible to build
intermediate public institutions to regulate and govern the market
economy; and constitutionalising public life should also improve
standards of conduct in the private domain. The British can have
a state that rules *for* them rather than *over* them.

Once the House of Commons starts to share its sovereignty
with other public institutions, new possibilities for the assertion
of common interests open up. We have seen how both TECs
and housing associations, for example, have been disabled by
their lack of autonomy, accountability and budgetary discretion.
They are potentially rich institutional instruments that could help
to upgrade British skills and social housing alike. But to break free
from the fetters in which they operate there has to be a wholesale
reconstruction of their constitutional basis.

All the time the need is to think systematically. Resources are
not limitless, but the profound reluctance of the Treasury ever
to concede the scale of social returns that can accrue from such
public investment is part of Whitehall's rentier culture. If this can
be broken, while intermediate institutions like housing associations

and TECs are given more autonomy and legitimacy, then the way is open to more creative public initiatives – especially if the users of their services, the public, begin to believe that those who are dispensing the services really represent 'us' rather than 'them'.

The principal obstacle within central government to such a course will remain the Treasury, the embodiment of the book-keeping nightwatchman view of the state. It has such power because it manages the economy and the budget within a system where all power flows from the centre. Decentralisation of power would be one blow to its position; another would be the placing of budgetary management with a new office of the budget; another the creation of a more democratic culture in which decisions are judged as much by their contribution to the common good as their impact on the financial markets. Reform of the Treasury is one pivot on which national renewal hangs.

Yet the Treasury itself is no more than an outgrowth of the British parliamentary system in which the executive holds extraordinary power and where the channels of accountability have become constitutional fictions. The questioning of the Prime Minister twice a week in the Commons is good political theatre but it rarely serves to illuminate the way power is used. More seriously, the capacity of Parliament to challenge the detailed clauses in bills is negligible; parliamentary committees reflect the composition of the House of Commons and the majority on the committee nec-essarily does the government's bidding, whatever inconsistencies bills contain. There is no requirement, when drafting bills, to con-sult with the relevant interests and not enough concession to good argument when the bill is scrutinised; the number of badly drafted laws mounts with each successive Parliament.[2]

Parliament's legislative function, and its role as the seat of executive government, need to be formally separated. The single most effective reform would be the recasting of the House of Lords as a proper revising second chamber. Its hereditary element must be abandoned and its membership elected; it must then have equal power with the Commons to block and amend legislation – legislation which itself should only be brought to Parliament after proper consultation and drafting. Scrutinising committees need to be properly financed and resourced so that representatives in either House have access to high-quality information and advice. Democracy cannot be run on a shoestring.

The many shades of opinion within the country can no longer be distorted by a first-past-the-post voting system based on single-member constituencies. Party strength in Parliament must become more proportional to the strength of the party in the country, both to respect elementary ideas of fairness and to improve the way parliamentary opinion reflects that of society at large. The current system, where most constituencies can be guaranteed to elect an MP from one of the two main parties, ensures a parliamentary seat to a candidate selected by his or her constituency caucus. British election results turn on votes in less than 100 constituencies where the result is genuinely indeterminate – the so-called marginals. As a result the Labour Party disproportionately represents the north of England, Scotland and Wales; the Conservative party dominates the south of England. Both parties become dangerously out of touch with sentiment outside their regional bases, further disabling the quality of national debate.[3]

The public realm must be reclaimed. Dialogue and inclusion must become political imperatives, and lines of accountability must be clear. The devolution of power within central government to executive agencies, trusts and quangos is not unreasonable as long as the appointment of their governing boards is transparent and their procedures open. Instead of mini-versions of the secret, centralised and powerful executive state they must become components of a more pluralist society in which power is devolved away from the centre.

There needs to be a new creativity as regards intermediate public institutions, where Britain's constitutional poverty is cruelly exposed. For example all British proposals for making the Bank of England independent[4] wrestle with the question of accountability and end up with a quasi-privatised Bank of England reporting to the House of Commons via the Treasury and Civil Service Select Committee and made accountable only to the Chancellor of the Exchequer. This, after all, is what parliamentary sovereignty demands. But how can the Chancellor answer for central bank decisions to which he is not party? And how can a committee, split along party lines and with no formal power, hold the Bank accountable in any effective sense? In the wonderland world of British democracy the choice is to give the Bank of England power without responsibility, which it currently enjoys, or to privatise it and make it nominally accountable to Parliament through the forms which supposedly represent democracy but in reality do not do so at all. An independent central bank that can be trusted with monetary policy must be a republican institution in the widest sense, in a system of federal government and delegated powers, or else it cannot work. To pass the control of interest rates to a quasi-private organisation run as an extension of one wing of the Conservative Party would be a disaster.

The same conundrum appears once you examine the regulation of privatised utilities. There is no tradition that utilities, as natural monopolies, are somehow held in common. Regulation was designed to be 'light' and 'flexible', mimicking what private competition would have achieved had the industries not been monopolies. As a regulatory concept this is woeful, allowing a wide range of views as to how the beast might be shadowed. One regulator may interpret the competitive model as an excuse for breaking up the industry into smaller competing parts; another for setting maximum rates of return; another for regarding pressure from the capital markets as a surrogate for competition and allowing the monopoly to remain intact. None of them have any clear idea of the national or common interest; some may feel that it is naturally achieved by competition, others that it has to be asserted.

Some regulators may involve consumers or their representatives; others effectively ignore them. The regulators' powers to acquire the information necessary to make effective judgements are strictly limited, dependent upon the co-operation of the utility which may or may not be forthcoming. The regulator is the British state in miniature; it has executive discretion but is uninformed by any republican sense of civil community and it supervises firms whose own constitutions insist that their only stakeholders are their owners. The privatised water industry has written off two-thirds of its £1.2 billion diversification programme, which the regulator was unable to prevent.[5]

There is a constant tension between the quest for economic efficiency measured by the stock market criteria, and wider considerations of efficiency in which some calculus of social return needs to be integrated, but which the regulators are unable to express. Perhaps the most famous example was government encouragement to build lots of gas-fired electricity generators in the search for lower energy prices, without considering the likely effect: a collapse in the demand for coal. The coal industry was given no chance to match lower gas prices. As a result Britain's energy policy became unbalanced, with expensive economic and social consequences for the mining industry and mining communities. The 'republican' regulator celebrated by Ian Ayres and John Braithwaite – flexible, negotiating, focusing on competence, imbued with a sense of wider interests, conscious that citizens have a right to participate in decisions – is conspicuous by its absence.[6]

Something similar could be said for all British attempts at regulation. In the law, the media, the police, financial services and even sport they are characterised by the same mix of self-regulation, with a spatchcock system of regulation bolted on here and there, usually as a result of some historic failure that required drastic action. But statutory regulation, when imposed from above, is not republican in spirit. It amounts to direct governance by the state, with no redress; and the state is still the party that commands a majority in the House of Commons. The City of London as much as the newspaper industry properly resists any extension of the state's unaccountable and partisan power – as unions did earlier. Yet there are areas that plainly require regulation and governance; but the only reasonable route is to establish such regulation as a system of rights that accompany obligations – and that in turn requires a wider constitutional framework. Newspaper regulation, for example, obliging newspapers to disseminate news with due impartiality and reasonable protection of individual privacy, would have to guarantee the press's right to information and its protection for the publication of material that was in the public interest. But without a constitutional settlement no such bargain is possible.

There also needs to be more delegation of political power to the constituent parts of the polity – again reflecting a republican sense that all parts of the state are equal and have the right, in so far as it is possible, to tailor their governance to their own specific needs. Scotland, Wales and Northern Ireland need more power to govern their affairs – as do English regions – as much because it would be efficient as because it would be more democratic. No enduring settlement is even possible in Northern Ireland, for example, until it governs itself within a state in which all citizens, Protestant and Catholic, have their rights constitutionally protected.

Devolution of political power makes for healthy cities. We have observed how in East Asia and social-market Europe the clustering of economic activity in cities has been an important factor in developing the co-operative relationships of successful capitalism. The German *Mittelstand* companies are clustered in one place: so are the Japanese *kigyo shudan*. Moreover public intervention has been imaginatively used to create supply-chains of sub-contractors, which makes for a virtuous circle of efficiency, growth and successful urbanisation. Urban areas have to be governed. Their transport, their recreation facilities, even the quality of their air require management and supervision; and this in turn requires autonomous political institutions.

In a republic there are city mayors, regional prime ministers and state governors; they compete for votes and govern their urban clusters to maximise their economic and social advantage. Their political power aids the formation and sustenance of the city; financial power follows political power. The extent to which a city or region governs itself helps companies to decide whether to locate these to be closer to power. Britain's poor, sad cities are denuded of such authority. They cannot express civic pride or act for themselves. All power is arrogated to the centre, with ministers decrying those political institutions that might express any republican communal and co-operative purpose as another layer of 'bureaucracy'. That the nearest London has to any form of governance is a committee of Conservative-supporting businessmen is an affront to any sense of democracy.

Paul Hirst has argued that the complexity of contemporary economic and social life requires more subtle, local and flexible forms of governance. The state can no longer be the vehicle for the top-down implementation of socialism or of free-market capitalism; instead society must be governed and regulated by a web of associations which have the moral authority of the state and which have democratic legitimacy. Cities, regulatory authorities, and a host of other institutions are the tools, but first they need the constitutional settlement which liberates them to do the job.

Constitutionalising civil society

Britain's institutional poverty is obvious even in the private sector. Here firms and pension funds are still operating under the aegis of nineteenth-century company and trust law. The City of London likes to boast that it is 'flexibly' regulated by itself in a system combining the best of statutory and self-regulation, so that it can get on with the business of deal-making without bureaucratic constraint. These are gentlemanly capitalists, unleavened by any republican or democratic sensibility, who have constructed an arena in which usury and avarice are excused because they represent 'market forces'. It is an ugly sight.

The constitution of the British firm, as we have seen, self-consciously reproduces the unwritten British constitution. Share-holders meet at the annual general meeting, to vote on how well the directors have executed their sole responsibility, which is to maximise their profits and the shareholders' assets. The chairman of the board, who may also be the chief executive, runs the enterprise with the same executive discretion as a prime minister. He (there are almost no shes in this position) can appoint whoever he likes to the board as a non-executive director to bolster his own position; can set the level of his own salary; need not consult nor communicate with his workforce; and can manipulate the firm's constitution to get his way – whether it be the treatment of pension fund surpluses, deciding on the level of tax payments or identifying the next takeover target.[7]

The mechanisms for challenging decisions are weak. For example, it is almost impossible for a dissident shareholder to query the board's strategy at an AGM: there is no legal provision for organising votes against the board. There isn't any obligation to vote, and many institutional shareholders do not bother to do so; generally they will endorse senior management and, if they don't, will sell their shareholding. This is the privilege they cherish, rather than encumbering themselves with the obligations that come from sharing in the development of a company's strategy. The litmus-paper of effectiveness is always the market test, which ideology insists is best.

Of course not all firms are run as the personal fiefdoms of their directors; but that is only because their institutional history has produced a different structure or because an enlightened board recognises that it is bad for business. But this is purely their own decision. There is nothing in company law that pushes them in this direction or mitigates the destructive, short-term behaviour to which the current system is biased.

There is, for example, no legal requirement for audit committees to provide alternative sources of financial information to the non-executive directors. There are no independent remuneration committees to assess directors' pay. There is no system for ensuring that the custodians of company pension funds are independent. Firms do not have to establish supervisory boards to monitor the performance of their executive board as they do in Europe; rather the board is judge and jury of its own performance. There is no formal incorporation of key stakeholders – trade unions and banks – in the constitution of the firm. There is no obligation to establish works councils or to recognise trade unions as partners in the enterprise. The public cannot easily obtain company information. Transparent and commonly accepted accounting guidelines are not enforced, and can vary hugely from firm to firm or from year to year; the annual report and accounts set out precisely what the board and its chairman decide they will set out. The firm is a law unto itself, sovereign of all it surveys. Its only job is to succeed in the marketplace.

Yet the success of British firms in the marketplace is very

idiosyncratic. They certainly succeed in making high real rates of return, so that nine of the world's fifty most profitable firms are British, but they do not in general win and hold market share. There is little innovation; the accent is not on investment. British enterprise is a trading culture; at the bottom it is the world of car-boot traders, dodgy second-hand dealers, estate agents and life insurance salesmen – at the top a world of ex-public schoolboys, or ex-grammar schoolboys apeing public school mores, running their companies as private preserves in which the object is to make the existing assets sweat harder. The key to success is too frequently seen as the capacity to exploit labour without let or hindrance, or fill a temporary market niche.

British companies need a fundamental change in culture and organisation. New standards should be codified into law. It is no longer enough to establish voluntary codes. For example the recommendations of the Cadbury Committee, setting out minimal standards of corporate governance, or the compromised attempts by the professional accounting bodies to devise more sophisticated accounting codes, are noble efforts to inculcate better practices but they rely on self-regulation and are stymied because they take place in a wider constitutional vacuum. Support for these reforms is tepid, undermined by charges that they obstruct 'enterprise'[8] – which in the British sense of course they do – and are always at risk from the possibility that those who fail to comply with them will reap competitive advantages. Voluntary adherence to the rules is therefore difficult to sustain. The Cadbury Committee's recommendations – hardly Draconian, given the scale of the problem – look set to become at best only a partial success.

If there is to be co-operative capitalism, management needs employee organisations with which to co-operate. Here British trade unionism requires a cultural and institutional revolution as much as British firms do. Unions have historically defined themselves as the permanent opposition to private companies; their internal constitutions confer considerable executive power on their general secretaries and executive committees. The ethos is that collective action secures collective goals; and partnership with companies used to be seen as limiting the freedom to pursue collective ends.

Under the pressure of the recent Conservative governments the culture began to change. Trade unions' capacity to maintain their old role was so enfeebled that they were compelled to rethink their relationship with their members, the companies with which they bargain and the Labour Party, the party which they founded. Rather than see themselves as the embodiment of a Labour movement dedicated to the transformation of capitalism, they have started to redefine themselves as social partners in the management of capitalism. They can still serve the individual interests of their members – ensuring proper pension rights and employment contracts – but within the framework of a capitalist economy. The withdrawal of labour in a strike, although a fundamental human right, is less and less seen as the principal objective or weapon of trade unionism.

These trends should be entrenched by arming trade unions with proper constitutions and constitutional entitlements. Union recognition should be mandatory where a majority of workers freely wish it. Consultation with unions and representation of unions on company boards should be compulsory. Unions themselves should accept reciprocal responsibilities, building upon the existing reforms and exposing companies to the risk of being sued for breach of contract. Social partners have rights; they also have obligations.

There can be no gold standard for private behaviour without a public domain more careful about its own constitution. A written constitution would set an example of checks and balances, of obligations accompanying rights. American capitalism is criticised for its excessive individualism, but it functions in a republican society and is at least modified by the existence of such qualities as openness, transparency and democratic regulation.

To allow the firm, the key animating force of the capitalist economy, to take as its constitutional model no better example than the sovereignty of the Westminster Parliament, is a grievous mistake. No reform in this field can be considered without reference to the whole – and the most crucial element is the financial system.

12. Stakeholder Capitalism

Keynes famously called for the socialisation of investment at the end of his *General Theory*, and many critics of the British financial system have echoed that call. But the task is a more subtle one, if the object of the exercise is to keep the merits of private ownership while reshaping the way it works. Thus the great challenge of the twentieth century, after the experience of both state socialism and of unfettered free markets, is to create a new financial architecture in which private decisions produce a less degenerate capitalism. The triple requirement is to broaden the area of stake-holding in companies and institutions, so creating a greater bias to longterm commitment from owners; to extend the supply of cheap, longterm debt; and to decentralise decision-making. The financial system, in short, needs to be comprehensively republicanised.

The first breach would be made by establishing a republican-style central bank which understood that its role was to recast the financial system as a servant of business rather than as its master. Financial freedom would no longer be taken as axiomatically good but as a privilege which has to be earned, and which carries obligations. As matters stand the current Bank of England is a permanent obstacle to financial reform: a precondition for any wider reconstruction of the financial system is a transformation of its constitution, mission and values.

The Bank's structure would match the new federal structure of the state. As the country began to be organised politically around its constituent regions, nations and cities, there would be a framework of regional public banks reporting to the Central Bank, whose chief executives would be appointed by the elected parliaments of the appropriate region. They would sit on the governing board of the Bank, replacing the current Court (which is staffed by placemen of the rentier state) and deliberate over monetary policy and the wider reform of the financial system. The extent to which the Bank had the final word over interest rates or the extent to which it fell to the Chancellor of the Exchequer could be decided after the new arrangements had bedded down for at least one complete economic cycle and the character of the Bank became clearer. If it became a social partner in the republican sense, running monetary policy impartially with a democratic awareness of the trade-offs between lost output and lower inflation, the presumption would be that it would gain independence along US lines. With new constitutional arrangements there would, finally, be a way of ensuring its democratic accountability.

In its conduct of monetary policy the Bank would be armed with a more complete array of financial instruments than short-term interest rates. Instead of conceding the financial institutions' argument that their balance sheets are their own concern and that the only legitimate tool of policy is the price of money, the Bank would have the power to influence directly the structure and profitability of banking business in pursuit of its wider public objectives. It would, for example, reintroduce reserve requirements to support its interest rate policy, and it would follow the Bundesbank and the Federal Reserve by regulating the markets in a wider public interest than that defined by the markets themselves.

One of the Bank's chief preoccupations would be to lower the cost of capital in Britain – the combination of servicing of bank debt and shareholders' funds – and to lengthen the payback periods that companies set for their investment projects. This is the core of the British supply-side problem and the single most important explanation for indifferent levels of investment. British companies need to borrow more longterm debt and lower their target rates of return from new investment. The Bank's objective, along with a reformed Treasury, must be to construct a financial system in which this can take place; the first time the British authorities will have played such a role since the Industrial Revolution.

In order for companies to borrow more, the banks have to lend funds that companies can afford to service. In the same way that purchasing a house on a three-year mortgage with a 20 per cent interest rate would mean that fewer houses would be bought, so very few companies can sustain high investment with three-year paybacks and 20 per cent nominal returns. The first task, then, is to change the conditions that give British clearing banks their short-term, anti-industrial lending policies.

But for the banks to lend longer term, they themselves need less demanding financial criteria because longterm loans are less profitable for them than short-term revolving credits. They need to have their own cost of capital lowered; they need access to longterm deposits; and they need better credit assessment techniques, with incentives to develop closer relationships with their industrial customers in order better to judge the viability of their investment proposals.

Britain should copy other industrialised countries and create a public agency that will act as a financial intermediary collecting longer term deposits and channelling them to lending institutions. The Japanese use their post office network to collect longterm savings, and their great public investment banks then lend directly or in partnership with Japan's commercial banks. The US has deployed their federal housing finance intermediaries, 'Fannie Mae' (Federal National Mortgage Association) and 'Freddie Mac' (Federal Home Loan Mortgage Corporation), to encourage direct and indirect longterm finance for home purchase and new home construction; while Germany has its *Kreditanstalt für Wiederaufbau* (the KfW or Bank for Reconstruction) which makes longterm loans in partnership with the commercial banks and a network of regional development banks. The UK has nothing.[1]

What it could have are regional banks collecting longterm deposits to recycle to clearing banks and other specialist lending institutions, like a housing bank to cater for housing associations, local authorities and the construction industry. A new benchmark for longterm bank lending would be established as more longterm bank loans were made. A specialist bank lending to small and medium-sized companies could support the same drive. In order to encourage longterm lending, the reformed Central Bank could offer assistance on favourable terms in the money markets to all longterm lenders – public and commercial banks alike. This would reassure them about the liquidity risk they were running.

But the banks are not charities and to entrench this new attitude the target rate of return on their own capital will have to be lowered. The Germans have two key mechanisms. First they exploit the stakeholder culture engendered by co-operative capitalism to lower the cost of capital for all enterprises, banks included. Shares are tokens of a longterm relationship rather than a trading asset, so that dividend payments can be lower and payback periods lengthened. Second, public banks at both state and regional level are constrained in their dividend distributions; profits build up as reserves and balance sheets are strengthened which gives a stable platform from which to lend longterm at keen rates of interest.

The combination is a potent one. Borrowers' loan packages, a mix of public and private loans, are cheaper because the private and public banks themselves need to earn lower financial returns. Nor do the commercial banks complain about this 'subsidised' finance, as their counterparts in Britain might be expected to do. As they are themselves shareholders in the borrowing companies, they benefit from the impact that cheaper loan finance has on the borrowers' trading prospects.

To lower the cost of capital, British banks and their customers need more patient, committed shareholders and less of a hunger for dividends. The entire system could then move into a virtuous circle in which more longterm bank lending was validated by improved economic performance resulting from higher investment. Lowering the cost of capital would also allow the banks to invest more in internal systems for information gathering and credit assessment; these are expensive and time consuming, but would help the banks avoid the lending mistakes they made in the 1980s boom. If, at the same time, they could share in the success of the companies in which they invested the rewards for lending would be higher.

One immediate move would be to insist that banks take equity stakes in enterprises, and that banks which did not do so would rank lower in claims on firms' assets than stakeholding banks. The banks' legal capacity to take a 'floating charge' on all of a company's assets should be abolished; this makes companies the prisoners of a single bank loan, prevents them from borrowing heavily to finance investment and encourages banks to look for property collateral to support their lending rather than offering finance for specific projects. It worsens the present disastrous arm's-length arrangements. A proper system of loan guarantees, run by a public institution, should be set up, allowing small firms in particular to borrow more aggressively. If these measures were combined with a legal requirement to regionalise the operations of the clearing banks, they would add up to a novel and important contribution to the creation of a British *Mittelstand* sector. Britain's small and medium-sized companies are damaged most by their inability to sustain high levels of longterm debt.

Perhaps, in the short run, bank dividends should be regulated and banks encouraged to build up cheaper internal reserves of capital. Banks will complain bitterly about any infringement of their 'freedom', but since the state is required to bail them out if they get into financial difficulties and to carry the wider social costs of their anti-industrial lending policies, such an initiative would create a proper symmetry of obligations.

The most important factor in reducing the cost of capital for banks and business generally is shareholder commitment. This should be fostered by exploiting the proposed new system of corporate governance and the role of non-executive directors, for banks and business alike. Groups of core institutional shareholders might be formed who would be represented on company and bank boards by non-executive directors with their own, information-gathering secretariats. Voting rights might be limited only to those shareholders who are represented on company boards, thus legally linking ownership with obligations to commitment. It might even be useful to split the functions of the supervisory and executive boards, as in Germany, with representatives of the core voting shareholders joining the supervisory board. They would engage in an ongoing dialogue with management about business strategy, with share options and bonuses only exercisable after a specified minimum period – say ten years' service – and with tax incentives for those who exercised options later. The current incentives for paper entrepreneurship, unlocking so-called shareholder value by asset manipulation and so boosting executives' share options, would be reduced. There would be a penal short-term capital gains tax for shareholders who took early profits, tapering to near zero for longterm shareholders. This would encourage shareholders to value future returns more highly than they do and so help companies to extend their payback periods.

This would only work if takeovers were made harder to mount. The tightening of lax accounting standards, setting new upper limits for advisers' fees (in particular removing their tax-deductibility) and allowing firms a 'public-interest' defence against hostile takeovers would all help. In addition the current obligation for any single shareholder to make a full bid if more than 30 per cent of the company is owned could be dropped. Large single shareholders can be sources of much needed stability. Although current doctrine is that effective stewardship of company assets requires the fear of takeover, this militates against the construction of longterm relationships within the company. Much of the so-called 'shareholder value' that is 'unlocked' by takeover amounts to no more than unravelling co-operative and committed relationships, which are priced above market-clearing levels, and reorganising them in a strictly price-mediated relationship. This lowers the company's variable costs which, taken together with the accountants' treatment of the financing costs of takeover, appears to make the acquisition profitable. But accounting fiddles are no route to industrial success, as Britain has discovered.

The approach to takeovers highlights another aspect of a properly constitutional democratic state – the role of audit. Without impartially prepared accounts that follow a transparent set of rules, the balance sheets and profits of firms are the playthings of private boards and their accountants. In their increasing anxiety to win business, accountants have been willing to bend accounting conventions to meet the short-term requirements of boards – so that accounts no longer offer a proper measure of company worth, failing to allow comparison of performance over time or with other firms. Corporate taxation becomes the quixotic result of whatever accounting standards are adopted, allowing boards in effect to choose their level of taxation. Audit needs to be regulated in the public interest, and auditors licensed like banks before they can go into business.

In the search for fees and commissions, investment and merchant banks have become ever more imaginative in their invention of financial assets that can be bought and sold, ranging from the sale of company bank debt to instruments that protect against future share price movements – with the Bank of England indulging the whole exercise as evidence of financial innovation. But this makes the system increasingly unstable, without increasing investment and innovation in the real economy. The system must be forced to exercise greater prudence and the financial institutions' balance sheets must be more strictly monitored. A balance needs to be struck between market contracts that protect against risk, and marketisation that destabilises longterm relationships between finance and industry.

The emergence of giant financial institutions, in particular pension funds, and their growing desire to hold company equity, paying dividends, has been one of the biggest motors of short-termism. Government and company bonds, of course, pay fixed rates of interest. Equity has offered a measure of protection against inflation, with profits and dividends tending to rise at least in line with inflation; but it has also been attractive because dividends have risen significantly in real terms. As a result pension funds hold 85 per cent of their assets in company shares, bringing their total holdings of shares to 40 per cent of the value quoted on the London Stock Exchange.

Dividends are meant to fluctuate with profits but pension funds, with their longterm liabilities to their pensioners, cannot afford such fluctuation. For them, dividends need to be as secure as fixed-interest investments with the extra bonus that they always rise – and companies are now yoked to this demand from their principal shareholders with all the adverse consequences. Pension funds and insurance companies have become classic absentee land-lords, exerting power without responsibility and making exacting demands upon companies without recognising their reciprocal obligation as owners.

Some funds have begun to exercise responsibilities, questioning some of the more outrageous executive pay deals, but typically the British savings institution is a supine accomplice of the board –

happy to go along with corporate strategy as long as the financial returns are high. Their power to affect the course of whole industries is extraordinary. For example, Mercury Asset Management, one of the largest City investment managers, settled the fate of London Weekend Television in its fight for independence from Granada and so set in train the spate of takeovers and mergers in the independent TV sector. Should one person in one investment management group have such power? Should the sole criterion for such decisions be the maximisation of short-term value for the funds which he or she manages? Although the funds will resist the limitations on their freedom that new proposals on takeovers and their participation in corporate governance would imply, in fact they need to be relieved of such awesome responsibilities – or at least be forced to treat them as would properly informed shareholders rather than institutional rentiers.

However, the power of pension funds and institutional saving has not grown in a vacuum; it is the direct consequence, as we have seen, of the explosion of home-ownership and the private provision for old age, with the state progressively abdicating its responsibilities in the name of 'choice' and 'self-reliance'. Pension fund contributions, the underlying fund and the final payment are all free of tax. The private has been privileged at least in part because of Britain's weaknesses in providing a solid state pension. That would demand a binding contract between the generations, but in Britain such contracts are expressed through Parliament whose guiding principle is that it cannot bind successors – a principle faithfully followed when the Conservatives carelessly debauched the SERPS scheme. Any inter-generational contract cannot be trusted - and the same is true for the provision of social housing.

As a result people have exploited tax privileges and protected themselves with private and occupational pensions, while even those for whom home-ownership is unsuitable have been forced to join the stampede into owner occupation, increasingly financed with an endowment insurance policy to pay off the mortgage. The consequence has been a flood of institutional savings, an acute demand for dividends and the foreshortening of investment time-horizons. These savings, if the wider financial system had been reformed to accommodate their new power and demands, could have been and still can be a fruitful source of finance for investment. Instead they have become destabilising.

The financial system is not an island. It is embedded in the wider British system – and at least some of the epidemic of short-termism and the hunger for dividends can be connected with the privatisation of the welfare state and growing importance of private insurance. But if welfare provision were on a sounder footing, the pressures would be less. Republicanisation of finance and the democratisation of welfare are intertwined.

The democratisation of the welfare state

At the heart of the welfare state lies a conception of the just society; a guarantee of some income for the disadvantaged against life's hazards, along with a roof over their heads, access to healthcare and, for their children, the education and training essential to improving their situation. The vitality of the welfare state is a badge of the healthy society; it is a symbol of our capacity to act together morally, to share and to recognise the mutuality of rights and obligations that underpins all human association. It is an expression of social citizenship.

Yet to function at all it has to be based on a series of income transfers between classes and generations underwritten by the recognition that social cohesion results from common endeavour, and is a good which benefits all. A welfare state cannot function independently of the wider economic and political structures; if they admit only a truncated notion of citizenship, then so will the welfare system.

There is, on the one hand, the hard, political requirement that the middle class and the top third of the income parade must have good reasons for accepting the progressive taxation upon which a welfare system depends. They need to get enough out of the system directly in terms of provision and indirectly in terms of social cohesion to make them support the principle of universal welfare to which they are disproportionately heavy contributors. That requires well-designed and high-quality welfare services that meet their needs as well. On the other hand, acceptance of such a settlement assumes that there is a wider public morality, which insists that universal participation is the only moral basis upon which the welfare system and society as a whole can be constructed.

But the basis for such an ethic has been corroded by the New Right requirement that the welfare system conform not to notions of citizenship and democracy but to the dictates of the market. People are urged instead to opt out into privatised provision – and the tax system is designed to help them; hence charitable status for private schools, and tax relief for private pensions and health insurance premiums. The delivery systems have been organised so as to mimic markets in the search for economic efficiency, and the welfare system shaped to reinforce a 'flexible' labour market. The resulting inequality is seen as the price of wealth creation.

But the argument should be stood on its head. What is in reality required from the welfare system is that it provide boundaries to the operation of markets, underwrites social cohesion and helps produce the values that sustain the co-operation without which successful economies cannot flourish. Instead of privatisation, the welfare state needs more democracy and more sensitivity to real needs. It must, as the Commission on Social Justice has argued, support people throughout their increasingly volatile lives' – dealing with periods of unemployment, retraining or changing family responsibilities.

It must confront the new role of women in the family and in the labour market. It cannot be indifferent to the structure of work. The higher skilled the labour force and the lower the unemployment, then the less the services of the welfare system are needed and the less expensive it will be. The system needs a new calculus in which welfare is seen to produce *social* returns, justifying the build-up of investment in skills, in education, in the transition between jobs, in the support of families.

In some respects the post-war welfare state was an attempt to strike a balance between welfare, social justice and efficiency that should not be jettisoned lightly. It has been undermined not because of its intrinsic irrationality, but because a conception of social citizenship without economic and political institutions to support it was never likely to endure. The post-war structures were never designed to deal with the scale of inequality and distress thrown up by letting rip the worst tendencies of British capitalism, while abandoning full employment as a policy aim. If these handicaps were removed the British welfare state remains a model to be modified and improved upon, rather than discarded and privatised.

For example, a reasonable state pension for all is an affordable, rational and democratic right in any society. It is targeted; for better-off pensioners pay more tax to the extent that their income is increased by the pension. It is universal. It is redistributive. Emasculating it does not reduce the claim that pensioners make on future national income, except to the extent it makes some pensioners poorer. For pensioners will still be there, whether or not they are provided for by the state, so that they will continue to have claims upon future generations. Privatisation merely forces them to hold those claims through the lottery of accumulating stocks and shares rather than through a proper measure of redistributive taxation to support a reasonable state pension.

This is not to argue that private saving should be discouraged; accompanied by the reforms outlined earlier it would boost investment and growth, making pension transfers more affordable. But it does mean that there is a balance to be struck. Without the reform of the financial system, pension funds are an unwitting accomplice in the hollowing out of the economy. Without some concept of social citizenship expressed as a guaranteed reasonable income for the old – which necessarily involves some measure of redistribution – many pensioners are simply going to be pauperised.

Pension funds themselves should be thoroughly democratised. As the Labour MP Frank Field has argued, it is absurd that the accumulated funds attributable to each individual cannot be used until they are of pensionable age.[2] Here are the resources that might finance training between jobs, allowing individuals the possibility of enhancing their life chances and earnings; here are the resources that might finance reduced working hours or improved child care for couples with young children, improving the quality of parenting. There are many possibilities, but pension funds remain locked up, the assets mercilessly traded in the quest for ever higher short-term returns.

It is this sensitivity to real need, along with the binding of society into a common project, that should be the goal of a universal welfare system. To boost welfare resources the contribution and insurance principle needs to be enhanced rather than diminished. The New Right's proposal to integrate tax with benefits is an attempt to move away from universalism and back to discretionary benefits for the 'deserving poor', making the generosity of the system wholly dependent upon its capacity to raise funds through taxes on higher earners – which in the present climate is extraordinarily difficult. The poverty of the system would thus compel it to resort to means-testing. Such discretionary means-tested benefits are incredibly divisive, driving a wedge between the mendicants and the tax-paying public for whom welfare becomes a 'burden'. They are also economically inefficient, the source of penal marginal rates of tax of 90 per cent or more – as well as discouraging women married to unemployed men from entering the labour market.

It is imperative both to avoid this trap and to bind the top third of our society into a system that embodies a morality of citizenship. There needs to be a sense, as with personal pension contributions, that individuals are contributing to their own well-being. The national insurance fund might be split into a fund for unemployment and for pensions. The SERPS principle could be extended to unemployment benefit, with individuals permitted to make additional payments above the minimum to assure themselves of higher levels of benefit. The argument that high unemployment benefit is a deterrent to work should be consigned to oblivion; but after eighteen months or so of unemployment the state should intervene to organise gainful work. Either it should train those out of work, or provide them with some form of subsidy to help lower their wage costs to an employer, or it should pay relocation costs for those who find work in a new area. One way or another, for

their own good and for that of the wider society, the longterm
unemployed cannot be allowed to rot.

In health there might be a tiered system of contributions
above the core contribution, assuring enhanced access to care
for non-life-threatening treatment. Critics may object to this as
the nationalisation of inequality, but the gains outrank the losses.
By incorporating inequality into the public domain at least it is
contained and managed, with increased resources placed at the
disposal of all. And, most importantly, the middle class is given
a vested interest in the effectiveness of the entire system; it opts in
rather than opts out, thus underpinning universality and common
purpose rather than privatisation and social fragmentation.

If the principle of inclusion is lost the welfare state perishes.
The idea of giving the young or the unemployed vouchers, cor-
responding to the value of their benefits, or their training costs,
or both, which they can spend either to make themselves more
attractive to employers or to buy customised training is a healthy
way of developing flexibility. In essence these are instruments of
inclusion. The voucher-holders are enabled to opt into the world
of work and training. Tax rebates, on the other hand, which
encourage opting out, have to be handled with more care.

This applies especially to education, where opting out and
exclusion have gone furthest. Throughout this book the persistent
theme has been the destructive role of 'gentlemanly capitalism' and
the privileged place occupied by finance and financial values in British society. Yet these do not appear out of a clear blue sky; they
are socially produced, and the principal transmission mechanism
is the British public school system. These schools, while generally
educationally excellent, are founded upon the very values of opting
out and distrust of the public domain that have proved so corrosive.

What is required is a republicanisation of that system's values.
If private schools could recognise that they were part of the
common realm, sharing in common endeavours, then one of
the main objections to them would fall away – and the extension of citizenship in the wider society would in itself trigger
a change in public school values. But that would need to be
accompanied by policies to break their present stranglehold on

education. Their tax incentives and public subsidies should be withdrawn. They should be compelled to form partnerships with the state sector, and charitable status made conditional on educating a high non-fee-paying proportion of children, who would gain from the massive educational infrastructure they support. Grammar schools and grammar school streams in com-prehensives need to be revived in order to attract members of the middle class back to the state system; nationalising inequality in education for the same reasons as in health. The league tables of school performance should reflect the catchment area of the school, but their continuing publication is an important demo-cratic gain and should not be withdrawn. Teachers should be better paid. Quotas should be set for public school entrants into Oxford and Cambridge.

For some this may be second best; but in constructing the welfare state the best has too frequently been the enemy of the good. To import the class divisions of the private sphere into the public sphere may seem a surrender to middle-class aspirations and values, but this is surely better than condemning public institutions to the second-class status that a middle-class exodus from them implies. In any case the aim is to imbue the middle class with a sense of their common citizenship, whilst recognising their impulse for self-advancement.

The increase in numbers going into higher education is expand-ing membership of the middle class – even if its work and salary experience is becoming increasingly insecure – while those left behind are more marginalised. It therefore becomes imperative to bind this expanding class into the system, and to win its support, for example, for the additional expenditure on edu-cation and training that is needed. Inequality is there whether we like it or not; an important means of tempering it is by empowering the disadvantaged with skills. That in turn rests on the public sector's capacity to deliver the appropriate training which is impossible if it is not rooted in the values of inclusion and citizenship.

The governance of 'abroad'

It is a paradox that the cult of parliamentary sovereignty has intensified at the very moment when economic and political sovereignty are ever more qualified by the rise of the global financial markets. Although a measure of national autonomy remains, the capacity to regulate the financial system, set minimum social standards and manage the national economy is increasingly constrained. Reform on the scale called for here is impossible without an international framework that prevents the destruction of such domestic initiatives.

The world financial system is spinning out of control. The stock of cross-border lending now exceeds a quarter of the GDP of all industrialised countries. International bank assets are double the value of world trade. The volume of business in the currency futures markets exceeds even that generated by daily trade flows. Groundless fears about what may happen in two or three years' time are moving current spot prices and interest rates, as traders in future prices hedge their bets in the spot markets. One month it can be the dollar that is being driven up or down to irrational levels; another month it may be world bond prices. The world has been turned on its head, with the real economy driven hither and thither by financial speculation.

Not even the US, German or Japanese governments have the financial clout to deal with the new volume of speculative flows – while many developing countries lack enough reserves to cover the purchase of eight weeks' imports. The right of exit coveted by financial operators has been converted into economic supremacy – with London's financial markets playing a pivotal role.

Yet all this financial activity has produced nothing like the high investment and growth of the post-war years; by allowing capital to look for the highest return, governments have raised its price and inadvertently caused investment to shrink. Britain and the US have the freest financial systems, demanding and receiving among the highest returns in the OECD; as a result they have the lowest levels of investment, and in consequence the lowest level of savings. But there has been a shortening of time horizons everywhere, and economies can only achieve low inflation with high levels of unemployment. The new instability is good for the brokers and currency traders, but bad for almost everybody else.

Indeed, as the financial markets exercise their veto over expansionary economic policy and drive up real interest rates, the trade-off between free finance and free trade that was so clear to the delegates at Bretton Woods in 1944 – when the post-war international financial system was designed – becomes more evident. Free trade results in massive dislocations of employment which can be more comfortably accommodated if economies are run at or near full employment. But if the policy framework is restrictive, then countries everywhere find that unemployment rises remorselessly – and the pressures to resort to protectionism may become irresistible.

What the world needs is to reinvent the bargain it abandoned in the early 1970s when the Bretton Woods system of fixed exchange rates, with the International Monetary Fund as its custodian, collapsed. Liberal trade, capital controls, fixed exchange rates and stable economic policies with an expansionary bias went together, creating prosperity and full employment for a generation. The US extended its domestic financial system to the world, offering dollars as the world currency backed by gold, but within an orderly international framework; a unique and possibly unrepeatable set of circumstances.

The growth of capital mobility, as Keynes had warned at Bretton Woods, undermined the system. In the early 1970s the combination of US trade weakness and currency speculation overwhelmed the central banks policing the fixed exchange rates.[3] Right-wing commentators hailed the collapse of the post-war system as signalling a new period of growth, with financial speculation rescuing the world from the grip of regulation, corporatism and government-led efforts to keep full employment. Instead, the world growth rate has halved and currency instability has exploded.

The world's financial markets need to be brought to heel. They themselves do not spontaneously provide international order; it has

to be created by public agency and then governed, which means
rule by some supranational authority. The world needs predictable
exchange rates that reflect economic realities. Countries need to
be able to manage their economies themselves, making what they
consider to be the right trade-offs between inflation, growth and
employment. Private capital needs to be able to move where it will,
but within a framework that respects justice; those who exploit
slave labour or the environment should not be permitted to trade
with those who do not simply because of the free trading world
order. The developing world needs access to the industrialised
countries' markets and resources.

The key to stability and recasting the system is to move
from a regime of floating currencies to some system of flexible
and adjustable bands in which currencies move predictably. The
world's leading states need to run their economies in support of
these exchange rates. The US and Japan in particular have to find
a way of mediating their increasingly tense relationship, built
upon two very different capitalist systems – and forcing them
to manage a fixed-exchange relationship between the dollar and
yen as part of a wider world agreement may be the only way of
compelling them to make the necessary adjustments. Neither the
dollar nor the yen is strong enough alone to be the pillar of the
world financial order; the two currencies must find some zones
of stability, with economic policies that back up the management of the currency. That would mean less consumption and
higher savings in the USA; in other words, tax increases – and
more consumption and less saving in Japan; in other words tax
reductions. This may be impossible to achieve – in which case
the world will continue to be unstable or stumble into competing
trading blocs.

Apart from relaxing the tension between the dollar and yen,
there will have to be formal policy co-ordination between the
major industrialised countries to encourage economic convergence. On occasion this will require unpleasant decisions on
public spending, taxes and interest rates; but they are better
taken in the context of a wider order, with the IMF holding the
ring in a system of semi-fixed exchange rates, than at the behest of

central bank governors and finance ministers suddenly appeasing the financial markets' latest whim.

Europe will have to reconstruct a parallel system of flexible exchange rate bands, and the destabilising speculative flows in the futures and options markets will need to be regulated. Mobility of capital is not an unqualified public good if it drives up the rates of return demanded from companies, destabilises macro-economic policy, and generates mass unemployment. Such initiatives will be deplored by those earning telephone number salaries in the financial markets and their supporters in the media, just as they were in the 1940s, 50s and 60s – but governments are, after all, in business to promote the general welfare.

The less developed world needs more buying power, more aid on generous terms and more intelligent support for efforts to alleviate chronic poverty and inequity. Its capacity to convert its own currencies into hard currency via the IMF system of special drawing rights should be greatly extended; and at the same time the world's rich countries need to recognise their interest in transferring many more resources to the people of the poorest countries. Above all, the terms on which the IMF and World Bank lend to distressed Third World countries, their so-called structural adjustment programmes, need to be radically overhauled. This is at present a lethal cocktail of belt-tightening and free market economics which everywhere promotes inequality, social upset and a collapse in investment.

For Britain is uniquely dependent upon the way the world economy develops. It exports a high proportion of its national output. It has one of the highest stock of overseas investments. It is one of the largest recipients of inward investment. Foreigners own a quarter of British shares, bonds and bank deposits. The capital markets' veto is particularly strong, and any British government will be imprisoned by their demands for fiscal and monetary caution. Britain therefore has a particular interest in the construction of a more stable international financial order. But the country cannot act on its own – and this is where the European Union and its potential for organising concerted action becomes crucial. The countries of the EU together have the power to regulate the financial markets and control capital flows, and to play a part in compelling the US and Japan to manage their relationship better, as part of a world deal. They have the potential jointly to manage demand, boosting and reducing it when necessary across the continent, without having their policies blown off course by the capital markets. Through the ERM, and possibly monetary union, they have the capacity to construct a system of international financial order. And if they choose they can act to weaken the speculative instruments available in the capital markets for betting against the currency parities they are defending. Europe is the third pillar, along with Japan and the US, on which any financial order must rest.

Europe can insist on common social rights across the continent, so that multinational firms cannot play one state off against another in an effort to bid down wages and working conditions. Europe can set common environmental standards, and common rules of corporate governance, establishing the concept of the stakeholder company. Indeed social-market Europe can formalise its rules and codes so that while there is enough latitude for countries to retain their particular institutions, there is still a larger framework within which a co-operative, more committed form of capitalism could be defended. If Europe wants to defend its idea of a welfare state and stakeholder, social capitalism – it will have to do so in a united way.

This, to an extent, is what the European Union has been attempting in the 1980s and early 1990s, but the process has been blocked by the British government at every turn. European Commission directives aimed at providing a longterm banking system, committed shareholders, worker participation and minimum social rights have been watered down and denuded of content by the British. Attempts to manage demand on a continental basis have similarly run up against British intransigence.

The extension of democracy upwards to the European Parliament has been as firmly resisted by the UK as local democracy at home has been attacked. The culmination of this campaign was the obstruction of the provisions for political, economic and monetary union in the Maastricht Treaty, leaving Europe with its commitment to a single currency without any of the democratic mechanisms to set common economic and social policies that would make such a single currency workable. Other factors derailed the movement, such as French and German reluctance to push integration any further – but British recalcitrance undoubtedly sealed its fate. For example, by negotiating an 'opt-out' of the tepid social charter, the British government undermined progress towards even a weak form of European social-market economy by making the other member states wary of establishing rules from which inward investors might shelter by locating in Britain.

It has been an astounding exercise in narrow nationalism and ignorance of contemporary realities and choices. The British objective has been to defend a state that will ensure that the market economy is run without any form of democratic regulation or constraint – at European or national level.

If the British rentier state succeeds in this, it will be seen as one of the great mistakes of the twentieth century. The 1980s was a unique moment in which Europe, still defined by the Cold War, might have developed the framework for a loose but continental-wide social-market economy, before the strains of German reunification weakened the alliance between France and Germany. The Delors white paper on Growth, Competitiveness and Employment in 1993 could be seen as the last gasp of the old order – trying to find support for Europe-wide Keynesianism and consensual capitalism even as the basis for that consensus was disappearing.

However, any British government interested in implementing the ideas in this book will need to revive that fading European idealism. If it is impossible to co-ordinate policy and build functioning supranational European institutions, then it is even more improbable that there will be any more success on a global scale. Any attempt to regulate the global capital markets – from a turnover tax on foreign exchange transactions, to scrutiny of the new speculative investment funds – needs to be global to be effective. The same is true for the environment, company taxation and even the management of trade: Europe must act together to act effectively.

For if the gentlemanly capitalists and international rentiers can operate offshore, with no democratic accountability, then democratisation of our national economy, polity and society will be permanently stymied. And if all governments can offer is to make their economies and societies conform to an ever less restricted market, narrowing the scope of welfare provision, reducing taxes while being unable to promote employment, and accepting an ever more degenerate capitalism, then this will strike at democracy itself across the industrialised West. If there are no real economic and political choices, then there is little point in voting – and the way is open for the return of totalitarian parties of right and left. It is a baleful prospect.

Conclusion

No state in the twentieth century has ever been able to recast its economy, political structures and society to the extent that Britain must do, without suffering defeat in war, economic collapse or revolution. Only traumatic events on that scale delegitimise the existing order to such an extent that a country concedes the case for dramatic change.

In this respect Britain's prospects must be viewed with great caution. The royal state is deeply embedded. The network of City institutions, public schools, regiments, landed estates, and board-rooms that forms the Conservative base is no less entrenched.[1] Opting out and the excuse of choice have become almost unchallengeable ideological pieties. The market-based financial system, unregulated labour market and minimalist welfare state now form an interlinked whole. The culture of the rentier governing class has the confidence that comes from being developed over generations.

The Conservative Party, the defender of this order, has become accustomed to power and has constructed an effectively hegemonic political position. Its supporters control most of the press and have a growing influence on television. The public schools turn out cohorts of Conservative supporters who staff the upper echelons of business and finance and are educated to believe in the superiority of the private, the self-regulated and the voluntary. They have little sense of the common weal or responsibility to their fellow citizens and they can be relied on to echo the general party line to the letter. The sense that civil society needs to be protected from 'bureaucratic' intervention and regulation is very strong. Any constructive suggestion involving public action or institution-building is dismissed as 'socialist'.

It must be admitted that the appeal of markets is that for some they do promote opportunity and efficiency – while for

others they create the illusion that prosperity is at least possible
for them too. Talk of democracy and accountability is all very
well, but most adult Britons simply want to go about their daily
business and are not worried about such abstract notions. If the
current system works, then let the Conservative Party get on with
it. The next lot will only be worse. Fatalism and stoicism combine
with credulity before the propaganda barrage mounted at general
elections – the only moment in a winner-take-all political system
when power can be effectively challenged.

Obviously, and fortunately, no catalytic event on the scale
of defeat in war or economic collapse seems likely to occur.
What this means, however, is that even if Labour alone or in
coalition with the Liberal Democrats took office and began to
implement the programme outlined in these pages, it would find
it hard to make any progress. The political base for change is
still weak, and the hysterical reaction of the highly politicised
business and financial community, allied with the conservative
media, to the reform of what they consider to be 'enterprise' can
easily be imagined. It would certainly be possible to slow down
the processes that are deepening inequality and gnawing away at
the internationally competitive part of the economy. Individual
acts of reform remain worthwhile. But to reverse the processes
of decline – to revitalise Britain's great cities, to reduce unemployment significantly, to rewrite the social contract; all that demands
a level of institutional change for which the political hunger is so
far lacking.

The problem is that although the current circumstances cannot and will not continue – objections to their incoherence and
irrationality will ultimately find expression even in a democracy as silted up as the UK's – the elements that make up
the Conservative hegemony would still have immense negative
power, even if they were no longer formally in control of the
state. Private financial interests, private schools, self-governing
professional groups all face major change if British capitalism is
to function effectively, but they can be relied upon to resist it to
the last, invoking every ancestral tradition and idea. Likewise, a
significant element if not a majority will resist playing any part

in the construction of a social-market Europe. Co-operative capitalism, intruding into the private networks of shareholders and the boardroom, and insisting on reciprocity of obligation, is an utterly foreign concept to them. The British officer class has been leaving its men in the lurch for a very long time.

Knowing this, the New Right may redouble its efforts to centralise power and accelerate the imposition of the market on society. For them, the failure of the project so far is not evidence that it is wrong; rather that it has been applied too weakly. Swingeing cuts in the welfare state could bring lower taxation. All inhibitions to the functioning of a free labour market could be removed, including a further limitation of trade unions' right to strike. There would be another round of business deregulation. Any reaction to these measures could be repressed by intensified policing and an increase in the prison population. The vestigial elements of public power lying outside the control of the state or the market could be removed. The country could opt out of all European institutions in order better to preserve the free market utopia.

Such an intensification of the Conservative programme cannot be excluded, but it would only worsen the adverse trends while revealing how weak the British political system is as an instrument of democracy – for however loyal middle England is to the Conservative cause it has no wish to create a brutish world in which all institutions representing a common interest are emasculated. Intensifying the revolution would be self-defeating at other levels. Lower taxes and a welfare system organised around means-testing would only deepen inequality and the malign economic and social consequences that flow from it. Further deregulation would not affect the lack of commitment and short-termism that plague the British economy. The consequences of high unemployment in social distress can be repressed for only so long, but finally even the instruments of repression – the police, army and prison service – would begin to recognise the hopelessness of their task. Leaving Europe, just when the world threatens to harden into competing economic blocs, could hardly come at a worse time. Nor is it convincing to trumpet a demagogic English nationalism while surrendering economic and financial control to foreign companies – the inconsistency will become clear even to the tabloid press and Conservative backbenchers. The New Right project has led nowhere; it can go nowhere.

This is the ground for a guarded optimism. It may be that Britain, the first country to establish parliamentary democracy and modern industry, could become the first country to transform itself peacefully without the spur of some national disaster. The conservative establishment may be hegemonic but its spectacular failure to create the good society may finally leave it defenceless against the forces of change. In any case the looming economic difficulties: rising inflation, systemic balance of payments deficits, high unemployment, constrained growth and the continuing disintegration of a chronically underfunded public infrastructure – while not as catastrophic as defeat in war, are going to be traumatic enough. If this is the best twenty years of Conservative government can do, then perhaps even middle England by the time of the next election will concede that there is a case for change.

Indeed the crisis of Conservatism is more deep-seated and threatening to its internal cohesion than is commonly recognised. Part of the reason for its extraordinary political dominance is that it has been extraordinarily successful. Until the 1990s the party managed to avoid the blame for the great devaluations of the century, and rode both the booms of the 1950s and the 1980s. Yet in the 1990s it too at last was stuck with the humiliation of devaluation when the pound dropped out of the ERM. It is obvious that the subsequent recovery has come despite, rather than because of, the policies of the Conservative Party. Suddenly it is no longer the party of economic competence.

The totems that lend it non-political appeal as the guardian of middle England – the royal family, Britain as Great Power, the aristocracy, the Church of England – are all themselves disintegrating. The party is even abolishing counties and county towns – an important source of its own social power – in its quest to centralise the state through unitary local authorities. It is becoming self-destructive.

The coalition that the party represents is under enormous pressure. The pro-European Christian-Democratic wing is uncomfortable with the grudging approach to Europe and the zeal to privatise everything, while many working-class supporters, plunged into poverty and distress, are recognising that the party of land and high finance is no friend of the working class. With the collapse of socialism, any excuse for the party's cynicism and lack of public morality is greatly reduced. The collapse of the 'Back to Basics' campaign revealed a deeper malaise.

At the same time the evidence that change is necessary becomes ever more compelling. The multiplying abuses of the political system – patronage, politicisation of the Civil Service, secrecy, poor scrutiny of legislation, centralisation – are all becoming actively dysfunctional. The patronage state has diminishing legitimacy, and the centralised state is overloaded.

Nor is the crown, which sanctifies the semi-feudal state, any longer wholly secure. Already this century, in the abdication crisis of Edward VIII, the system has come close to failure as an individual monarch fails to match the impossible moral standards of the institution. That episode may prove to have been the forerunner of greater change. Without a set of written constitutional obligations or democratic legitimacy, the royal family has to rely on its unimpeachable behaviour for its continuing legitimacy – and this is beyond the capacity of any human family to guarantee. The enchantment radiated by the institution has been shattered by the all too human failings of Elizabeth II's children and their spouses, and it seems unlikely that the monarchy can survive unchanged into the next century. It is difficult to see how renewed legitimacy for the dynasty can be achieved without a new constitutional settlement.

Social cohesion is deteriorating year by year. The combination of repression, poorly-paid work and moral sermons offered by the right as a solution is no answer to reasonable demands for decent working and living conditions, whose erosion is indissolubly linked with the rise of crime, drugs and violence. There comes a point, as with the collapse of apartheid, where even the theorists of a bankrupt ideology are compelled to recognise its non-correspondence with reality.

In this respect the country is at a turning-point like that of the 1630s, 1680s, 1830s, 1900s and 1940s. In each of these periods there was a conflation of economic, social and political crises which forced the decaying network of institutions to admit new demands for inclusion and participation. Indeed, after the great exception of the Civil War, the hallmark of English life has been the capacity to organise such transformations peacefully – forming an historical memory of reformist change that passes subliminally from generation to generation and which may still exist today.

For the opposition parties, especially the Labour Party, this is both an opportunity and fearful responsibility. They must continue the progressive tradition in British life. But the demands of the present situation are very great, and require unusual imagination and subtlety. The limited constitutional reforms of the Liberal government at the turn of the century, and the economic and social reshaping of British capitalism by the 1945–51 Labour government, have to be reprised, but this time simultaneously and in contemporary guise – for the two are interdependent necessities.

With sufficient political creativity the coalition to sustain such a momentous political initiative could be constructed. In industry and commerce there is growing support for a focus on the values of production rather than finance. At the time of writing, one or two major companies are considering donations to Labour – unheard of for a generation. Every English region outside the Home Counties, together with Scotland and Wales, wants more power to govern its own affairs. Within the 30/30/40 society, there is a comfortable majority that would benefit from a less unfair, less insecure and more equitable society who might be prepared to enter a new social compact. Within the ranks of the marginalised and insecure, who together comprise nearly 60 per cent of the population, the majority for change is overwhelming, and it is extending into the privileged 40 per cent, alarmed by the society they see around them. Women, of whom a majority have consistently supported the conservative cause, are being radicalised by the struggle to reconcile the responsibilities of work and family with little support – and younger women especially are recognising that Conservatism is no ally in their growing conviction that society could be shaped to meet their needs as much as men's.

This groundswell of dissent is diffuse and so far has no clear political voice. Yet the Labour Party cannot hope to articulate it merely by inviting each element of the dissident coalition to sink its differences and sign up to be members of Labour's still tribal identity. Instead each component of a new coalition needs to be respected for its own integrity. This is the politics of pluralism, which would be difficult enough even in a new constitutional order – but even more difficult to organise in the winner-take-all world of contemporary British politics.

Reconstructing the state and economy cannot, for these reasons, be the preserve of one political party with a simple majority in the House of Commons; it needs many allies in Parliament and in society at large. Already the Labour Party, in signalling its willingness to change its own constitution and rewrite its famous Clause 4 calling for wholesale public ownership, has made an important step towards widening its appeal. A party that cannot rewrite and modernise its own constitution can hardly pretend to do the same for the state. But there is still more to be done. Labour has to organise strategic alliances to broaden its political base as much as it can. The Liberal Democrats are one obvious ally, and before the next election both parties must seek to find as much common ground as possible. There is even a case for a formal electoral alliance, if only to make clear the nature of their common project. If voters back such an honest pact, a democratic mandate would truly have been given for the renewal of Britain – a prize for which bold politicians should surely aim.

For that is the measure of the task, and this book is both a definition of its urgency and a demand for its fulfilment. Its themes are not new to Britain – they were at the heart of Keynes' and Beveridge's position and before them of Tom Paine's – but they have been buried by twentieth-century socialism and New

Right conservatism. A written constitution; the democratisation of civil society; the republicanisation of finance; the recognition that the market economy has to be managed and regulated, both at home and abroad; the upholding of a welfare state that incorporates social citizenship; the construction of a stable international financial order beyond the nation state. These feasible and achievable reforms must be accomplished if the dynamism of capitalism is to be harnessed to the common good.

Notes

1. The State We're In

1 Jonathan Wadsworth, 'The Terrible Waste', *New Economy*, vol 1, Spring 1994.

2 *The Justice Gap*, IPPR, July 1993.

3 At the time of writing the Scott Inquiry had finished its deliberations but not published its report. During this investigation into how the government had allowed its own arms embargo to Iraq to be broached by Matrix Churchill and then subsequently prosecuted the company's directors, the evidence by law officers and the head of the Civil Service, Sir Robin Butler, showed the degree to which party and government interest had intertwined. Officials attempted to throw a mantle of utmost secrecy around the disclosure of documents, while Sir Robin Butler defended what he acknowledged were only half-true comments by ministers to the House of Commons.

4 'The Quango Explosion', *Guardian*, 19 November 1993.

5 Office of Fair Trading's report on Insurance Companies, June 1994.

6 Roger Levitt, former chairman of the Levitt group of companies which collapsed with debts of £34 million and who misled the regulatory authority, Fimbra, received only 180 hours community service.

7 *Independent on Sunday* 12 June 1994.

8 Department of Trade and Industry R & D scoreboard, 16 June 1994.

9 'Tomorrow's Company: the role of business in a changing world', Royal Society of Arts Interim Report, February 1994.

10 Martin Ricketts in *Britain's Economic Performance* (eds) Tony Buxton, Paul Chapman and Paul Temple, Routledge, p. 177.

11 Bob Woodward, *The Agenda: Inside the Clinton White House*, Simon and Schuster.

12 Richard Freeman in *New Economy*, Spring 1994, p. 22.

13 Quoted by Robert Reich, US Labour Secretary in a seminar at the Guardian on 5 June 1994.

14 This term was invented by Cain and Hopkin in *British Imperialism*.

2. The Conservative Supremacy

1 The Chairman of the Funding Agency for Schools is Sir Christopher Benson, head of Sun Alliance, Costain and director of MEPC – all

important contributors to the Conservative Party. Other members include Sir Robert Balchin, chairman of the Conservatives in the South-East and Edward Lister, Conservative leader of Wandsworth Council.

2 Helena Kennedy, 'A New Gunpowder Plot', Violations 14, Charter 88, 1994.

3 Voting figures supplied by Commoners.

4 Nigel Lawson, *The View from No 11*.

5 Ian Gilmour, *Dancing with Dogma*.

6 ibid.

7 ibid. p. 203.

8 'Ego Trip: Extra-governmental Organisations in the UK and their accountability', edited by Stuart Weir and Wendy Hall, Democratic Audit and Charter 88 Trust.

9 ibid.

10 In *Good Times, Bad Times* Harold Evans, editor of the *Sunday Times* at the time of the takeover insists that Mrs Thatcher engineered the waiver. The predictions of imminent bankruptcy of Times Newspapers on which the waiver was justified were wholly unjustified, he says.

11 In *Britain's Economic Performance*, edited by Tony Buxton, Paul Chapman and Paul Temple, Routledge, 1994.

12 Helena Kennedy, *Eve was Framed*, Vintage, p. 268.

13 Richard Tomlinson, *Independent on Sunday*, 20 December 1992.

14 Figures supplied privately to the author.

15 See para. 383, the Beveridge Report on full employment.

3. Finance Unbound

1 From 'Taming International Finance: Controls, Policy coordination or Convergence', Yilmaz Akyuz, delivered to the 'Managing the Global Economy' Conference in Cambridge, May 1994.

2 UN-TCMD World Investment Report, 1993.

3 Michael Kitson and Jonathan Michie compute that the world economy became more open than in the pre-1914 period in the early 1960s and openness is now more than 50 per cent higher than it was then. See *Managing the Global Economy*, edited by Kitson and Michie, Cambridge University Press.

4 Richard Kozul-Wright in *Managing the Global Economy* op cit.

5 John Plender and Paul Wallace, *The Square Mile*, Century, 1985, p. 64.

6 In today's capital markets the equivalent to printing money is to issue Treasury Bills, short-term IOUs, which are bought by the banking system. The banks part with cash which the government can spend, and now hold an asset – a Treasury Bill – which counts as cash as far as banks are concerned. They can use the bills to settle accounts with each other, and they are always realisable for a predictable amount of cash in the London

money markets. In effect the government has printed money.

7 'Good Housekeeping', Will Hutton, IPPR, 1991.
8 Christopher Johnson, *The Economy under Mrs Thatcher*, Penguin, 1991.
9 Nic Crafts, 'Can Deindustrialisation Seriously Damage your Wealth?' IEA Hobart Paper 120, London 1993.
10 *The Future of UK Competitiveness and the Role of Industrial Policy*, edited by Kirsty Hughes.
11 Author's calculations.
12 Goldman Sachs calculations for the IFS 'Green Budget', 12 October 1994.
13 Evidence by the Cambridge-Harvard Research Group to the Trade and Industry Select Committee, p. 22.
14 Figures supplied by Bill Martin, chief economist of UBS, in advice to the Treasury and Civil Service Select Committee, November 1993.
15 Trade and Industry Select Committee, op. cit.

4. The Revolution Founders

1 For a good survey of the literature on unions in the 1970s, see Richard Cockett, *Thinking the Unthinkable*, HarperCollins, 1994.
2 See Ben Pimlott's account in his biography of Harold Wilson.
3 How government borrowing boosted the money supply was more complicated (recall Chapter 3) but this was the essence of the story.
4 There was a lively debate about what constituted the correct measure of the money supply, with varying definitions supposedly producing a better statistical fit with inflation. For a useful account see David Smith's *The Rise and Fall of Monetarism*, Penguin, 1987.
5 *Employment Gazette*, June 1994, HMSO.
6 Blanchflower and Freeman, in the *UK Labour Market*, edited by Ray Barrell, NIESR, p. 58.
7 Neil Millward *The New Industrial Relations?*, Policy Studies Institute.
8 Janet Walsh, 'Developments in Private Sector Pay Determination', presented to Cambridge Conference on Pay in 1991.
9 See OECD *Employment Outlook*, July 1994, pp. 137–64.
10 Patrick Minford and Jonathan Riley in the *UK Labour Market*, op. cit.
11 *The Bank of England Inflation Report*, February 1994, p. 27.
12 See David Metcalf in the *UK Labour Market*, op. cit.
13 See Ray Barrell, op. cit.
14 *Department of Employment Gazette*, quoted in Colin Ley.
15 See Colin Ley's 'Politics in Britain' citing a contemporary assessment by the Department of Employment.
16 For a good account of the insider/outsider relationship see Assar Lindbeck and Dennis Snower in 'The Insider–Outsider Theory of Employment and Unemployment', MIT, 1988.
17 Neil Millward, op. cit., pp. 78–9.

18 See the National Association of Citizens Advice Bureaux publication 'Job Insecurity'. Employment-related enquiries to advice bureaux between 1987 and 1991 increased by over 50 per cent from just under 60,000 to just under 100,000.

19 These computations, unless otherwise sourced, come from the LSE data bank compiled from the Labour Force and General Household Surveys. Many thanks to Paul Gregg for his help, advice and computer runs.

20 See Joan Brown, *Escaping from Dependence*, IPPR, 1994, p. 19.

21 See Millward, op. cit.

22 See Mary Gregory and Veronique Sandoval in Barrell, op. cit.

23 Paul Gregg and Jonathan Wadsworth, 'Job Tenure and Job Security in the 1980s', NIESR, (forthcoming).

24 See Paul Gregg, *Guardian*, 23 May 1994.

5.   Proud Finance

1 Maxine Berg, Frank Cass, 'Small Producer Capitalism in Eighteenth-Century England' in *Business History* vol. 35, No 1, 1993.

2 Maxine Berg, *The Age of Manufacturers*, Routledge, 1994, p. 242.

3 William Kennedy, *Industrial Structure, Capital Markets and the Origins of British Economic Decline*, Cambridge University Press, 1987.

4 Charles Goodhart (*The Business of Banking*, 1891–1914, Weidenfeld & Nicolson, 1972) shows how the banks held extraordinarily high proportions of cash to deposits, running at some 15 per cent, and as assets held 40 to 45 per cent in very liquid form such as balances on call with the London discount houses.

5 See Kennedy op. cit.

6 Quoted in Kennedy op. cit.

7 Geoffrey Ingham, *Capitalism Divided*, Macmillan, 1984.

8 E.H.H. Green, 'The Influence of the City over British Economic Policy 1880–1960', in Y. Cassis (ed.) *Finance and Financiers in European History 1880–1960*, Cambridge University Press.

9 Quoted in Sidney Pollard, *The Development of the British Economy 1914–1980*, Edward Arnold, 1991.

6.   Tomorrow's Money Today

1 Forrest Capie and Michael Collins, *Have the Banks Failed British Industry?* IEA, 1992.

2 Michael Porter, 'Capital disadvantage: America's falling capital investment system', *Harvard Business Review*, September 1992.

3   Robert Reich, 'Bailout; a comparative study in law and industrial structure', *Yale Journal of Regulation*, vol. 2, 1985, p. 163.

4   1993 figures, see *The Bank of England Quarterly Bulletin*, February 1994.

5   ibid.

6   ibid.

7   Jonathan Charkham, *Keeping Good Company*, Oxford University Press 1993. Figures supplied by the Bank of England. Record foreign equity turnover in the UK in 1993 at £290.7 billion, with the US ranking second with £170.8 billion.

8   Stephany Griffiths-Jones with Vassilis Papageorgiou, 'Globalisation of Financial Markets and Impact on Flows to LDCS; new challenges for regulation' – paper presented to Fonad Conference, June 1993.

9   Yao-su Hu quotes the author L.C. Mather, 'Requirements for capital outlay are not desirable banking business because they tend to be longterm advances repayable only gradually from surplus profits after tax and the satisfaction of the proprietors.'

10 Form 20-F submitted by NatWest to the Securities and Exchange Commission, year ending 1992.

11 Deutsche Bank.

12 Cranfield European Enterprise Centre, quoted in E.P. Davis 'Whither corporate-banking relations?' in *The Future of UK Competitiveness and the Role of Industrial Policy*, edited by Kirsty Hughes, PSI 1994.

13 Final report for study on international differences in the cost of capital for the European Commission, Coopers & Lybrand, April 1993.

14 ibid.

15 John Muellbauer and Anthony Murphy, 'Is the UK Balance of Payments Deficit Sustainable?', *Economic Policy*, October 1990.

16 Yao-su Hu, *Industrial Banking and Credit Institutions*, PSI, 1984.

17 *Realistic Returns*, CBI, 1994.

18 Colin Mayer, 'Promiscuity and the UK Financial System', lecture at University of Warwick, November 1993.

19 Robert Frank, *Passions Within Reason*.

20 Colin Mayer, op. cit.

21 John Scott, 'Corporate Control and Corporate Rule', *British Journal of Sociology* no. 41, September 1990.

22 David Miles, 'Testing for Short Termism in the UK Stock Market', *The Economic Journal*, November 1993.

23 Paddy Linkaker, chief executive of the unit trust group M&G, wrote in the *Financial Times* in May 1994 that dividend payments were proper returns for risk and that it was not the business of government to intervene – a point made even more forcibly by Lord Hanson in an open letter to the Prime Minister, John Major, in June 1994 saying that any government examination of the level of dividend payments was a socialist measure!

24 See Martha Prevezer in *Britain's Economic Performance*, p. 202.

25 Colin Mayer, op cit.

26 Bank for International Settlements Annual Report, 1994, p. 100.
27 ibid., p. 98

7. Why Inequality Doesn't Work

1   C. Giles and P. Johnson, 'Taxes down, taxes up', IFS, February 1994.
2   Alison Goodman and Steven Webb, 'For Richer, For Poorer', IFS, 1994.
3   Amanda Gosling, Stephen Machin and Costas Meghir, 'What has happened to wages?', IFS, 1994.
4   The OECD estimates that in textiles and apparels between 1986 and 1990, the UK trade balance deteriorated by 24 per cent and employment fell by 3 per cent. See the OEDC Employment Outlook 1994.
5   The examples are legion. In 1994 London International closed its plants manufacturing surgical gloves in Britain and moved production to Asia. Amstrad manufactures its personal computers in Taiwan. British Aerospace unsuccessfully negotiated to move production of its short-range jet, the 146, to Asia – in particular to Taiwan.
6   Both ICI and Rolls-Royce for example have moved some production out of the UK for this reason.
7   Gregg and Machin in the *UK Labour Market*, op. cit.
8   Amanda Gosling et al, op. cit.
9   Stephen Jenkins, *Winners and Losers, A portrait of income distribution during the 1980s*, Rowntree Foundation.
10 Both quoted in David Vincent's *Poor Citizens* – see References.
11 Author's estimates.
12 C.V. Brown et al, 'Taxation and Family Labour Supply in the UK', Department of Economics, University of Stirling.
13 *Sunday Times*, 10 July 1993.
14 Bill Robinson, 'Britain's Borrowing Problem', Social Market Foundation, 1993.
15 *Transport 2000, Myths and Facts*, Transport 2000, July 1994.
16 Maurice Mullard, *The Politics of Public Expenditure*, Routledge 1993, and calculations for the *Guardian*.
17 John Hagan in 'Paying for Equity', IPPR.
18 'Oxford Review of Economic Policy', vol. 4, no. 3, 1988.
19 OECD Employment Outlook 1994, op. cit., p. 28.
20 S.J. Prais and Elaine Beadle, 'Pre-vocational schooling in Europe today', NIESR, 1991, p. 36.
21 ibid.
22 Robert Bennett, Peter Wicks and Andrew McCoshan, *Local Empowerment and Business Services*, UCL Press, 1994.
23 ibid.
24 Francis Greene, 'Training: Inequality and Inefficiency' in *Paying for Inequality*, see References to Chap. 8.

25 Bennett, Wicks and McCoshan, op. cit., pp. 139–41.
26 R. Bennett, H. Glennerston and Nevison 'Investing in Skills: To stay or not to stay on', *Oxford Review of Economic Policy*, vol. 8, no. 2, pp. 130–45.
27 G. Psacharopaolus and R. Layard (see References), pp. 485–503.

8.   Divide And Rule

1   Stephen Jenkins and Frank Cowell, 'Dwarves and Giants in the 1980s', Department of Swansea Discussion Paper No. 93–03.
2   Eithene McLaughlin, 'Jobs in Jeopardy', *Political Quarterly*, vol. 65 no. 2, pp. 179–90.
3   'Snow White Ideology and the Thirty Million Dwarves', the *Guardian*, 27 December, 1993.
4   Not all pensioners would need their money simultaneously, so that the pensioners' fund could be approximately halved. On the other hand there will be future pensioners all trying to build up their funds, which would double the volume of necessary assets again. For ease of exposition I have let the calculation stand.
5   John Hills, *The Future of Welfare*, Rowntree Foundation, 1993.
6   'Pensioners exploited on annuities', *Sunday Times*, 24 July 1994.
7   Duncan Maclennan, *A Competitive UK economy, the challenges for housing policy*, Rowntree Foundation, June 1994.
8   Building Society Association, 1989.
9   Duncan Maclennan, op. cit.
10 The BMA report that in a survey of 247 hospitals 4 out of 10 give preference to patients of GP fundholders, *Financial Times*, 10 December 1993.
11 Bradford NHS Trust won the contract to look after the records of Surrey Mental Health Department in 1994.
12 46 per cent of parents said they would educate their children privately if they could afford it, reported a MORI poll for ISIS in 1994.
13 Anthony Sampson, *The Essential Anatomy of Britain*.
14 BBC Radio 4 'File on Four', 1 March 1994, transcript made available by BBC Current Affairs.
15 Mike Power, *The Audit Trail*, Demos 1994.
16 Anthony Bottoms and Paul Wiles, 'Crime and Insecurity in the City', private paper.
17 Richard Wilkinson, *Unfair Shares*.
18 *Guardian*, 29 August 1994.

9. Why Keynesian Economics Is Best

1 Gary Becker's articles in the *Journal of Political Economy*, (81, 1973 and 82, 1974) are typical of this type of market rationalism.

2 In *Social Change and the Experience of Unemployment* (edited by Duncan Gaillie, Catherine Marsh and Carolyn Vogler, Oxford University Press, 1994, pp. 115–53) Duncan Gaillie and Carolyn Vogler demonstrate in an examination of attitudes from the 1986 Work Attitudes Survey and the 1987 Household and Community Survey that the 'unemployed were even more likely than the employed to show a strong longer-term commitment to employment.'

3 Quoted from Pandora's marketplace in the *New Scientist* supplement, 6 February 1993, p. 6.

4 Leon Walras, *Elements d'économie pure*, translated by William Jaffe, Allen and Unwin, 1954.

5 Keynes, 'The General Theory of Employment, Interest and Money', *Quarterly Journal of Economics*, February 1939, p. 213.

6 ibid, p. 163.

7 Keynes, *The General Theory of Employment, Interest and Money*, Royal Economic Society, 1978, p. 46.

8 ibid, p. 219.

9 Both quotes in this paragraph are from Chapter 12 of *The General Theory of Employment, Interest and Money*, Macmillan, 1973, pp. 159 and 164.

10 Gregory Mankiw and David Romer, 'Keynesian Economics Today', *Journal of Economic Perspectives*, vol 7, no 1, winter, 1993.

11 Stanley Fisher, 'Longterm contracts, rational expectations, and the optimal money supply rule', *Journal of Political Economy 85*, 1975, pp. 191–205.

12 Blanchard and Kiyotaki produce an interesting example of such a model in 'Monopolistic Competition and the Effects of Aggregate Demand' in the *American Economic Review*, September 1987, pp. 647–66.

13 Stiglitz, 'Capital Markets and Economic Fluctuations in Capitalist Economies', *European Economic Review*, April 1992, pp. 269–306.

14 Quoted to the author from a 1994 internal Treasury memorandum.

15 George Akerlof in 'The Market for Lemons; Quality, Uncertainty and the Market Mechanism', sets out the case that availability may in itself be a signal of poor quality. See the *Quarterly Journal of Economics*, August 1970, pp. 488–500.

16 There are a variety of models of so-called efficiency wages. Shapiro and Stiglitz ('Equilibrium Unemployment as a Worker Discipline Device', *American Economic Review*, June 1984, pp. 434–44) argue that higher than market-clearing wages prove an incentive not to engage in behaviour that might lose them their jobs. Aberlof and Yellen (*Efficiency Wage Models of the Labour Market*, Cambridge University Press 1986) suggest that they are a means of an employer signalling that wages are fair and that non-market rules apply within the firm. Bulow and Summers ('A Theory of Dual Labour Markets', *Journal of Labour Economics*, July 1986,

pp. 376–414) argue that they are means of ensuring effort and minimal shirking.

10. The Political Economy
Of The World's Capitalisms

1   Richard Freeman, 'Jobs in the USA', *New Economy* (Dryden Press for IPPR), Spring 1994, vol. 1, issue 1, pp. 20–4.
2   ibid.
3   John Scott, *Capitalist Power and Financial Power*, Harvester Wheatsheaf, 1986, pp. 146–54.
4   The Defence Science Board's memorandum to the Pentagon on Semi-conductor Dependency (31 December 1986) is a good example of US industry's expectations of the Pentagon. The response was to organise US manufacturers in a loose coalition to share R&D costs for the next generation of products, which allowed US industry at least to hold the line.
5   Richard Ferlauto, 'Community Capital: Delivering jobs from the bottom-up', delivered to the International Seminar on Growth and Employment, Magdalen College Oxford, 13–15 April 1994.
6   De Tocqueville, *Democracy in America*, p. 393.
7   Cited in David Goodhart's *The Reshaping of the German Model*, IPPR 1994.
8   Quoted in *The Seven Cultures of Capitalism*, by Charles Hampden-Turner and Alfons Trompenaars, p. 229.
9   Wolfgang Streeck, *Industrial Relations in West Germany: a case study of the car industry*, Heinemann, 1984.
10 *The Seven Cultures of Capitalism*, op. cit.
11 Hiroyuki Itami, cited by Weiichi Masuyama in a paper for the National Economic Development Office City and Industry Conference, November 1991.
12 *Japan in the Passing Lane* by Satoshi Kamata (Unwin) gives a very sobering account of life in a Toyota car factory.
13 In *The Japanese Firm*, Clarendon Press, 1994.
14 ibid.
15 Kamekichi Takahashi, 'The Stock Company: a cause of national decay', quoted in *The Japanese Firm*, op. cit.
16 Guy de Carmoy and Jonathan Storey, *Western Europe in World Affairs*, Praeger, p. 140.
17 Lester Thurow, *Head to Head*, Nicholas Brealey, 1994, p. 62.
18 Andrew Walter, *World Power and World Money*, Harvester Wheatsheaf, pp. 204–8.

11. The Republican Opportunity

1 Quoted from Lord Radcliffe's 1951 Reith Lectures 'Power and the State' pp. 25–7 in Ferdinand Mount's *The British Constitution Now*.

2 For a good account of the case for parliamentary reform see *Citizens and Subjects* by Tony Wright, Routledge.

3 Martin Linton and Mary Georghiou, 'Labour's Road to Electoral Reform', Labour Campaign for Electoral Reform.

4 See the Centre for Economic Policy Research, and the Treasury and Civil Select Committee which both published reports in 1994 advocating Bank of England independence.

5 See the National Consumers Council's report on the Water Industry, July 1994.

6 Ian Ayres and John Braithwaite, *Responsive Regulation*, Oxford University Press, 1992.

7 Jonathan Charkham, *Keeping Good Company*, Oxford, 1993.

8 The chief executive of the oil company Lasmo, Jonathan Agnew, for example, criticised the Cadbury code for interfering with wealth creation; when he and his co-directors had been awarded additional share options the same week as a bid was made from Enterprise Oil.

12. Stakeholder Capitalism

1 Only the Agricultural Mortgage Corporation continues to play a public role, albeit small.

2 Frank Field, *An Agenda for Britain*, Penguin, 1993.

3 Eichengreen, *Institutions of World Economic Growth*, CEPR.

Conclusion

1 Anthony Barnett in an important essay calls this network of state and conservative institutions 'The Empire State'. See *Power and the Throne*, ed. Anthony Barnett, Vintage 1994.

References

Chapter 1

Martin Linton, 'Money and Votes', IPPR, 1994
Kevin Morgan and Ellis Roberts, 'The Democratic Deficit, A guide to Quangoland', October 1993, University of Wales
Amitai Etzioni, *The Moral Dimension*, Free Press, 1988
J.K. Galbraith, *The Culture of Contentment*, 1992
Charles Hampden-Turner and Alfons Trompenaars, *The Seven Cultures of Capitalism*, Piatkus, 1994
David Marquand, *The Unprincipled Society*, Jonathan Cape, 1988
Tony Wright, *Citizens and Subjects*, Routledge, 1993
David Held, 'A new International order', IPPR, 1993
Karl Polanyi, *The Great Transformation*, Octagon, 1972
Tony Buxton, Paul Chapman and Paul Temple (eds), *Britain's Economic Performance*, Routledge 1994
Edward Balls and Paul Gregg, 'Work and Welfare', Commission of Social Justice Working Paper No 3
Commission on Social Justice, 'The Justice Gap', IPPR, 1993
Bob Woodward, *Agenda: Inside the Clinton White House*, Simon and Schuster, 1994

Chapter 2

Ian Gilmour, *Dancing with Dogma*, Simon and Schuster, 1992
P.J. Godfrey Hodgson, 'A Squint at Democracy', Charter 88
Shirley Robin Letwin, *The Anatomy of Thatcherism*, Fontana, 1992
M. Cain and J.K. Hopkin, *British Imperialism*, Longman, 1993
Hansard Society, 'Making the Law', the report on the Hansard Society of the Legislative Process, 1993
A. Giddens, *Beyond Left and Right*, Polity Press, 1994
Nigel Lawson, *The View from No 11*, Bantam, 1992
Harold Evans, *Good Times, Bad Times*, Coronet, 1983
R.N. Berki, *Socialism*, Dent, 1987
Helena Kennedy, *Eve Was Framed*, Vintage, 1994
Helena Kennedy, 'A New Gunpowder Plot', Violations 14, Charter 88, 1994
John Saville, *The Labour Movement in Britain*, Faber, 1988

Gregory Elliott, *Labourism and the English Genius*, Verso, 1993
Ferdinand Mount, *The British Constitution Now*, Heinemann, 1992

Chapter 3

Kenichi Ohmae, *The Borderless World*, HarperBusiness, 1990
John Plender and Paul Wallace, *The Square Mile*, Century, 1985
E.P. Davis, *Debt, Financial Fragility and Systemic Risk*, Oxford University
   Press, 1992
J.C.R. Dow and I.D. Saville, *A Critique of Monetary Policy*, Oxford University
   Press, 1988
Duncan Maclennan, *A Competitive UK economy: The challenges for housing
   policy*, Joseph Rowntree, 1994
'The Competitiveness of UK Manufacturing Industry', Trade and Industry
   Committee, April 1994
Maurice Scott, *A New View of Economic Growth*, Oxford University Press, 1989
John Wells, 'The UK Record since 1979', *New Economy*, vol 1, no 1, IPPR, 1993
Michael Kitson and Jonathan Michie, *Managing the Global Economy*, Oxford
   University Press, 1994
Peter Warburton, 'Low national savings rate leaves UK economy and gilts
   at risk', Flemings Research, May 1994
A.P. Thirlwall and Heather Gibson, *Balance of Payments Theory and the
   UK experience*, Macmillan, 1992
Bill Martin, Evidence to the Treasury and Civil Service Select Committee,
   January 1994. Also 'Invisible, visible, risible', UBS Economic Commentary
   March 1994 and 'Debt by Misadventure', UBS Economic Commentary,
   March 1994
Andrew Walter, *World Power and World Money*, Harvester Wheatsheaf, 1993
Christopher Johnson, *The Economy under Mrs Thatcher*, Penguin, 1991
Jeffrey Frieden, 'Invested Interests: the politics of national economic policies
   in a world of global finances', International Organisation, Autumn 1991

Chapter 4

Henry Pelling, *A History of British Trade Unionism*, Pelican, 1979
Colin Leys, *Politics in Britain*, Verso, 1983
Keith Middlemass, *Politics in Industrial Society*, Deutsch, 1979
David Blanchflower and Richard Freeman, 'Did the Thatcher reforms
   change British labour market performance?', *The UK Market Labour
   Market*, Cambridge University Press, NIESR, 1993
David Metcalf, 'Transformation of British industrial relations? Institutions,

Processes and Outcomes 1980–1990.' in *The UK Labour Market*, Cambridge University Press, NIESR, 1993

Employment Gazette, Department of Employment, 1981

Robert H. Frank, *Choosing the Right Pond*, Oxford University Press, 1985

Robert Lane, *The Market Experience*, Cambridge University Press, 1991

Ben Pimlott, *Harold Wilson*, HarperCollins, 1993

'Job Insecurity', National Association of Citizens' Advice Bureaux, 1993

Milton Friedman, *The Counter-Revolution in Monetary Theory*, IEA, 1970

David Smith, *The Rise and Fall of Monetarism*, Penguin, 1987

Richard Cockett, *Thinking the Unthinkable*, HarperCollins, 1994

Mary O'Mahoney and Karin Wagner with Marcel Paulsen, 'Changing fortunes: an industry study of British and German productivity growth over three decades', NIESR, Report Series 7, 1994

Neil Millward, 'The New Industrial Relations', Policy Studies Institute, 1994

Robert Solow, *The Labour Market as a Social Institution*, Blackwell, 1990

Truman Bewlay, Research findings presented to the Happiness Conference, LSE, November 1993

OECD Employment Outlook, July 1994

'Performance pay fails to motivate', Institute of Manpower Studies, November 1993

Carey Oppenheim, *Poverty: the Facts*, Child Poverty Action Group, 1990

Joan Brown, 'Escaping from Dependence', IPPR, 1994

Chapter 5

Maxine Berg and Frank Cass, 'Small Producer Capitalism in Eighteenth-century England' in *Business History* volume 35, no 1, 1993

Maxine Berg, *The Age of Manufacturers; 1700–1820*, Routledge, 1994

William Kennedy, *Industrial Structure, Capital Markets and the Origins of British Economic Decline*, Cambridge University Press, 1987

Geoffrey Ingham, *Capitalism Divided*, Macmillan, 1984

The Report of the Committee on Finance and Industry, (1931 Cmnd. 3897): Minutes of Evidence 2 Vols (1931)

Sidney Pollard, *The Development of the British Economy 1914–1980*, Edward Arnold, 1991

W.D. Rubinstein, *Capitalism, Culture and Decline in Britain; 1750–1990*, Routledge, 1994

Peter Matthias, *First Industrial Nation*, Methuen, 1978

C.A.E. Goodhart, *The Business of Banking; 1891–1914*, Weidenfeld & Nicolson, 1972

Steven Tolliday, *Business, Banking and Politics; the case of British steel, 1918–1936*, Harvard University Press, 1987

Forrest Capie and Michael Collins, 'Have the Banks failed British Industry?' IEA, 1992

Michael Collins, *Banks and Industrial Finance in Britain 1800–1939*, Macmillan, 1991

Corelli Barnett, *The Audit of War*, Macmillan, 1986

David Edgerton, 'The Prophet Militant and Industrial, Twentieth-century British History', vol 2, no 3, 1991, pp. 360–79

E.H.H. Green, 'The influence of the City over British economic policy, 1880–1960', in Y. Cassin (ed), *Finance and financiers in European History 1880–1960*, Cambridge University Press

Chapter 6

'Investing for Britain's future', report of the City/Industry task force 1987

'Minimum Reserve Requirements Abroad', Bundesbank monthly report, Bundesbank, March 1990

Richard Hernstein, 'On the law of effect', *Journal of Experimental Analysis of Behaviour*, 1970, pp. 242–66

Robert Frank, *Passions Within Reason*, Norton, 1988

David Miles, 'Testing for Short Termism in the UK Stock Market', *The Economic Journal*, vol 103, no 421

Colin Mayer, 'Stock markets, Financial Institutions and Corporate Performance', NEDO Conference on capital markets and corporate success, November 1991

Robert Reich, 'Bailout; a comparative study in law and industrial structure', in *Yale Journal on Regulation*, vol 2, 1985, p. 163

Paul Marsh, 'Short-termism on trial', Institutional Fund Managers Association, 1990

John Muellbauer and Anthony Murphy, 'Is the UK Balance of Payments Deficit sustainable?' in *Economic Policy*, Cambridge University Press, October 1990

Stephen A. Zimmer and Robert N. McCauley, 'Bank Cost of Capital and International Competition', in *Federal Reserve Bank of New York Quarterly Review*, Winter 1991

Yao-su Hu, 'Industrial Banking and Special Credit Institutions', Policy Studies Institute, 1984

Michael E. Porter, 'Capital Disadvantage: America's failing capital investment system' in *Harvard Business Review*, September–October 1992

John Kay, *The Foundations of Corporate Success*, Oxford University Press, 1993

Forrest Capie and Michael Collins, 'Have the Banks failed British industry?' IEA Hobart Paper, No 119, 1992

John Scott, 'Corporate control and corporate rule' in *British Journal of Sociology*, no 41, September 1990

Martha Prevezer, 'Capital and Control: an overview of City-industry relations' in *Britain's Economic Performance*, Routledge, 1994

Cooper & Lybrand, 'The Middle Market Survey', 1994

Cooper & Lybrand, 'Final report for study on international differences in the cost of capital for the European Commission', April 1993

E.P. Davis, 'Whither Corporate Banking Relations?' in *The Future of UK Competitiveness and the Role of Industrial Policy*, edited by Kirsty Hughes, PSI, 1994

Alex Brummer and Roger Cowe, *Hanson*, Fourth Estate, 1994

Michael Porter, *The Competitive Advantage of Nations*, Macmillan, 1990

CBI, 'Realistic Returns: how do manufacturers access new investment?' July 1994

'Investment appraisal and corporate investment' in *Bank of England Quarterly Bulletin*, vol 34, no 3, August 1994

Chapter 7

Adrian Wood, *North-South Trade, Employment and Inequality*, Oxford University Press, 1994

C. Giles and P. Johnson, 'Taxes down, Taxes up: the effects of a decade of tax changes', in The Institute for Fiscal Studies *Commentary*, no 41 February 1994

Mick Dunford and Tony Fielding, 'Greater London, the south-east region and the wider Britain: metropolitan polarisation, uneven development and interregional migration', University of Sussex, 1993

David Vincent, *Poor Citizens; the state and the poor in twentieth-century Britain*, Longman, 1991

Arthur Okun, 'Equality and Efficiency; the big trade-off', Brookings, Washington, 1975

Andrew Glyn and David Miliband, 'Paying for Inequality', IPPR/Rivers Oram Press, 1994

John Hagan, 'Crime Inequality and efficiency' in 'Paying for Inequality' pp. 80–99

Bill Robinson, 'Britain's borrowing problem', Social Market Foundation Report, no 4, 1993

Alex Bryson and Stephen Mckay, 'Is It Worth Working?', Policy Studies Institute 1994

C.V. Brown et al, *Taxation and Family Labour Supply in Great Britain*, University of Stirling, 1986

David Finegold and David Soskice, 'The Failure of Training in Britain: Analysis and Prescription' in *Oxford Review of Economic Policy*, vol 4, no 3, 1988

Robert Bennett, Peter Wicks and Andrew McCoshan, *Local Empowerment and Business Services*, UCL Press, 1994

A. Dilnot and M. Kell, 'Top rate tax cuts and incentives; some empirical evidence', in *Fiscal Studies*, vol 9, 1988, pp. 70–92

A.B. Atkinson and G.V. Mogensen, *Welfare and Work Incentives*, Clarendon Press, 1994

Mark Blaug, 'The Rate of Return on Investments in Education in Great
    Britain', in *The Economics of Education and the Education of an Economist*,
    New York University Press, 1987
Amitai Etzioni, *The Parenting Deficit*, Demos, 1993
Stephen P. Jenkins, 'Winners and Losers: A portrait of the UK Income
    Distribution during the 1980s', Joseph Rowntree Findings Series, 1994
Amanda Gosling, Stephen Machin and Costas Meghir, 'What has happened
    to wages?' IFS, 1994
Alisa Goodman and Stephen Webb, 'For Richer, for Poorer', in *Commentary*,
    no 42, IFS, 1994
R. Bennett, H. Glennerster and D. Nevison, 'Investing in Skill; To stay
    on or not to stay on', in *Oxford Review of Economic Policy*, vol 8, no 2,
    1992
G. Psacharopoulus and R. Layard, 'Human Capital and earnings; British
    evidence and a critique', in *Review of Economic Studies*, vol 46, 1979, pp.
    485–503
Maurice Mullard, *The Politics of Public Expenditure*, Routledge, 1993

Chapter 8

Richard Wilkinson, 'Health, Redistribution and Growth' in *Paying for Inequality*
    edited by Andrew Glynn and David Miliband, IPPR, 1994, pp. 24–43
Amitai Etzioni, *The Parenting Deficit*, Demos, 1993
Amitai Etzioni, *The Moral Dimension*, Free Press, 1990
Steve Wilcox, Housing Finance Review, Joseph Rowntree Foundation, 1993
Julian le Grand and Will Bartlett (eds.), *Quasi-markets and social policy*,
    Macmillan, 1993
John Hills, 'The Future of Welfare, a guide to the debate', Joseph Rowntree
    Foundation, 1994
'Securities and Investment Board, Pension Transfers', Report to the SIB
    by KPMG Peat Marwick, December 1993
Jeremy Paxman, *Friends in High Places*, Penguin, 1991
Anthony Sampson, *The Essential Anatomy of Britain – Democracy in Crisis*,
    Hodder and Stoughton, 1993
Richard Wilkinson, *Unfair Shares*, Barnados, 1994

Chapter 9

Paul Krugman, *Peddling Prosperity*, Norton, 1994
Daniel Kahneman, 'New Challenges to the Rationality Assumption', paper
    delivered to the LSE Happiness Conference in November 1993 and to the

11th International Seminar on the New Institutional Economics

Robert Lane, *The Market Experience*, Cambridge University Press, 1991

Will Hutton, *The Revolution That Never Was*, Longman, 1986

Paul Ormerod, *The Death of Economics*, Faber, 1994

M. Mitchell Waldrop, *Complexity, the emerging science at the edge of order and chaos*, Simon and Schuster, 1992

Roy Radner, 'Competitive Equilibrium under Uncertainty', in *Econometrica*, vol 36, 1968

Axel Leijonhufvud, *On Keynesian Economics and the Economics of Keynes*, Oxford University Press, 1968

Allan Meltzer, *Keynes Monetary Theory*, Cambridge University Press, 1988

Robert H. Frank, *Passions Within Reasons*, Norton, 1988

Mark Casson, *Enterprise and Competitiveness*, Clarendon Press, 1990

Edwards Deming, Joseph Stiglitz and Andrew Weiss, 'Credit Rationing in Markets with Imperfect Informaton', in *American Economic Review*, June 1981 pp. 393–410

Chapter 10

Michel Albert, *Capitalism against capitalism*, Whurr, 1993

Ezra Vogel, *Comeback*, Simon and Schuster, 1985

Wolfgang Stutzel et al, *Standard Texts on the Social Market Economy*, Gustav Fischer, 1982

David Goodhart, 'The Reshaping of the German Model', IPPR, 1994

Wolfgang Streeck, *The Social Institutions of Economic Performance*, Sage, 1988

Philip Cooke, Kevin Morgan and Adam Price, 'The Future of the Mittelstand', Regional Industrial Research Report no 13, University of Wales

Philip Cooke et al, 'The Challenge of Lean Production in German Industry', Regional Research Report No 12, University of Wales

Colin Crouch and David Marquand, *Ethics and Markets*, Blackwell, 1993

Masohiko Aoki and Ronald Dore (eds), *The Japanese Firm*, Clarendon Press, 1994

Alan Blinder, 'Should the Former Socialist Economies look East or West for a model?', presented to the 10th World Congress of the International Economic Association in Moscow, August 1992

James Abbeglen, *Sea Change*, Free Press, 1994

Charles Hampden-Turner and Alfons Trompenaars, *The Seven Cultures of Capitalism*, Piatkus, 1994

Andrew Walter, *World Power and World Money*, Harvester Wheatsheaf, 1993

Guy de Carmoy and Jonathan Storey, *Western Europe in World Affairs*, Praeger, 1986

Toshihiro Nishiguchi, *Strategic Industrial Pricing, the Japanese Advantage*, Oxford University Press, 1994

Lester Thurow, *Head to Head*, Nicholas Brealey, 1994

Chapter 11

Paul Hirst, *Associative Democracy*, Polity, 1994
Ian Ayres and John Braithwaite, *Responsive Regulation*, Oxford University
    Press, 1993
Stephen Haseler, *The End of the House of Windsor*, IB Tauris, 1993
Ferdinand Mount, *The British Constitution Now*, Heinemann, 1992
Martin Linton and Mary Georghiou, 'Labour's Road to Electoral Reform',
    Labour Campaign for Electoral Reform, 1993
Tony Wright, *Citizens and Subjects*, Routledge, 1994

Chapter 12

Frank Field, *An Agenda for Britain*, Penguin, 1993
Jonathan Charkham, *Keeping Good Company*, Oxford University Press, 1993
John Banham, *The Anatomy of Change*, Butterfield, 1994
Kirsty Hughes (ed), 'The Future of UK Competitiveness and the Role of
    Industrial Policy', Policy Studies Institute 1994
Barry Eichengreen, 'Institutions and Economic Growth: Europe after World
    War II', CEPR 1994
Report of the Bretton Woods Commission, IMF, 1994
Social Justice, The Report of the Commission on Social Justice, Vintage, 1994
John Williamson, Stephany Griffith-Jones and Arjun Sengupta, *Fragile Finance*,
    Fondad, 1992
European Commission, The White Paper on Growth, Competitiveness,
    Employment, Brussels 1993
Ruth Kelly, 'Taxing the Speculator', Fabian Discussion Paper 15, 1993

Conclusion

Anthony Barnett (ed) *Power and the Throne*, Vintage, 1994

Index